Philosophy and Education

Written for education studies students, this accessible text offers a clear introduction to philosophy and education. Skilfully guiding readers through this challenging and sometimes complex area, it brings key philosophical ideas and questions to life in the context and practice of education. There is also a companion website to accompany the book, featuring weblinks for each activity, which can be visited at www.routledge.com/cw/haynes.

The authors consider the implications of educational trends and movements through a variety of philosophical lenses such as Marxism, utopianism, feminism and poststructuralism. The book explores enduring themes such as childhood and contemporary issues such as teaching critical thinking and philosophy in schools. Features include:

- a range of individual and group activities that invite questioning and discussion
- case studies and examples from a variety of formal and informal education settings and contexts
- reference to philosophically informed practices of research, reading, writing and teaching
- overviews and key questions for each chapter and suggestions for further reading.

Drawing on readers' experiences of education, the book reveals the connections between philosophical ideas and educational policy and practice. Part of the *Foundations in Education Studies* series, this engaging textbook is essential reading for students coming to the study of philosophy and education for the first time.

Joanna Haynes is Associate Professor in Education Studies at Plymouth University Institute of Education, UK.

Ken Gale is Lecturer in Education at Plymouth University Institute of Education, UK.

Melanie Parker is Lecturer in Education Studies at Plymouth University Institute of Education, UK.

WITHDRAWN FROM
THE LIBRARY

UNIVERSITY OF
WINCHESTER

D0322644

Foundations of Education Studies Series

This is a series of books written specifically to support undergraduate education studies students. Each book provides a broad overview of a fundamental area of study exploring the key themes and ideas to show how these relate to education. Accessibly written with chapter objectives, individual and group tasks, case studies and suggestions for further reading, the books will give students an essential understanding of the key disciplines in education studies, forming the foundations for future study.

Philosophy and Education, An introduction to key questions and themes,
Joanna Haynes, Ken Gale and Melanie Parker

Research and Education, Will Curtis, Mark Murphy and Sam Shields

Policy and Education, Paul Adams

Forthcoming titles

Sociology and Education, Richard Waller and Chrissie Rogers

Philosophy and Education

An introduction to key questions and themes

Joanna Haynes, Ken Gale and Melanie Parker

UNIVERSITY OF WINCHESTER
LIBRARY

 Routledge
Taylor & Francis Group

LONDON AND NEW YORK

First published 2015
by Routledge
2 Park Square, Milton Park, Abingdon, Oxon OX14 4RN

and by Routledge
711 Third Avenue, New York, NY 10017

Routledge is an imprint of the Taylor & Francis Group, an informa business

© 2015 Joanna Haynes, Ken Gale and Melanie Parker

The right of Joanna Haynes, Ken Gale and Melanie Parker to be identified as authors
of this work has been asserted by them in accordance with sections 77 and 78 of the
Copyright, Designs and Patents Act 1988.

All rights reserved. No part of this book may be reprinted or reproduced or utilised in
any form or by any electronic, mechanical, or other means, now known or hereafter
invented, including photocopying and recording, or in any information storage or
retrieval system, without permission in writing from the publishers.

Trademark notice: Product or corporate names may be trademarks or registered trademarks,
and are used only for identification and explanation without intent to infringe.

British Library Cataloguing in Publication Data
A catalogue record for this book is available from the British Library

Library of Congress Cataloging-in-Publication Data
Haynes, Joanna, 1953-
Philosophy and education : an introduction to key questions and themes / Joanna
Haynes, Ken Gale and Melanie Parker.
pages cm—(Foundations of education studies)
Includes bibliographical references and index.
1. Education—Philosophy. I. Gale, Ken. II. Parker, Melanie, 1969- III. Title.
LB14.7.H38 2014
371.001—dc23
2014020863

ISBN: 978-0-415-53617-2 (hbk)
ISBN: 978-0-415-53618-9 (pbk)
ISBN: 978-1-315-74215-1 (ebk)

Typeset in Bembo Std and Helvetica Neue LT Pro
by Swales & Willis Ltd, Exeter, Devon, UK

UNIVERSITY OF WINCHESTER

MIX
Paper from
responsible sources
FSC
www.fsc.org   FSC® C013056

Printed and bound in Great Britain by
TJ International Ltd, Padstow, Cornwall

Contents

Author biographies

Joanna Haynes is Associate Professor at the University of Plymouth, where she leads the PhD programme in the Institute of Education, as well as teaching on the BA Education Studies programme. Following undergraduate studies in philosophy, Joanna taught in primary schools in inner-city Glasgow and Bristol, before moving into teacher education and professional development and completing a Master's degree in education at Bristol University. Her PhD (University of Exeter) is in philosophy with children. She is author of *Children as Philosophers* (Routledge 2002, 2008), which has been translated into several languages. Joanna co-authored *Picturebooks, Pedagogy and Philosophy* (Routledge Research in Education Series, 2012) and co-edited *Engaging Education: Perspectives on Participation and Inclusion* (published by Continuum in 2009). She is co-editor of a special issue of *Studies in Philosophy and Education* on the theme 'child as educator' (published by Springer, 2013). She was recently invited to contribute a chapter for the forthcoming *Routledge International Handbook of Young Children's Thinking and Understanding*. Joanna has been involved in writing, presenting, teaching and leading courses on philosophical enquiry and philosophy with children for over twenty years and is a member of the national and international philosophy for children networks, SAPERE and ICPIC. She belongs to the Philosophy of Education Society (PESGB). Her research interests are in the ethics of teaching and learning relations, troublesome knowledge and critical and transformative pedagogies. Joanna enjoys being part of a much-loved extended family. She lives in Devon with her partner Jonie and Roly the lovely lurcher. She is a proud mother to daughter Georgia and son Louis and delighted grandmother to two-year-old twins Jimmy and Jacob.

Ken Gale works in the Institute of Education at Plymouth University. His main teaching and research interests can broadly be contextualised within the philosophy of education. Ken has published widely and presented at a number of international conferences. He was part of a Higher Education Academy-funded project to develop online resources on collaborative writing for early career researchers and faculty: www. writeinquiry.org. He is co-author, with Jonathan Wyatt, of the book *Between the Two: A Nomadic Inquiry into Collaborative Writing and Subjectivity* (Cambridge Scholars Publishing, 2009). With Bronwyn Davies, Susanne Gannon and Jonathan Wyatt he co-authored the book *Deleuze and Collaborative Writing: An Immanent Plane of Composition* (Peter Lang, 2011) and, recently, with friends and colleagues Jonathan

Wyatt, Tami Spry, Ron Pelias and Larry Russell, he has co-authored the book *How Writing Touches: An Intimate Scholarly Collaboration* (Cambridge Scholars Publishing, 2012). More recently, with Jonathan Wyatt, he has edited a Special Edition on collaborative writing for the journal *International Review of Qualitative Research*, published in 2013. With some of the above colleagues Ken has been invited to contribute a chapter on approaches to collaborative writing to the fifth edition of the *Sage Handbook of Qualitative Research*. He is an associate member of the Higher Education Academy and a member of the International Association of Qualitative Inquiry and the Narrative Inquiry Centre at the University of Bristol, where he is also a Visiting Fellow. Ken has three children, Katy, Reuben and Phoebe, is a proud grandfather to Rohan James and lives, nurtures and sustains his soul in Cornwall in the UK.

Melanie Parker is a Lecturer in Education Studies in the Institute of Education at Plymouth University. On the BA Education Studies Programme she leads modules on Inclusive Education and Alternative Education as well as teaching on postgraduate programmes and supervising doctoral research students. Melanie won the Plymouth University Student and Staff Teaching and Representation Award for 'Most Inspirational Teacher' in 2012. Prior to taking up her current post Melanie was Deputy Director for the Centre for Excellence in Placement Learning at Plymouth University. She is also the branch coordinator for the Devon and Cornwall branch of the Philosophy of Education Society (PESGB). A very experienced education researcher, Melanie has been involved in a number of funded research projects. Melanie has given presentations and published academic papers and online resources in the field of inclusive practice in higher education teaching and learning (http://cpdoer.net/about/team/). She has also carried out community-based research with refugees and asylum seekers and disabled people. Melanie is very active in involving her students in local community education projects, for example in adult literacy. Her teaching and research interests, as reflected in her chapters for this book, are in critical and revolutionary pedagogy, utopias and education, and social and educational inclusion. An enthusiastic festival goer, Melanie lives in Tavistock with her family, which includes her lovely husband Mark and their fantastic children Sabrina, Emily and James, not forgetting their two dogs, Aila and Lorna.

Acknowledgements

We would like to thank all our students, past and present. The writing in this book has been informed by keeping our students in mind. Many of the activities have been part of our teaching and developed for the book in the light of students' responses. Particular thanks are extended to second-year education studies student John Walker, who read some of the material and gave us valuable feedback. We are fortunate to work with an exceptional group of academic and support staff at Plymouth University Institute of Education and we would like to express our special appreciation for our colleagues in the education studies team.

Acknowledgements

Introduction

This book aims to bring philosophical ideas and questions to life in the contexts and practices of education. It seeks to provoke critical thinking and engage readers in the interpretation of philosophical ideas and approaches to education research. The book sets out to speak directly to readers' experiences of education and to their future roles as educators or postgraduate students, in making connections between philosophical ideas and familiar or new education policy and practice contexts. We have made reference to examples from a wide variety of informal and formal educational settings throughout the life course.

The book considers the implications of educational trends and movements through a variety of philosophical lenses. We are living in a time when many educational discourses and texts seem to be very prescriptive and to present too many unquestioned 'givens' that students of education are expected to accept as 'best practice' or professional obligations. Ball (1998) made an important argument for such a position which also provides a helpful supporting comment for the rationale underlying the rhetoric and intent of this book. In making a case for the urgent role of theory in educational studies, he challenges the performative cultures and pervasiveness of their ensuing practices in pedagogy and research. Ball claims that by subordinating and diminishing theory in relation to practice, performative cultures not only serve to reduce the critical and qualitative nature of such practices but also to challenge the professional status and abilities of those who are committed to the enhancement and promotion of education in the future.

This book seeks to subvert and disrupt some of these discourses and texts by inviting readers to be philosophically active and explore methods of critical thinking, reasoning and enquiry. As authors we hope that the doubt, uncertainty and creative disturbance that sometimes go together with such critical methods will enable students to engage in meaningful discussion with one another about significant educational matters. We hope the experience of working with the material will give readers the confidence to question and debate, perhaps with a sense of rigour and purpose, perhaps with a sense of playfulness and subversion.

Invitation to philosophise

The book has been written with students of education particularly in mind, whether interested in education as a subject of critical study or out of a desire to work with children, young people or adults, perhaps as a teacher or education practitioner in schools or informal settings. The nature of the book has originated from our discussions about the role of philosophy in education, from our perspectives as tutors working with Education Studies students. We have taught on a range of different programmes and in a variety of higher education institutions. We also bring our experience of teaching in nurseries, schools, colleges and informal and community settings.

We have set out to offer an introduction to what we consider some of the most interesting, important or relevant topics in education. In philosophy concepts are contested, so we set out to open concepts up for exploration rather than define them. The intention is to give a flavour – but not a full digest of the topics, philosophers or works in question. The book is not designed to offer a full or representative history of philosophical ideas in education but to provide an introduction to a selection of leading philosophical thinkers and ideas.

A core idea driving our work and the approach of this book is that philosophising is an essential part of the practice of studying education. The ideas included here have emerged from and been tried out with our students. The material is designed to be engaging and a springboard to further reading and personal and collaborative enquiry. We aim to bring about a politicisation of students' experience in education, to encourage readers to move from personal opinions to informed positions that can be articulated as part of an ongoing dialogue with others in the field. As tutors we particularly relish those moments when our students get stuck into hearty discussion and contentious debate.

The selection of topics

Through our experience of working together on the Education Studies programme in our setting, as authors we chose to write chapters on particular topics or philosophers that have been significant in our teaching and thinking. The topics reflect our interests, research, professional expertise and other publications. It is our view that these chapters are highly pertinent to current and future Education Studies programmes. We have distinctive and complementary philosophical interests and knowledge that we bring to the text. All three authors are philosophers in education, through their scholarship/degree studies and professional backgrounds, committed to drawing on philosophy to enrich the study of education.

Our shared place of work has allowed the writing of this book to develop through our dialogue with one another and through our commitment to trying out a wide selection of the book material with students and redrafting the material on the basis of students' responses and feedback. The coherence of the book is achieved through this active approach to its creation and through our positioning as 'activist philosophers'. By this we mean educators who are seeking to apply philosophical ideas and methods in our teaching and in our professional and personal lives. There is a story behind each of the selections of chapters we have written. These reflect our professional lives in the teaching and development of a very dynamic Education Studies curriculum in our own establishment. We are fortunate to be part of what we believe to be a very distinctive programme – involving the study of formal, informal and life-long education. By playing to the interests, experience and strengths of staff, the programme has evolved to include studies of education in a wide variety of settings and explores enduring and contemporary themes. From this position we have created opportunities to draw on philosophical ideas and methods in our teaching. The work we include here emerges from the active theorising in which we engage with our students.

Melanie Parker's selection of chapters emerges from her education and community work with historically 'oppressed' groups including disabled people, refugees and asylum seekers, and people who are materially poor. It has been her quest to locate and deploy theories that illuminate and challenge inequalities. She seeks to question systems that favour a few over the many, in education and society. As a critical pedagogue, her goal is to bring about emancipation and social change.

The chapters written by Ken Gale have emerged from his ever-present activist tendencies. As a philosophy graduate of the 1960s, his scholarly, pedagogical and research-based intentions have been designed to trouble, question and subvert dominant and dominating educational theories, practices and policies. Consequently, his radical and creative tendencies have led to the selection included in this book.

Joanna Haynes' selection of chapters is shaped by her studies in philosophy and her interest in the theory and practice of philosophy with children. Her involvement over many years in inter-generational philosophical dialogues and exploring the methodology of collaborative communities of philosophical enquiry is connected to her broader research on the ethics of teaching and learning relationships, the education philosophy of Matthew Lipman and critical theories of dialogue and communicative action.

Using the book

This book brings philosophers, both past and contemporary, onto the educational stage to ask philosophical questions and carry out philosophical analyses of educational policy and practice. At the macro level, for example, Karl Marx might ask us to explain the economic and political forces at play in maintaining the hegemony of capitalist discourses today. At the micro level Foucault might be nudging us into thinking about the influence of technologies of the self.

The book can be used by individuals or tutors working with groups of students in class. We have set out to insist and rely on readers' engagement and participation in these discussions through a series of imaginative exercises and scenarios, to be carried out independently and in groups. Each chapter includes activities to help make sense of and interrogate our take on things. For us, the philosophy of education has consequences for action. Its role is integral to a research-based approach to teaching and learning. The final chapter opens up the potentially contentious concept of research and offers ideas and practices that can enrich Education Studies as scholarly activity.

There are a number of valuable texts introducing the philosophy of education and we have provided a short list of recommended introductory sources for students of education at the end of this book, in a brief section on further reading.

Reference

Ball, S. (1998) Intellectuals or Technicians? The Urgent Role of Theory in Educational Studies, *British Journal of Educational Studies* 43 (3): 255–71.

1

Enduring messages from utopias

Melanie Parker

Overview

This chapter aims to provide a conceptualisation of utopian and dystopian thinking. It also gives an overview of Plato's influence on education through his seminal work *The Republic*, which serves as a powerful example of utopian thinking and remains a legacy for education today. Finally, through the work of two very different scholars, I will be making a case for utopias, as a means to vision and change education for the better.[1]

Questions

- How can utopia and dystopia be used to help us think and re-vision?
- What role does utopia play in helping us understand knowledge?
- How can Plato's *Republic* illuminate the issues facing education today?

Welcome to utopia!

ACTIVITY 1

A good way to start thinking about utopia is by entering the term into Google Images. What sort of world is captured in the images displayed?

The concept of utopia has many different and contested meanings:

> There is a huge literature on utopianism, spanning fiction, literary criticism, political theory, philosophy, sociology, theology and architecture. Definitions are contested, or more frequently simply presumed or neglected. At its broadest, utopia may be defined as the expression of a desire for a better way of living, which may take many forms.

> (Levitas, 2013: 122)

Generally, utopia combines the ideas of good and no place. It is an imaginary perfect world, an expression of desire where possible alternative societies and transformational futures become realised. Bloch (1986) argued that the utopian impulse to long for and imagine a life otherwise is a natural human characteristic.

A traditional feature of utopia is that it represents an exemplary society projecting values and morals that elevate the whole of society. Generally credited with being one of the earliest utopias and certainly influencing many subsequent utopias was Plato's expansive narrative, *The Republic*, written in 373 BC. The title *Republic* represents a 'poor' translation of the Greek word, 'politeia' (Plato, 1998: xi), which basically means political and government system. Plato's *Republic* is more than just a political work as it also re-visions education and society, the results of which provide us with both a methodology and legacy for thinking about knowledge and learning today.

Plato – life and influences

> **ACTIVITY 2**
>
> For a great three-minute introduction to the impact of Plato:
> www.youtube.com/watch?v=q34MHpBu0Oo
>
> What arguments are given for Plato's enduring significance and relevance?

Plato was born to a noble family in Athens during 427 BC and grew up during the Peloponnesian War (431–404 BC), which was to engulf the whole civilised world in its turbulent struggle between democracy (Athens) and oligarchy (Sparta). In 399 the war ended with the restoration of democracy in Athens. By familial position Plato's political preferences would have leant towards oligarchy and this outlook would no doubt have been reinforced when this newly reformed democracy of Athens condemned Socrates, the decisive philosophical influence of Plato's life, to death. Socrates was charged with irreligion and corrupting the minds of the city's youth, and this charge marked an irreversible disenchantment in Plato with the democratic political system of Athens. In 388 BC, still interested in politics at the request of the tyrant rulers, Dionysius the elder and younger, Plato took a disastrous trip to Sicily to share his utopian philosophy for an ideal world. However, this conquest failed and Plato was forced to flee Sicily and return to Athens where he committed the rest of his life to philosophy. This included establishing a philosophical community in Athens known as the Academy, which attracted students and philosophers from across the Greek world and became both a research university and religious community – a transcendental *utopia* by intention and design! The term *transcendental* utopia refers to utopias that have been realised on earth. Richard Francis (2007) used the term to describe the New England community movement that undertook utopian experiments during the 1840s: Brook Farm, Fruitlands and Walden's community of one. Their attempts to reconcile the world with history, nature and their community represented a re-birth for utopia from metaphysical realms into contemporary reality.

Plato's *Republic* – enduring metaphors of interest

The structure of Plato's *Republic*

> Plato's ideas on the subject of education are living doctrines in constant use.
>
> (Brumbaugh, 2009: 95)

In this section we will be exploring some of Plato's key ideas relating to structure, knowledge and education in *The Republic. The Republic* is both a narrative and political monologue and Plato's key ideas are presented through analogy and metaphor, which require us to stop and think about their function and meaning. Later we will be applying some of Plato's key ideas contemporarily to explore their significance and relevance for us today. The final point I want to make is that *The Republic* is a rich, complex text and the following section gives the briefest of insights into some of his ideas. I would encourage all readers to go find and read Plato's *Republic*, because there is so much more to be discovered.

Platonic scholars (Rosen, 2005; Pappas, 2003) have identified the work as a treatise on justice and the human spirit and flourishing. However, I agree with Waterfield (1998) who states that the work requires a more encompassing term, like *morality*. This is because in *The Republic* morality represents and connects so many of Plato's key ideas like 'Morality is a good mental state, and that immorality is a bad state' (Plato, 373 BC/1998: 428).

Morality in the Platonic sense is not drawn from a singular individualist basis, but is actually considered in terms of the stability and good of the whole community: 'The happiness of the whole is more important than of any of its parts' (Plato, 373 BC/1998: 415).

Plato's social structure is formulated around ensuring the stability and continuity of the state and in some ways provides a striking similarity to today's system, which as we will be considering in Chapters 2 and 3 is in many ways formulated around sustaining the capitalist status quo. Also not unlike our social class system today, Plato achieves this stability by dividing the population of his republic into three classes, likening this tripartite structure of society to that of a tripartite psychology: 'We've reached the reasonable conclusion that the constituent categories of a community and of any individual's mind are identical in nature and number' (Plato, 373 BC/1998: 152).

ACTIVITY 3

What arguments is Plato putting forward through his connecting metaphor of the tripartite society and psychology?

Metaphors are a handy tool for philosophers; take a look at these slides:
http://slideshare.net/bcole/teachers-and-teaching-metaphors-presentation

See if you can you suggest any others relating to teaching and learning.

UNIVERSITY OF WINCHESTER
LIBRARY

Plato's views on morality, education and society depend considerably upon this tripartite psychology, which is primarily founded on the mind being split into the rational and non-rational:

> So it wouldn't be irrational of us to expect that these are two separate parts,' I said, 'one of which we can describe as rational, and the other as irrational and desirous. The first is responsible for the mind's capacity to think rationally and the second – which is an ally of certain satisfactions and pleasures.
>
> (Plato, 373 BC/1998: 440b)

From these two parts Plato identifies three main sources of motivation that manifest themselves in individuals. First, there is a desire to satisfy basic instincts; second, there is the desire for oneself, which can show itself through anger, courage, sexual desire and the like; and finally there is a desire for truth and understanding. Each part of the mind has cognitive skills, such as recognising hunger and holding beliefs and views, but only the most rational part of the mind can express the sort of reason that imparts pure truth and understanding. Synonymous with this analogy of the mind is the metaphor of the human form as representative of the political and social (class) structure. The workers form the body and limbs of the state; the auxiliaries its heart; and philosophers its head. As Plato's philosophers are the only social class that have all three dimensions of Plato's tripartite psychology, it therefore falls to them to rule as they have 'gained a clear enough impression of the madness of the masses. . . .' (Plato, 373 BC/1998: 219). To ensure stability and continuity in Plato's republic it is necessary for the majority of the population to remain in their given social class. The philosopher rulers therefore 'lie for the good of the community' (Plato, 373 BC/1998: 83) and Plato presents this as a 'noble lie':

> We'll continue by telling them . . . God included gold in the mixture when he was forming those of you who have what it takes to be rulers (which is why rulers have the greatest privileges), silver when he was forming the auxiliaries, iron and copper when he was forming the farmers and other workers.
>
> (Plato, 373 BC/1998: 415a)

Despite the 'noble lie', there are opportunities for social mobility through talent and intellect, which is rather similar to our contemporary aspirations to meritocracy.

> If a child born to a worker or a farmer has a nature tinged with gold or silver, they should honour it and elevate it to the rank of either guardian or auxiliary, because of an oracle which states that the community will be destroyed when it has copper or iron guardian.
>
> (Plato, 373 BC/1998: 415 c–d)

You may well be sceptical of the presumed intellect of the philosopher kings, who knowingly accept a '(noble) lie' without question, but this links to the earlier idea of the role of morality in ensuring the continuation of a stable society.

Knowledge and education in *The Republic*

The notion of human flourishing is at the heart of the education system in *The Republic*. The first responsibility of the philosopher kings lies with protecting the 'plasticity' of the young souls from false and ignoble beliefs for fear the young will assimilate themselves with the worst kind of model of morality, which would weaken their reason and character:

> if young men of our community hear this kind of thing and take it seriously, rather than regarding it as despicable and absurd, they're hardly going to regard such behaviour as despicable in human beings like themselves and feel remorse when they also find themselves saying or doing these or similar things. Instead, they won't find it at all degrading to be constantly chanting laments and dirges for trivial incidents, and they won't resist doing so.
>
> (Plato, 373 BC/1998: 388d)

ACTIVITY 4

Do you think the recent evidence from the American Psychological Association (2013) (www.apa.org/research/action/protect.aspx) which suggests the behaviour of children and young people is influenced and shaped by computer games and television is an example of Plato's notion of plasticity of the young soul?

What do you think the impact of television and computer games is upon their reason and character?

Do you think educational policy and the curriculum have a role in shaping the reason and character of the young soul?

The point that Plato is making is that the arts have a definite function in the development of character, which in turn shapes the society we have as a result. Similarly, and in the same way that simplicity and temperance in the arts produce a rational healthy mind, sport and gymnastics produce a healthy body, which has a preventative role in combating sickness in the physical body and spiritual soul. This is a significant point, as Plato's notions of the ideal and well-rounded human being also function as a broader metaphor for his ideal education system and society.

We are beginning to see a Platonic curriculum emerging, which is made up of dimensions, sports and arts similar to what we have today. However, I would argue that it is Plato's claims for knowledge that are most illuminating, as they act as a methodology for exploring the type of knowledge we have today. The 'noble lie' apart, Plato's knowledge is based on truth, reality and authenticity, which requires rejecting unsubstantiated claims and accepting things at face value. This he identifies as the difference between holding *beliefs* rather than having true *knowledge*.

Plato argued that true knowledge comes from the principles and properties of ideas. Properties of ideas are drawn from their nature and essence, which are enduring and provide us with a fixed basis of how to understand them. For example, I might call my daughter beautiful, because of our mutual love and understanding, but I couldn't then use this description to describe the idea of beautiful itself, because beauty is not a property of my daughter alone, but of all beautiful things. To be able to make these distinctions Plato argues we need to look and see from a true unclouded vision, which actually comes from goodness. Once again this connects to Plato's ideas of morality, which we met at the beginning of this section, and in the same way that the sun generates light, growth and seeing, goodness is the origin of truth and reality, which generates sight through true knowledge.

The sun is the child of goodness I was talking about, then. It is a counterpart to its father, goodness. As goodness stands in the intelligible realm and the things we know, so in the visible realm the sun stands to sight and the things we see.

(Plato, 373 BC/1998: 508c)

Plato uses the simile of the sun to further illustrate his point about beliefs, which can only provide a partial sight, as they do not provide true enlightenment. Note how in the quote below Plato uses the simile of the sun to liken the loss of sight in darkness to a dimming of the mind and soul:

Well, here's how you can think about the mind as well. When its object is something which is lit up by truth and reality, then it has – and obviously has – intelligent awareness and knowledge. However, when its object is permeated with darkness (that is, when its object is something which is subject to generation and decay), then it has beliefs and is less effective, because its beliefs chop and change under these circumstances it comes across devoid of intelligence.

(Plato, 373 BC/1998: 508d)

The distinction between belief and knowledge is further expounded through Plato's analogy of the divided line. Plato describes an unequally divided line with each part re-divided. The top two divisions relate to the application of reason and intellect, which in turn correspond to goodness and enlightenment. The bottom two divisions relate to beliefs in the temporal world, which are merely understood at face value and without any true application of the mind.

ACTIVITY 5

Take a look at the following links:

www.mc.maricopa.edu/~barsp59601/graph/charts/dividedline.jpg

www.hermes-press.com/dialectic_being.htm

These provide a pictorial representation of the analogy of the divided line. What points do you think Plato is making in terms of beliefs and true knowledge?

Rosen (2005) provides a useful way of understanding the relationship between the simile of the sun and the analogy of the lines. He states that the simile is primarily ontological (Plato's cognitive position) and the analogy is epistemological (the knowledge constructed as a result). He identifies that human life is missing from these two metaphors and that this final element is secured in the cave analogy.

Analogy of the cave

Plato describes a cave in which humans are chained by the neck and ankle from birth facing a wall. On the other side of the wall are puppet masters who carry 'all sorts of artefacts' (Plato, 373 BC/1998: 515b) that cast shadows on the wall in front of the prisoners who mistake these shadows to be reality binding them to the lowest experience of the divided line analogy. The chains represent a shackling of the mind and soul from which a prisoner becomes released by nature. Once released, he is drawn immediately to the light of a fire as his psyche slowly sharpens and his vision develops from seeing shadows and reflections to discerning objects both natural and artificial of the visible domain (reality) and onwards towards sunlight and its associated knowledge and goodness: 'If you think of the upward journey and the sight of things on the surface of the earth as the mind's ascent to the intelligible realm, you won't be wrong' (Plato, 373 BC/1998: 517b).

However, we learn that should the ex-prisoner descend back into the cave, he would be blinded by the lack of sun and unable to discern the shadows that occupy the captives, who would ridicule and threaten his failure. This imagery has been constructed to show the radical discontinuity between everyday life and wisdom. Metaphorically speaking, those who do not seek liberation from their bondage remain with their thoughts and minds shackled in darkness. However, those who have 'made the ascent and see goodness' (Plato, 373 BC/1998: 519c) have experienced 'the reorientation of the mind from a kind of twilight to true daylight and this orientation is an ascent to reality or in other words true philosophy' (Plato, 373 BC/1998: 512d).

ACTIVITY 6

To illustrate the points made above, listen to the following commentary of the cave analogy: www.youtube.com/watch?v=UQfRdl3GTw4

Over the years, I have enjoyed sharing this commentary with the students that I work with and we have had fun applying it contemporarily. Students have likened the puppet masters to modern-day politicians who are confining what young people learn to the political and economic aims of the day! Another group likened the shadows to the images cast by television and computer games far removed from reality and a distraction from the real pursuit of learning.

It is fair to say that the cave analogy is used to illustrate the effect of knowledge and education upon our being. Our power to learn is like that of the ex-prisoner: within our soul. It is necessary to break the shackles that contain us to move our whole body towards the light and its brightest part, goodness. Turning the soul around begins the process of philosophy to enable the realisation of Plato's *Republic* – the blueprint for an ideal society.

What does Plato's *Republic* mean for education and society today?

In applying some of the ideas from Plato's *Republic* contemporarily, we have a methodology for diagnosing the ills and challenges facing education and society today. In *The Republic*, morality is based upon unity of the state, but this is a faulty stability formed out of a ('noble') lie. Equally faulty is neoliberal capitalism, the contemporary 'noble lie' that attempts to provide a stability of almost global proportions; a stability that manages to keep the poorest poor through third-world debt, and in the UK elicits an unquestioning loyalty and apathy from its citizens during a recession (2014) that reduces the basic rate of tax for the very rich and allows cuts to public services that leave society's most vulnerable at risk (*The Guardian*, 2011: www.theguardian.

com/society/patrick-butler-cuts-blog/2011/may/12/cutswatch-help-us-tell-the-momentous-story-of-the-cuts). Furthermore, contemporary mainstream education does little to challenge such notions and beliefs, far too preoccupied with educating the contemporary 'noble lie', neoliberal capitalism. 'Employability' and 'links and partnerships with business' have become the accepted language and pursuit of higher education, and are also increasingly emerging in secondary and primary education as commercial corporations move in to run our schools.

Plato saw the physical human body as a representation of society; contemporarily this body has become weakened by inactivity and gluttonous excesses like binge drinking, smoking and obesity, which diagnose a sickly and deteriorating society – a metaphor that can be extended to represent global warming and environmental decay.

Plato was determined to point out the properties behind knowledge as being true reality and not those that we would identify as resonating from inauthenticity. He teaches us to think about beauty in terms of a concept that can be applied to all beautiful things and not as something unstable and shifting that can be determined by popularist notions of the day. Therefore, contemporary thinking appears to be at odds with true Platonic knowledge with our ideas of beauty being constructed from the high-profile celebrities of the moment like WAGs (wives and girlfriends of sportsmen) and pop and film stars, whose reinvented looks and air-brushed appearances seem far removed from 'ordinary' people. Society's obsession with recreating and copying celebrities' 'look(s)' and lifestyles has made these individuals the accepted role models for today's society – a realisation of Plato's foresight, ' . . . they're deluded into imagining that they're true statesmen simply because the masses think highly of them . . . ' (Plato, 373 BC/1998: 426e).

This exposes the contemporary human condition as being confined and restricted by affectation. In the same way as the cave analogy presents its prisoners shackled to the walls, seeing only the shadows in front of them cast by the puppet masters and believing this to be reality, we have become shackled to the darkness by the puppet masters of popular and virtual culture. The views depicted by the tabloids, television and computer games now form our basis of reality. If, like the prisoner in the cave, we seek freedom from this, we face ridicule from mainstream thinking and society.

Finally, and in the spirit of Marx, we have not moved so far from Plato's social class-based education system – the higher the class, the better the educational opportunities! Contemporary independent schools remain accessible only to a few; middle-class/upper working-class education is purchased by postcode; and the lower/working classes have no other option but to take what is made available to them. These urgent analyses are revealed to us using a utopian methodology, Platonic thinking, as a way of critically exploring contemporary education and society.

The legacy of Plato and utopia

Jean-Jacques Rousseau's educational utopia *Emile* (1762) visions a different type of education process, formulated around an anthropological approach to pedagogical freedom, which has non-intervention and self-direction at the heart of the educational process. This would have provided a stark alternative to the more common instrumental approaches of the day. Like Plato, Rousseau has provided us with both an educational legacy still relevant and in place today, based on a student-centred rather than subject or teacher-centred ethos, involving self-discovery and experimentation and like Plato, a methodology for critiquing existing and current educational systems. See Chapter Ten on 'Philosophy's children' for further discussion of his ideas.

ACTIVITY 7

Plato's *Republic* and Rousseau's *Emile* are both concerned with the creation of an 'ideal' education system. What would your ideal education system be? What would be the foci of your curriculum? What kind (if any) of assessment would you have? What would the environment be like? Would it be a school? Who would attend? Who would provide the teaching/facilitation? How would the classrooms/learning spaces be organised (age, gender, diversity)? What pedagogical approaches would be deployed? What would be the ethos of the education system?

By examining your education system, what does it tell us about existing systems in the UK?

Dystopia, the underside of utopia

So far in exploring utopian writing we have explored places or ideas that are generally considered as ideals by their authors. However, utopia has a dark underside known as dystopia. Classical dystopian texts include: Aldous Huxley's *Brave New World* (1932), George Orwell's *Nineteen Eighty-Four* (1949) and Margaret Atwood's *The Handmaid's Tale* (1985). These stories are of totalitarian states and sites of universal despair and are far removed from the societies striving for the educational and human flourishing presented in Plato's *Republic* and Rousseau's *Emile*.

However, at this juncture it is important to make two points about the concepts of utopia and dystopia. First, determining what is utopia and what is dystopia is often merely a matter of personal opinion! The second point is that there is often an ambiguity between what is utopia and dystopia. This is a deliberate juxtaposition and disguise by the author who seeks to use this juxtaposition as a methodology for critical illumination, which is what we will be exploring next in this chapter, through *Summer in Algiers* (1955) by Albert Camus.

Summer in Algiers is similar to *The Republic* in that it explores the human condition and capacity for flourishing. Camus, an existentialist, uses rich visual and symbolic imagery to present a normalised perfect world:

> In Algiers one loves the commonplace: the sea at the end of every street, a certain volume of sunlight, the beauty of the race . . . Here, at least, man is gratified in every wish and, sure of his desires, can at least measure his possessions.
>
> (Camus, 1955: 1)

However, the juxtaposition comes from this ideal utopian environment, which in actual fact obscures the real 'absurdity' of the human condition, 'one has to live in Algiers for some time to realize how paralysing an excess of nature's bounty can be. There is nothing here whoever would learn, educate himself, or better himself' (Camus, 1955: 2). The notion of the 'absurd' in Camus' writing reflects the fundamental disharmony and tragic incompatibility in our existence. On the one hand we live in a seemingly perfect and prosperous society, but when we examine things closer we realise the human condition is not based on the authenticity and truth that Plato associated with true knowledge, but instead a superficiality and ignorance, which Plato would identify as belief. This comes from being conditioned by the dominant political, cultural and educational thinking of the day; and the ultimate absurdity for Camus is our unquestioning acceptance of this situation.

ACTIVITY 8

To illustrate the above point further, listen to the prophetic dystopia, Zooropa (1993) by U2. Available at: www.youtube.com/watch?v=wlPGlDm-Bvc

Similarly to Camus' *Summer in Algiers* (1955), Zooropa provides a phenomenological description of the absurdity of modern life by channelling the medium of European television into techno music, creating a nihilistic commentary on consumerism and commercialism. Reminiscent of Plato, it acknowledges the power and influence of 'representational' culture (i.e. poetry, painting and songs) in persuading and shaping minds.

Utopian positioning and visioning

The above discussion of utopia and dystopia shows how the field of utopian studies has developed into an 'eclectic' (Goodwin, 2001: 1) rather than an esoteric field of academia. It is not only us with our interest in philosophy and education, but sociologists, artists, architects, musicians and economists who have used the genre to critique the existing status quo by exploring and visioning different forms and alternatives, which makes it a vibrant but impossible field to define.

The following section will continue with the general themes of education, politics and society to consider the use of utopia in the work of Ruth Levitas and David Halpin. Like Albert Camus and U2, Ruth Levitas is critical of capitalism and consumerism, which has shaped our education system and society. She seeks to transform knowledge and society to create a fairer UK; this is her utopian project. David Halpin is more tolerant of capitalism and consumerism and his utopian project is based upon bringing a 'utopian imagination' (Halpin, 2005) to education and society.

David Halpin – 'The role of the (grounded) utopian imagination'

I have sought to articulate a conception of education that links it inexorably with the idea of hope, indicating concurrently the degree to which a distinctive vocabulary of optimism about schooling and teaching and learning is capable of being fostered through specific exercises of the utopian imagination.

(Halpin, 2005: 1)

David Halpin's work sets out to explore the significance of hope and the utopian reflection in an educational climate of 'social, moral and educational despair and disaffection' (Carr, 2004: 373). In 2010 *The Guardian* reported that nearly half of newly qualified teachers are leaving the profession (www.theguardian.com/education/2010/nov/16/teaching-problem-schools). Therefore, Halpin's utopian project appears to be urgently required. Halpin's utopian impulses are underpinned by love (2003a) and heroism (2010), yet he is keen to avoid utopianism's more coercive and provocative associations and instead adopts a 'utopian realist' (Webb, 2009: 743) approach, which confronts an education system affected by the inevitable bedfellows of capitalism, marketisation and managerialism, with a utopian imagination that is grounded in the current context, reasonableness and practicality. Thus his utopian vision deliberately avoids the totalitarian blueprint advocated by Plato. Instead he subscribes to incremental social and educational reforms with an emphasis on creating 'a more equal and more democratic education system and society' (Halpin, 2003b: 5).

> hard answers to the more difficult questions about education can be envisaged through exercises of the utopian imagination. Such positive imaginings, which seek to relativise and offer a critique of the present, by conjuring images of alternative futures, provide both an antidote to depressive inaction and prompt to think progressively about and act for the better upon one's world.
>
> (Halpin, 2003b: 16)

ACTIVITY 9

Can you think of a time when a 'utopian imagination' (Halpin, 2005) would have helped you through a difficult period or a challenging educational practice?

Furthermore, Halpin provides four illustrative examples of possible and successful utopian projects. These include, first, 'a reformed curriculum' (Halpin, 2009: 763) based around enabling children to live a good life rather than the economic priorities of government; second, Tim Brighouse's collegiate approach to secondary education that engages all the current secondary education providers (state, independent) in pooling expertise and resources in one new re-visioned comprehensive approach; third, a case study of a 'dynamic headteacher' (Halpin, 2009: 763) in the West Midlands who re-conceives a leadership approach based on mutual trust, respect and support rather than managerialism and performativity; and finally, 'cited as a utopian exercise in spatial organisation' (Webb, 2009: 745), the award-winning 'space-age' building design of Great Notley Primary School in Essex, which marks utopia's ongoing engagement with architecture (Halpin, 2007; Levitas, 2013).

However, I would argue that David Halpin's vision of hope and utopianism has its limitations, which are the 'limits placed on imagination by historical and institutional contexts' (Levitas, 2004: 269). David Halpin's ready acceptance of neoliberal capitalist policy inhibits the radical visions and possibilities usually associated with a utopian imagination. It also fails to expose and challenge the power relations that exist in society, which is a fundamental part of critical education. Other critical responses (Webb, 2009) have accused his realist approach to utopia as being 'oxymoronic' (Webb, 2009: 746).

Wherever you stand on the efficacy of David Halpin's utopian realism, it can provide a type of 'militant optimism' to what can be difficult situations and circumstances in education. I think we could all benefit from deploying a utopian imagination from time to time!

Ruth Levitas – 'Utopia as method'[2]

> My own interest in utopia (and indeed sociology) has always been driven by the conviction that the world could and should be other than it is.
>
> (Levitas, 2000: 26)

In this section we will be exploring Ruth Levitas' ongoing political and social engagement with utopia, which has come to determine both her ontological position and methodological application. The concept of utopia has shaped both the knowledge and application she has deployed in her research and writing for over thirty years. The utopian project Ruth Levitas engages in is future orientated and politically and socially motivated:

> I am still searching for a route to a just and sustainable future. And as part of this critical or even utopian project the idea of an inclusive society might yet inform a further more radical discourse and even, eventually a more radical politics.
>
> (Levitas, 2005a: 6)

Levitas' application of the utopian form is far removed from Halpin's 'militant optimism'. Instead, her method is more critical and sociopolitical to expose and 'address more effectively the major problems that confront us' (Levitas, 2005b: 15). Indeed, Levitas' utopian method has been deployed in varying political and social contexts that she has found herself working in and has been primarily informed by her ongoing political economic and social engagement. In 1999 she became part of the team that undertook the Poverty and Social Exclusion survey of Britain (PSE). This survey represented the most comprehensive review of poverty and social exclusion ever undertaken in Britain at that time. The survey measured poverty in terms of deprivation from goods, services and activities considered necessary to live an everyday life. The survey linked directly to the new labour government's own utopian visioning to eradicate child poverty and reduce social exclusion through increased participation with the labour market and of course the authors' own utopian visions for reducing national and international poverty:

> The UK Government and others have committed themselves to the aim of eliminating poverty throughout the world during the twenty-first century. The UK Government has a key role to play not only by investigating and putting policies in place to reduce poverty but by influencing scientific standards of investigation, analysis of causes and reduction of poverty in other parts of the world.
>
> (Gordon et al., 2000: 68)

Critical utopian approach

However, Levitas was soon to replace these utopian aspirations for the new labour government with a more critical utopian approach, which was to realise her earlier prophecy that 'the Labour Party is less utopian in office than in opposition' (Levitas, p. 28, 1979). Furthermore, it demonstrated how her methodological engagement with utopia adapts according to the different social and economic conditions of the time. Thus her subsequent work reveals a more sceptical response to the visioning of new labour than that of the authors of the PSE (1999):

> In Blair's fantasy land, the rich deserve their wealth and are not resented. The poor have presumably abolished themselves through the saving grace of working in McDonald's and call centres, ventures indirectly subsidised through tax credits. Children have stopped playing truant partly through fear of police sweeps, and partly because they understand the consequences of educational failure. Teenagers

do not have unprotected sex. People accept their obligation to maintain their employability, so that they can exploit the changing opportunities provided by markets, make individual provision against risk, discharge their obligations as parents and active citizens when they have done earning a living. (They are too tired to protest on May Day, and know anyway that all demonstrators are anarchists, meaning mindless thugs, or anti-capitalists, meaning much the same.) Continuing growth ensures a rising tax take without increased tax rates. Public funds can thus be used to underwrite essential services, mainly contracted out to the private sector where successful businesses (or, increasingly, multi-national concerns) make profits subsidised out of taxation.

(Levitas, 2001: 459)

Like me, you may be struck by the relevance of the description of 'Blair's fantasy land' fifteen years on, and despite the change to a coalition government, Levitas claims the social situation has deteriorated further:

The formation of the Coalition government in 2010 has resulted in unprecedented spending cuts presented as necessary austerity, together with the promotion of the 'Big Society' as the panacea for social ills. This article argues that the cuts continue a thirty-year process of redistribution to the rich.

(Levitas, 2012: 320)

ACTIVITY 10

Summarise the main points Levitas is making from the two quotes above, which provide a social and political picture of the last fifteen years in the UK.
    What part do you think education has to play in responding to the points you have made?

Although Levitas' utopian vision adapted to fit the political outcomes of the day, her overarching utopian aim remains fixed upon transformation through the eradication of poverty and social exclusion:

I wanted, and still want, the world to be changed. Our current social arrangements condemn most of the world's population to poverty and premature death, and subject even those of us who are very affluent to forms of alienation, repression, competition and separation from each other, which are incompatible with a full human existence.

(Levitas and Sargisson, 2003: 13)

Furthermore, unlike Halpin's compliant approach, her visioning of such a society requires the overhaul of existing economic and political systems:

. . . a vision of a good society needs to use a more utopian method, in the sense that it needs to define the principles of such a society independently of short term politics, and without the assumption that a good society is in fact, compatible with global (or any other kind of) capitalism.

(Levitas, 2004: 69)

Positioning on utopias/dystopias

Ruth Levitas' utopian project seeks radical social change to end social exclusion, establish equality and mark the end of national and international poverty. Her utopian methodology exposes the shortcomings of politics and economics in achieving this, but like so many utopian imaginings, could be accused of being 'fanciful' and 'unrealistic' (Webb, 2009: 746). Furthermore, there is no engagement with the moral implications of the process for achieving the desired utopian outcome, which would inevitably represent suppression for some social groups and a threat to the equality she intends utopia to bring. Utopias, like those imagined by Levitas, Plato and Rousseau, are expressions of dreams for an improved political, social and educational process. However, it is from this position of dreaming, rather than realising, that the troubles stem, because whether it is Karl Marx's communism or Plato's perfect society, utopias rarely consider the process, implications and human and economic cost of realising their vision. They simply provide 'a blueprint' (Popper, 1990: 166) of an ideal alternative state that generally requires the mass reconstruction of society as a whole.

Ruth Levitas' aims for her utopian project are admirable, her work and research into utopianism, politics, poverty and social exclusion is extensive, and her future-orientated projects have commendable social aims. David Halpin's intention is to bring the utopian imagination to education, which he sees as an intrinsically hopeful and transformational process. Furthermore, like Plato, Rousseau and Camus, what they have in common is a commitment to the utopian methodology as a process that goes some way to re-imagining and transforming education and society from current conditions. This is similar to my aspirations for education which I will be sharing with you in Chapter 3, 'Critical and revolutionary pedagogies', which leads me to ask: what will be your utopian project?

Notes

1 This chapter draws from my thesis, Utopias of Education, in which I argued urgently for utopias to have a place in contemporary education and society, as a response to capitalist agendas and priorities.
2 This phrase comes from Ruth Levitas' book title *Utopia as Method: The Imaginary Reconstitution of Society* published by Palgrave Macmillan in 2013.

References

Bloch, E. (1986) *The Principle of Hope*, Cambridge, MA: MIT Press.
Brumbaugh, R. S. (2009) The Republic Afterword in Cahn, S. M. (2009) *Philosophy of Education*, London: Routledge.
Camus, A. (1955) *Summer in Algiers*, London: Penguin Short Classics.
Carr, D. (2004) Book Reviews, *Cambridge Journal of Education*, 34: 3, 373–81.
Francis, R. (2007) *Transcendental Utopias: Individual and Community at Brook Farm, Fruitlands, and Walden*, New York: Cornell University Press.
Goodwin, B. (2001) *The Philosophy of Utopia*, London: Routledge.
Gordon, D., Levitas, R., Pantazis, C., Patsios, D., Payne, S., Townsend, P., Adelman, L., Ashworth, K., Middleton, S., Bradshaw, J. and Williams, J. (2000) *Poverty and Social Exclusion in Britain*. York: Joseph Rowntree Foundation.

The Guardian (16 November 2010) Why are New Teachers Leaving in Droves? Available at: www.theguardian.com/education/2010/nov/16/teaching-problem-schools [Accessed on 6 July 2014].

The Guardian (12 May 2011) Cutswatch: Help Us Tell the Momentous Story of the Cuts. Available at: www.theguardian.com/society/patrick-butler-cuts-blog/2011/may/12/cutswatch-help-us-tell-the-momentous-story-of-the-cuts [Accessed on 6 July 2014].

Halpin, D. (2003a) Hope, Utopianism and Educational Renewal', the Encyclopedia of Informal Education. Available at: www.infed.org/biblio/hope.htm [Accessed on 16 March 2014]. (A fuller version of this paper was presented at Charterhouse School, 6 January 2003.)

Halpin, D. (2003b) *Hope and Education – The Role of the Utopian Imagination*, London: RoutledgeFalmer.

Halpin, D. (2005) Search for the Hero Inside Yourself: Why a Romantic Conception of Education Matters (Professorial Lecture) in Parker, M. (2011) Utopias of Education, Doctoral Thesis University of Sheffield.

Halpin, D. (2006) Why a Romantic Conception of Education Matters, *Oxford Review of Education*, 32 (3): 325–45.

Halpin, D. (2007) Utopian Spaces of 'Robust Hope': The Architecture and Nature of Progressive Learning Environments, *Asia-Pacific Journal of Teacher Education*, 35 (3): 243–55.

Halpin, D. (2009) Pedagogy and Romantic Love, *Pedagogy, Curriculum and Society*, 17 (1): 89–102.

Halpin, D. (2010) Heroism and Pedagogy, *Pedagogies*, 3 (3): 265–74.

Levitas, R. (1979) Sociology and Utopia, *Sociology*, 13 (1): 19–33.

Levitas, R. (2000) For Utopia: (The Limits of the) Utopian Function in Late Capitalist Society in Goodwin, B. (2000) *The Philosophy of Utopia*, London: Routledge.

Levitas, R. (2001) Against Work: A Utopian Incursion into Social Policy, *Critical Social Policy*, 21: 449–65.

Levitas, R. (2004) Hope and Education, *Journal of Philosophy of Education*, 38 (2): 269–73.

Levitas, R. (2005a) *The Inclusive Society? Social Exclusion and New Labour*, Basingstoke: Palgrave Macmillan.

Levitas, R. (2005b) The Imaginary Reconstitution of Society or Why Sociologists and Others Should Take Utopia More Seriously, Inaugural Lecture, University of Bristol.

Levitas, R. (2012) The Just's Umbrella: Austerity and the Big Society in Coalition Policy and Beyond, *Critical Social Policy*, 32: 320–42.

Levitas, R. (2013) *Utopia as Method: The Imaginary Reconstitution of Society*, Basingstoke: Palgrave Macmillan.

Levitas, R. and Sargisson, L. (2003) Utopia in Dark Times: Optimism/Pessimism and Utopia/Dystopia in Baccoline, R. and Moylan, T. (2003) *Dark Horizons Science Fiction and the Dystopian Imagination*, London: Routledge.

Pappas, N. (2003) *Plato and the Republic*, London: Routledge.

Plato (373 BC/1998) *The Republic*, translated by R. Waterfield, Oxford: Oxford World Classics.

Popper, K. (1990) *The Open Society and Its Enemies: Volume Two: Hegel and Marx*, London: Routledge.

Rosen, S. (2005) *Plato's Republic – A Study*, London: Yale University Press.

Rousseau, J. J. (1762/2003) *Emile*, London: Everyman.

Webb, D. (2009) Where's the Vision? The Concept of Utopia in Contemporary Educational Theory, *Oxford Review of Education*, 35 (6): 743–60.

2

Structures of education and society
Karl Marx and Marxism
Melanie Parker

Overview

> Philosophy is the head of human emancipation and the proletariat is its heart.
>
> (Marx, 1845)

The philosophy of Karl Marx is often received as problematic due to the political failure associated with communism and the subsequent and meteoric rise and dominance of capitalism. However, this chapter espouses that Karl Marx's work and in this instance, *Capital* (1867), does not merely provide observations on politics and economics, but an examination of the impact of capitalism and the arising struggle upon the modern world. *Capital* requires us to ask questions of the structures of education and society that we have in place as a result of this. This chapter explores the implications of such structures upon humanisation and social being. Later in the chapter we will be exploring the work of Marxist scholars Louis Althusser, Antonio Gramsci and Jacques Derrida to deconstruct capitalism and rethink education and society today.

QUESTIONS

- What is the relevance of Marxism for education and society today?
- How does deploying a Marxist lens help us to understand the consequences of capitalism?
- How will you be taking Marxist thinking forward?

Introduction

You may well be sceptical of the relevance of a scholar writing nearly 150 years ago, but like many others, I would argue that Karl Marx is a thinker for the world today. His work poses critical questions and revolutionary alternatives and projects that are highly relevant to contemporary education and society. Indeed, Terry Eagleton (2011) observes:

> There is a sense in which the whole of Marx's writing boils down to several embarrassing questions: Why is it that the capitalist West has accumulated more resources than human history has ever witnessed, yet appears powerless to overcome poverty, starvation, exploitation, and inequality? What are the mechanisms by which affluence for a minority seem to breed hardship and indignity for the many? Why does private wealth seem to go hand in hand with public squalor? Or is it more plausible to maintain that there is something in the nature of capitalism itself, which generates deprivation and inequality . . . ?
>
> (Eagleton, 2011: B7)

These questions couldn't be more pertinent at the current time and this chapter attempts to tackle these issues, as it is important for those who care about education and society to understand the work of Karl Marx and not retreat from challenging hegemonic orthodoxies that allow inequality, social exclusion and poverty to prevail. Anyon (2011), reading Marx, claims that 'capitalism is a primary source of systematic, social, economic and educational inequality' (Anyon, 2011: 5). It is therefore imperative to reconsider and re-vision any system that does not promote social and educational justice. Therefore, I would argue that everyone should be reading Marx, as a timeless revolutionary thinker advocating an education system for social justice.

Marx undertook a very close analysis and investigation into capitalism and this chapter represents my favourite bits from his extensive writing. These have developed and shaped my own knowledge and understanding and contributed to how I position myself within and understand the world. Marxism, to me, is a 'lived' (Althusser, 2005: 10) philosophy, and in this chapter I will be actively engaging with key ideas from his writing and re-presenting them in terms of education and society today. In sharing some of my thinking with you, I hope to demonstrate the Marxist lens that I bring to my day-to-day life. You will see later in the chapter that it is not only me who makes claims for the timeliness and relevance of Marx today, and we will be exploring some of these perspectives later on as well. Therefore, I hope you will engage with this chapter in an open, critical and reflexive way and use it to rethink, reconsider and re-vision the education system and society that we have today.

Marx's life and works

Before we get started on some of Marx's key ideas, I think it is important to share three significant contextual points with you. First, I will present a brief biography of Marx's life and in doing so I hope to give you a few insights into the experiences and influences that were to shape his writing. Karl Marx was born in 1818 in Trier, Rhineland and was the eldest son in a family of eight children. He attended the University of Berlin from 1836 until 1841 to study philosophy. In 1842 he was appointed editor of the newspaper *Rheinische Zeitung*, which brought him into conflict with the government through his criticism of social conditions and the existing political structures. In 1843 he resigned from the newspaper and moved to Paris, where he met and married Jenny Von Westphalen with whom he was later to have six children (sadly, three died during childhood).

In 1844 Marx met Friedrich Engels, with whom he began a lifelong collaboration. During this period Marx's radicalism became recognisably communistic to the point that his revolutionary analysis in 1845 led to him being ordered to leave Paris. Settling in Brussels, he wrote *Theses on Feuerbach* and *The German Ideology* as well as organising Communist Correspondence Committees in a number of European cities. This led to the development of the Communist League and the writing of the *Communist Manifesto* with Engels. 1848 marked the Year of Revolutions and Marx was forced to leave Brussels, returning first to Paris and then to the Rhineland. While in Cologne he set up and edited the *Neue Rheinische Zeitung*, which led in 1849 to him being arrested and tried on an incitement to armed insurrection, a charge for which he was found guilty; he was then expelled from Germany. Marx spent the remainder of his life in London, arriving in 1849 and living in poverty until he died in 1883. *Capital* formed the focus of his intellectual work during these years. The first part was published in 1867 with parts two and three published posthumously in 1885 and 1894 by his lifelong friend and collaborator, Engels.

Karl Marx's work is often criticised as being gender-blind (in terms of women)[1] and 'unreadable', but I would argue that this is typical of the historical period and does not make his work any less relevant. The point is to embrace the effort and try and get beyond the challenge of the language, as the insights his work brings makes it well worth the trouble! I hope to further convince you of this later in the chapter when we will be working with some Marxist scholars to apply some of his ideas to contemporary educational and societal contexts. Further, I think it is important to acknowledge that my methodological approach for this chapter could be considered an 'epistemological break' (Marx, 1845 in Althusser, 2005: 28) with traditional philosophy, seeking objectivity through the sort of *true* knowledge Plato espoused in Chapter 1. This chapter acknowledges Chapter 6 and the Deleuzian notion of creativity, in which philosophy is part of a continuous process of inquiry and expression. Others have also contended that 'strictly speaking, Marxist philosophy is not to be found in Marx's writing, but emerged retrospectively, as a more general and more abstract reflection on the meaning, principles and universal significance of his work' (Balibar, 2007: 2). Therefore, and after Derrida, Gramsci and Althusser, who brought their own unique interpretations to the writings of Karl Marx, this chapter attempts to go beyond orthodox interpretations to apply many of the writings and commentaries of and on Marx to explore contemporary education and society.

Karl Marx on capitalism

In this section, I will outline Karl Marx's theory of capitalism, which will form the basis of our subsequent discussions. This is because the ideas Marx presents through capitalism expose the acute inequalities that have to exist for this economic system to prevail. Furthermore, Marx identified capitalism as an overwhelming force that does not stop at economics but infiltrates every part of human life. Therefore, a significant consequence of capitalism is that it 'creates a world after its own image' (Marx and Engels, 1848: 7), and education is invariably part of this world. As comrades passionate about education, we should be aware of our possible or future part in capitalism's ongoing reign!

First, let us consider what a world created in the image of capitalism actually looks like. I think McLaren and Farahmandpur's (2002) description can help us here:

> Mesmerized by the scent of money, we wilfully ignore the ramifications of capitalism's current flight; its elimination of multiple layers of management, administration

and production; and processes such as deindustrialization, the ascendancy of financial and speculative capital, the expansion of transnational circuits of migrant workers, and the casualization of the labour force. We ignore the monopolies, the oligopolies, the cartels, the new corporate carpetbaggers, the prophets of privatization, the Wal-Martization of the global lifeworld, and the transfer of capital investments to cheaper markets offering higher rates of exploitation. We pretend we don't see the reduced social expenditures in health, education and social services, the business counterattack against labour, the state's growing indebtedness to corporate bondholders, the privatization of municipal services, the assault on trade unionism and the draconian attacks on the social safety net.

(McLaren and Farahmandpur, 2002: 61)

ACTIVITY 1

On capitalism:

Write down your thoughts concerning the world McLaren and Farahmandpur describe.

Watch Tristram Hunt, 'Marx was clear about the social consequences of Capitalism', from the debate 'Karl Marx was Right! Capitalism post 2008 is falling apart under the weight of its own contradictions', filmed at the Royal Geographical Society on 9 April 2013:
www.youtube.com/watch?v=FWc2eFYKh4I

Take a look at the following clip from Question Time with Russell Brand:
www.youtube.com/watch?v=RH_DJXoufNY

How do these sources support the claims made by McLaren and Farahmandpur (2002)?

Do you think these resources present an accurate description of the western capitalist world?

As Tristram Hunt claims, engaging with the work of Karl Marx can help us understand how we have come to have the world described by McLaren and Farahmandpur (2002) and Russell Brand. These standpoints also describe the historical basis from which Marx undertook his analysis of capitalism. Marx claimed that in the same way that feudal society had been a phase in human development and history, capitalism represents just another phase from which society will inevitably progress from.

Capitalism and production

Marx claimed that capitalism is organised around the relationship of human beings to the mode of *production*. He believed that the organisation of society is structured around the production of economic goods. In other words, what is produced, who produces it, how it is produced and how it is exchanged. This in turn determines the lives human beings have.

Marx claimed that production has inevitable outcomes: most obviously some kind of product, referred to by Marx as a commodity, which has come about as a direct result of human labour. Marx identified that this commodity has both a 'use-value' (Marx, 1867: 54) in terms of satisfying a human need, like food for hunger or clothes for warmth, and an 'exchange-value' (Marx, 1867: 55) in terms of exchanging it for something else, generally money/capital.

Commodities

Marx developed this analysis further and connected this two-fold understanding of commodities to the production of labour. He claimed there is 'concrete' (Marx, 1867: 22) labour, which relates to the *use-value* of the commodity and denotes that there are types of basic skills and practices necessary to produce the commodity; and there is 'abstract' Marx, 1867: 21) labour, which relates to the commodity's *exchange-value*.

ACTIVITY 2

Marx's use of the idea of the abstract is significant, but does make his theories a little more complex to understand and work with! He often uses visual and metaphoric imagery to bring further depth to the points he is making.

In the following sections, look closely at the words and language Marx uses and think about the effect that it has on your understanding of the arguments he is making.

Exchange-value and commodity fetishism

It is through *exchange-value* that labour becomes *abstract*, because if it no longer has a clear *use-value* alone, it becomes something that can be used and exchanged for something else, generally money. Marx identified that labour at this point 'assumes a social form' (1867: 42), as human beings enter into a relationship with one another to sell and purchase this labour. Marx terms this idea of labour as a product/commodity 'fetishism' (1867: 44).

ACTIVITY 3

Humour aside, there are other understandings of fetishism. Marx's interpretation is drawn from anthropological understandings and the Enlightenment where 'fetishism is a . . . irrational, phenomenon . . . that produces illusions' (Osborne, 2005: 16).

If you get a chance, read section 4, Part One of Karl Marx's seminal work *Capital*, which is rich with metaphoric language, like 'hieroglyphic', 'mist' (45), 'mystery', 'super-natural', 'magic' and 'necromancy' (46), that promotes the idea of an illusion where labour becomes reduced to the form of a commodity, open to sale and purchase in the same way an inanimate object like a packet of biscuits is.

Marx (1867) claimed that in a capitalist society it is commodities above human labour that carry (social) value. For Marx, this was the real mystery and illusion. He argued that inanimate goods/commodities have a kind of visible intrinsic value to the purchasing public, while the human labour and skill expelled to create them remain unseen and unconsidered: 'value by labour-time is therefore a secret, hidden under the apparent fluctuations in the relative values of commodities' (Marx, 1867: 46).

ACTIVITY 4

It is important to think of Marx's understanding of fetishism in terms of understanding the concept of commodities today.

When we see an item of clothing (it could be anything – electrical goods, furniture, etc.), do we consider the human labour involved – do we think of how it was made? Who made it?

What conditions did the workers operate in? What were they paid? Or are the workers invisible and the object alone an embodiment of the price?

Does this explain why in western societies people knowingly continue to purchase their goods from outlets that use child labour and provide poor working conditions and low pay?

Would you agree with Marx – do you think inanimate commodities/goods (clothes, electrical goods, furniture) are valued above human beings in capitalist societies?

What are the consequences of this for today's society?

If you would like further explanation and illustrations, take a look at the film 'Law of Value 2: The Fetishism of Commodities', available at: www.youtube.com/watch?v=D4MbUx-il6c

Marx extended his analysis of labour-time through the concept of 'surplus value'. Surplus value is the difference between the value of the products of labour and the cost of producing that labour power. Inevitably, some people work faster and more skilfully than others, which determines that there must be a 'socially necessary' (Marx, 1867: 150) labour-time, a kind of average value that enables the capitalist, the individual who has purchased the labourer/employee's time in exchange for money/capital, to achieve a good profit. Marx further identified that this profit can be extended by the capitalist lengthening 'the working day' (Marx, 1867: 151).

ACTIVITY 5

In *Capital* (1867) Marx paints an evocative picture of the consequences of surplus value and capitalism. Try reading the following extract then summarising the arguments Marx is making.

'The capitalist has bought the labour-power at its daily value. The use value of the labour-power belongs to him throughout one working day. He has thus acquired the right to make the worker work for him during one day. But what is a working day? At all events, it is less than a natural day. How much less? The capitalist has his own view of this point of no return, the necessary limit of the working day. As a capitalist he is only capital personified. His soul is the soul of capital. But capital has one single life-force, the drive to valorise itself, to create surplus-value, to make its constant part, the means of production, absorb the greatest possible amount of surplus labour. Capital is dead labour which, vampire-like, lives only by sucking living labour, and lives the more, the more labour it sucks. The time during which the worker works is the time during which the capitalist consumes the labour-power he has bought from him. If the worker consumes his disposable time for himself, he robs the capitalist.'

(Marx, 1867: 149)

Do you agree/disagree with the points Marx is making?

Alienation

Marx identified that the result of such a system was 'the process of alienation of man's own labour' (Marx, 1867: 384), which means that men and women become increasingly disconnected from their own work and employment, as the commodity being produced is merely to generate profits for their employer/the capitalist and not for themselves: 'Capital uses the worker, the worker does not use capital: and capital is only composed of the objects which employ the worker and thus have an existence, a will and a consciousness personified in the capitalist' (Marx, 1867: 385).

However, the capitalist is not safe from alienation; on the contrary, Marx identified that the capitalist is already 'rooted in his process of alienation' and this has come about 'through the domination of the capitalist over the worker' (Marx, 1867: 383), which has reduced the capitalist to 'the personification of capital, capital in person' (Marx, 1867: 383).

ACTIVITY 6

On alienation: two very different thinking points!

How many times have you felt yourself or have observed people at work or study who appear to take no pleasure or pride in their employment?

Do you think purchasing, wearing and owning expensive branded goods (like Polo, Mercedes, Ralph Lauren, Chanel, etc.) is an example of the 'personification of capital, capital in person' (Marx, 1867: 383)?

The result of alienation is dehumanisation, which comes about through the system of wage-labour/capital relations. As a result, both the capitalist and the worker experience a shift/change in their 'species-being' (Marx, 1844: 91). Marx understood 'species-being' as a dialectical and relational understanding that humans have in terms both of themselves and as part of a social group. Therefore, the workers would see themselves as part of the wage-earning class, and the capitalists part of the ownership class, and thereby not of the same species.

Marx's theory of labour-value identified that there will be those that create the commodity and those that organise and profit from it, thereby creating a two-tier social system. Marx identified this as 'material production, the true process of social life' (Marx, 1867: 384). Marx further recognised that *material production* is bound up with the existence of social class, which in turn is determined by your relationship to the means of production.

Social classes

Marx identified two main classes characterising the capitalist system. First there is the bourgeoisie, who are the capitalists and the owners of capital, purchasing (and sometimes) exploiting labour power through surplus value to make the best possible profit. 'The essential condition for the existence, and for the sway of the bourgeois class, is the accumulation of wealth in the hands of private individuals, the formation and augmentation of capital; the condition of capital is wage labour' (Marx, 1848: 15). Second, there is the proletariat, who are the owners of the labour power who need to sell their labour to live. They are 'the modern working class – a class of labourers, who live only so long as they find work, and who find work only so long as their labour increases capital. These labourers, who must sell themselves piecemeal, are a commodity, like every other article of commerce, and are consequently exposed to all the vicissitudes of competition, to all fluctuations of the market' (Marx, 1848: 9).

In addition to these two groups, Marx also identified a number of other classes, but felt over time these would phase out and society would be organised around the two main classes of the bourgeoisie and the proletariat.

In considering the impact of social class upon society, we return once more to the beginning of this section, Karl Marx on capitalism, and the claim that capitalism 'creates a world after its own image' (Marx, 1848: 7), to consider what and whom it is that influences and shapes the world we live in:

> The ideas of the ruling class are in every epoch the ruling ideas, the class which is the ruling material force of society, is at the same time its ruling intellectual force. The class which has the means of material production at its disposal has control at the same time over the means of mental production, so that thereby, generally speaking, the ideas of those who lack the means of mental production are subject to it. The ruling ideas are nothing more than the ideal expression of the dominant material relationships, the dominant material relationships grasped as ideas.
>
> (Marx and Engels, 1846: 192, in McLellan, 2004)

Marx understood this as a deterministic economic conception that inevitably divides society into two levels: *the base*, which is the tangible world we live in where everything is composed around the relationship to material production; and *the superstructure*, 'the reflection of the ensemble of the social relations of production' (Gramsci, 1999: 192). In other words, the political and ideological institutions of society (this includes education) are shaped by and reproduce the spirit of capitalism.

This is a significant claim and important for us comrades in education to investigate further and contemporarily, which leads us on to the next section.

Exploring education and society with the Marxist scholars

> The Philosophers have only interpreted the world, in various ways; the point, however, is to change it.
>
> (Marx, 1845: 173)

It was Lenin who pointed out that revolutionary change in society is the function of creative ideas and the critical consciousness attained by the proletariat (working classes). However, despite Marxism being considered the 'working class bible' (Rius, 1999: 34) and generating the most 'profound revolution' (Salamini, 1974: 359) in western social and educational theory and political movements, it has to a certain extent proved 'incapable of revolutionizing the consciousness of the masses' (Salamini, 1974: 359). This huge dilemma was to occupy the early educational thinking of the Italian revolutionary, Antonio Gramsci (1891–1937), one of the protagonists of this section. I think the following claim by French Marxist philosopher Louis Althusser (1918–1990), another of our protagonists, can help us understand why 'no production is possible which does not allow for the reproduction of the material conditions of production: the reproduction of the means of production' (Althusser, 1971: npn).

In other words, capitalism has become so successful in 'creating a world in its own image' (Marx, 1848: 7) that we receive and accept it without question through a process not unlike osmosis! However, after Gramsci (1988: 39), it is time for us to 'be stronger in our thinking and to act better'. Therefore, this section is about using Marxist theory to think more critically about the world and, in particular, education. As desired by our final protagonist, French philosopher and major force in the postmodern/structuralist movement Jacques Derrida (1930–2004), it is time for us to conjure up the 'spirit of Marxism' (Derrida, 1993: 109) and deploy it to interrogate how capitalism and its prevailing structures like education and society are shaped and constructed.

ACTIVITY 7

Individuals' narratives play an important part in shaping how we make sense of theory and the world around us. Take a look at the links below, which provide biographical information on Althusser, Gramsci and Derrida. This will help to illustrate the influence of Marxism on their lives.

    www.marxists.org/glossary/people/a/l.htm
    www.marxists.org/archive/gramsci/intro.htm
    www.critical-theory.com/derrida-documentary-proves-derrida-answer-simple-god-damned-question
    www.derridalabiographie.com/en

So let us return to the start of this chapter and Marx's claim that capitalism 'creates a world after its own image' (Marx, 1848: 7), as we start to explore the means and *apparatus* that enable such a thing to occur and be sustained. This was also the starting point for French philosopher and communist intellectual Louis Althusser's (1971) seminal work, *Ideology and Ideological State Apparatus*.

Louis Althusser – 'For Marx' (Althusser, 2005: 9)

Louis Althusser (1971) identified that capitalism reproduces itself through *ideology*, which is a 'system of ideas and representations that dominate the mind of a man or a social group' (Althusser, 1971: npn). Ideology is able to achieve this through two mechanisms: *Ideological State Apparatus* (ISA) and *Repressive State Apparatus* (RSA).

> The ideology of the ruling class does not become the ruling ideology by the grace of God, nor even by virtue of the seizure of state power alone. It is by the installation of the ISAs in which this ideology is realized and realizes itself that it becomes the ruling ideology.
>
> (Althusser, 1971: npn)

ISAs operate in society through cultural and social institutions such as the church, family, media, culture and even education. RSAs achieve obedience from the public through repressive means and physical coercion, which functions in society through institutions like the police force, military, courts and prisons.

ACTIVITY 8

On ideology, ISA and RSA:

For an example in education, take a look at the following YouTube clips of the student protests of 2011. Can you relate these events to Althusser's theories of ideology, RSA and ISA? Write down your thoughts and reactions.

    www.bbc.co.uk/news/education-15646709
    www.bbc.co.uk/news/uk-15654585

Althusser on education

Althusser (1971: npn) claimed that 'ideologies are not "born" in the ISAs, but after Marx, from the social classes at grips in the class struggle; from their conditions of existence, their practices, their experience of the struggle, etc'. They have 'no history', are 'nothingness', an 'imaginary construction', and a mere 'illusion'. Althusser is arguing that ideology has no historical or intellectual basis; it is merely a representation of the world we live in, which becomes 'integrated into our everyday consciousness' through ISAs, like the education system.

ACTIVITY 9

On schooling: what points does Althusser raise regarding the role of schooling?

What do children learn at school? They go varying distances in their studies, but at any rate they learn to read, to write and to add – ie: a number of techniques, and a number of things as well, including elements (which may be rudimentary or on the contrary thoroughgoing) of 'scientific' or 'literary culture', which are directly useful in the different jobs in production (one instruction for manual workers, another for technicians, a third for engineers, a final one for higher management, etc). Thus they learn know-how. They also learn the 'rules' of good behaviour, the attitude that should be observed by every agent in the division of labour, according to the job he is 'destined' for: rules of morality, civic and professional conscience, which actually means rules of respect for the socio-technical division of labour and ultimately the rules of the order established by class domination.

(Althusser, 1971: npn)

Althusser understood *know-how* as a reproducing form of knowledge that ensured submission to the rules of the established order; in other words, capitalism. The claim that capitalism is reproduced in education is a bold and significant one and worthy of closer examination. Let's think about Althusser's claim in terms of education today.

At the time of writing, we are currently experiencing a bewildering period of policy change in education. Schooling in particular is experiencing a radical (re)-presentation in language and is re-emerging in a varying array of forms, presented under the banner of 'free schools and academies'. These schools include 'philanthropic start-up sponsored; charity/university sponsored, converter, multi-academy chain' (Bassey, 2013: 15). Within these emerging structures, schools can operate free from local community accountability and therefore determine their own pay and conditions for staff, including employing unqualified teachers; increasing flexibility around the curriculum; and developing their own operating and admissions policies. In other words, schooling is being re-presented as a (free) open marketplace and mirroring many of the features of capitalism.

Furthermore, Althusser's above claim of differentiated social class pathways in education developed to meet the requirements of the labour market was recently reconceived through Michael Gove's (failed) attempt to introduce the English Baccalaureate (EBac):

> with results that will inevitably be class-biased. The EBac for the top layer, destined for higher education, itself increasingly hierarchised in class terms. A middle technical layer for whom the new University Technical Colleges (a vocational 14–19

academy) are designed. And for the bottom layer, a basic academic education coupled with what Gove calls 'practical learning'.

(Hatcher, 2012: 254)

Despite Gove's failure to introduce the EBac (at the time of writing), differentiated curriculum pathways remain in secondary education; and education remains positioned towards the interests of the middle classes and capitalism. Furthermore, 'it is widely believed that if the Tories are re-elected in 2015 they will allow schools to be owned and run by private companies for profit' (Hatcher, 2013: 26). Althusser (1971) would claim this as another example of capitalism reproducing itself through the ISA of education. He identified that this situation is 'heavy with consequences', as education is part of a process that 'transforms individuals into subjects' of capitalism. This is conducted through the practice of 'rituals of ideological recognition' (Althusser, 1971: npn), which are explored below.

ACTIVITY 10

Thinking about 'rituals of ideological recognition'

- What are the consequences and for whom of having both state and private education systems?
- What is the significance of school uniform – what does it look like and why?
- Happiness is clearly important to society, so why is this not on the curriculum while GCSE and A Level Business Studies are?
- What is the significance of competition through league tables to schooling and education?

'Everyone is a bit of a Marxist' (Gramsci, 1988: 36) – Antonio Gramsci

At the heart of Antonio Gramsci's writing was a commitment to Marxism as a force for change. He considered Marxism as an ideology 'useful in guiding the masses towards cultural and political hegemony and continually subject to change and reformulation in emerging new historical contexts' (Salamini, 1974: 360). Gramsci understood hegemony as presupposing 'the interests and tendencies of the groups of which hegemony is to be exercised' (Gramsci, 1999: 211), and identified that the bourgeoisie achieved this through economic determination and intellectual leadership. Therefore, the basis of Gramsci's revolutionary thought comes from a commitment to the creation of intellectuals from the proletarian class, which he felt would contribute to a counter-hegemony and a post-revolutionary period where the proletariat would unite to develop a new and different ideology to that of capitalism. Therefore, much of Gramsci's early educational thinking revolves around the problem of how to establish this new and organic intellectual class, which would be distinctive from 'traditional' (Gramsci, 1999: 308) bourgeoisie intellectuals who merely maintain and reproduce the capitalist social order (through the exercise of hegemony).

'The notion of "the intellectuals" as a distinct social category independent of class is a myth. All men are potentially intellectuals in the sense of having an intellect and using it, but not all are intellectuals by social function' (Gramsci, 1999: 131). For Gramsci, 'all men are intellectuals, but not all men have in society the function of intellectuals' (Gramsci, 1988: 304). He saw this as due to the organisation of schooling and the division of the 'vocational school for the instrumental (subordinate) classes and the classical school for the dominant classes and the intellectuals', this being a system of schooling that determines a 'pupil's destiny and future activity in advance' (Gramsci, 1999: 166).

ACTIVITY 11

How different are Gramsci's ideas in relation to the organisation of the current UK system?

Explore: www.education.gov.uk/schools/leadership/typesofschools

Are there any similarities to how education is currently organised?

Do you think grammar schools represent Gramsci's notion of the 'classical' school?

Gramsci identified instead a common education as an alternative to the above stratified system, 'imparting a general, humanistic formative culture; this would strike the right balance between development of the capacity for working manually (technically, industrially) and development of the capacities required for intellectual work' (Gramsci, 1999: 166).[2] It would be a 'system in which the child is allowed to develop and mature and acquire those general features that serve to develop character . . . A school that does not force the child's will, his intelligence and growing awareness to run along tracks to a predetermined station. Instead a school of freedom and free initiative . . . where manual labour and intellectual labour are to be joined in the schools and thus create a new educational tradition' (Gramsci, 1988: 72).

Gramsci believed this would enable the development of a new class of intellectuals to emerge developed from an education system that forges a strong relationship between 'theory, practice, consciousness and action' (Mayo, 2008: 432). This would represent a true social pedagogy that would transform education and society into a fairer and more equal landscape, far removed from existing stratified systems.

Jacques Derrida and *Specters of Marx*

> Enter the ghost, exit the ghost, re-enter the ghost.
>
> (Hamlet in Derrida, 1993: xix)

I hope this chapter has demonstrated the many readings and illuminations that can come from the theories of Karl Marx. It therefore feels fitting to bring this chapter's journey to a close with a book that was all about demonstrating that there are many different ways of thinking and deploying Marx.

This is what is argued in *Specters of Marx* (1993) by Jacques Derrida. After Shakespeare's *Hamlet*, the text operates around the idea of a 'rotten state' (capitalism) (Derrida, 1993: 3), which is haunted by a ghostly apparition (Marx). As a poststructuralist (see earlier links to biography), Derrida was keen for readers to apply his thinking in different ways to create a multiplicity of possible readings and meanings, and this is what we turn to now.

First, the notion of the ghostly 'spectre' is at the heart of Derrida's work as after Marx[3] Derrida reminds us that Marxism/communism provides an alternative to capitalism, and the ghost(s) of Marx are set to continually haunt and remind capitalism of this fact! Derrida called this 'hauntology' (1993).

UNIVERSITY OF WINCHESTER
LIBRARY

ACTIVITY 12

How do the following articles relating to Michael Gove's claim of 'Marxist teachers' in the education system illustrate the above hauntology argument?

www.theguardian.com/education/2013/may/06/academics-against-gove-national-curriculum

www.dailymail.co.uk/debate/article-2298146/I-refuse-surrender-Marxist-teachers-hell-bent-destroying-schools-Education-Secretary-berates-new-enemies-promise-opposing-plans.html

http://internationalsocialist.org.uk/index.php/blog/michael-gove-a-marxist-teacher-responds

Second, the spectre, which is both of this world and the 'other', represents the 'inherent instability of reality', which connects to our earlier discussions in the chapter concerning the 'illusions' generated by capitalism.

Third, a spectre is neither dead nor alive, real nor unreal, and somewhat signifies the 'ghostly and monstrous qualities' (Gibson–Graham, 1995: 27) that are the inevitable outcomes of 'selfish capitalism' (James, 2008).

Finally, and somewhat reminiscent of Chapter 1, the spectre is the prophecy of social, political and educational possibility. 'This question arrives, if it arrives, it questions with regard to what will come in the future-to-come. Turned toward the future, going toward it, it also comes from it, it proceeds from the future' (Derrida, 1993: xix).

In the next chapter we will be exploring how critical and revolutionary pedagogues deploy Marxism in their work, but for now we return to Chapter 1 once again in finishing with Derrida (1993) who claimed that Marxist knowledge was the natural heir to Platonic thinking, because it provides us with a situational and contemporary methodology for critical analysis, which we have engaged in throughout this chapter. So let us 'return to Marx, let's read him again as a great philosopher. We have heard this and we will hear it again' (Derrida, 1993: 38).

ACTIVITY 13

How will you be taking the spectre(s) of Marx forward in your thinking and work?

Notes

1 This claim overlooks Karl Marx's précis (www.marxists.org/archive/marx/works/1884/origin-family/marx-conspectus.htm) of Lewis Morgan's *Ancient Society* (1877) (www.marxists.org/reference/archive/morgan-lewis/ancient-society/index.htm), which was then further developed by his 'alter-ego', lifelong friend and collaborator, Frederick Engels, into the work, *The Origin of the Family, Private Property and the State* (1891) (www.marxists.org/archive/marx/works/1884/origin-family). In this work, Engels identified that the origin of female oppression could be located in the rise of the class-based society.

2 Gramsci (1999) wrote that culture is 'organization, discipline of one's inner self, a coming to terms with one's own personality; it is the attainment of a higher awareness, with the aid of which one succeeds in understanding one's own historical value, one's own function in life, one's own rights and obligations' (Gramsci, 1999: 57).

3 The Communist Manifesto (1848) opens with 'A spectre is haunting Europe'; as noted previously in this chapter, Part One, section 4 of *Capital* (1867) is rich with the language of the supernatural.

References

Althusser, L. (1971) Ideology and Ideological State Apparatus: Notes Towards an Investigation in *Lenin and Philosophy and Other Essays*, New York: Monthly Review Press. Available at: www.marxists.org/reference/archive/althusser/1970/ideology.htm [Accessed on 19 July 2014].

Althusser, L. (2005) *For Marx*, London: Verso.

Anyon, J. (2011) *Marx and Education*, London: Routledge.

Balibar, E. (2007) *The Philosophy of Marx*, London: Verso.

Bassey, M. (2013) Academies: The Willing, the Pressured and the Forced, in Fisher, T. (ed.) *Schools at Risk! Gove's School Revolution Scrutinised*. Stafford: Socialist Educational Association.

Derrida, J. (1993) *Specters of Marx*, London: Routledge.

Eagleton, T. (2011) In Praise of Marx, *Chronicle of Higher Education*, 57: 32, B6–B9.

Engels, F. (1884) *The Origin of the Family, Private Property and the State*, Peking: Foreign Language Press. Available at: http://www.marx2Mao.com/M&E/OFPS84.html [Accessed on 19 July 2014].

Gibson-Graham, J. K. (1995) Haunting Capitalism in the Spirit of Marx and Derrida, *Rethinking Marxism*, 8 (4): 25–39.

Gramsci, A. (1988) in Forgacs, D. (ed.) *The Antonio Gramsci Reader, Selected Writings 1916–1935*, London: Lawrence & Wishart.

Gramsci, A. (1999) *Selections from the Prison Notebooks* edited and translated by Hoare, Q. and Smith, G. N. (1971) London: Lawrence & Wishart.

Hatcher, R. (2012) Social Class and Schooling, in Cole, M. (ed.) *Education, Equality and Human Rights*, London: Routledge.

Hatcher, R. (2013) Two Ways to Make Profits: Run the Schools, Sell the Teaching, in Fisher, T. (ed.) *Schools at Risk! Gove's School Revolution Scrutinised*, Socialist Educational Association.

James, O. (2008) *The Selfish Capitalist – Origins of Affluenza*, London: Vermilion.

Marx, K. (1844) Economic and Philosophical Manuscripts, in McLellan, D. (2004) (ed.) *Karl Marx Selected Writings*, Oxford: Oxford University Press.

Marx, K. (1867/1999) *Capital*, Oxford: Oxford World's Classics.

Marx, K and Engels, F. (1845) Theses on Feuerbach, in McLellan, D. (2004) (ed.) *Karl Marx Selected Writings*, Oxford: Oxford University Press.

Marx, K. and Engels, F. (1846) The German Ideology, in McLellan, D. (2004) (ed.) *Karl Marx Selected Writings*, Oxford: Oxford University Press.

Marx, K. and Engels, F. (1848/1998) *The Communist Manifesto*, Oxford: Oxford World's Classics.

Mayo, P. (2008) Antonio Gramsci and His Relevance for the Education of Adults, *Educational Philosophy and Theory*, 40 (3): 418–35.

McLaren, P. and Farahmandpur, R. (2002) Breaking Signifying Chains: A Marxist Position on Postmodernism, in Hill, D., McLaren, P., Cole, M. and Rikowski, G., *Marxism Against Postmodernism in Educational Theory*, Lanham, MD: Lexington Books.

Morgan, Lewis (1877) *Ancient Society*, London: Macmillan & Co. Available at: www.marxists.org/reference/archive/morgan-lewis/ancient-society/index.htm [Accessed on 19 July 2014].

Rius (1999) *Introducing Marx*, Cambridge: Icon Books.

Salamini, L. (1974) Gramsci and Marxist Sociology of Knowledge: An Analysis of Hegemony – Ideology – Knowledge, *The Sociological Quarterly*, 15: 359–80.

3

Critical and revolutionary pedagogies for today's education and society

Melanie Parker

Overview

Philosophy raises critical questions about how we live and why; and theory not only develops our knowledge and thinking, but can also inspire our actions and give greater direction to our practice. This theory action combination in philosophy is associated with critical, revolutionary pedagogy. This pedagogy bases education on personal and social liberation, and argues for all pedagogy to be a call for action against an education system formulated to support the accumulation of wealth for the few at the expense and suffering of others. This chapter will focus on a major thinker of this approach, Paulo Freire, whose work has also inspired Peter McLaren's thinking in the field of critical revolutionary pedagogy. I will argue that never has this critical educational movement been needed more than at this political and educational moment, and I would encourage you to think about how this educational philosophy can inform your own developing ontology and practice.

> **QUESTIONS**
> - Can critical and revolutionary pedagogy transform education society?
> - How can this pedagogy be situated contemporarily?
> - Is critical revolutionary pedagogy the antidote to an education system formulated out of market forces?

Introductions – returning to Karl Marx to introduce Paulo Freire

Without hope there is no way we can even start thinking about education.

(Freire, 2007: 87)

Irwin (2012) writes that 'the intimate connections between life and philosophy are no more apparent than in an exploration of Paulo Freire's work' (Irwin, 2012: 1) and I hope that this notion will remain with us throughout this chapter and beyond. To this end, and for the purposes of this introduction, I will be sharing small windows of my narrative with you. Like bell hooks (1994) who drew her notions of engaged pedagogy from Paulo Freire's work, 'Paulo was one of the thinkers whose work gave me a language' (hooks, 1994: 46). For me, this is the language of hope for human beings and educators alike; hope for the classroom, hope for society and hope for the world. Paulo Freire's narrative has resulted in the development of a critical pedagogy shaped from a deep love for the poor and society's marginalised. Paulo Freire (2007) invites educators to bring their hopes and dreams to educational spaces. My dreams are for a kinder and more including world and for an education system to work ethically and compassionately towards these ends. I long for an education system that is firmly based on an uncompromising desire to transform the lives of individuals for a fairer and more just society. In this chapter I invite you to think about economic and social inequity and to consider the role of education in bringing an end to such injustice. Critical and revolutionary pedagogy is clear in its intentions to bring about social transformation, through its active critique of society and the ways in which the education system reproduces inequality, and through its empowering *pedagogy of hope* (Freire, 2004).

To Freire via Marx

I came to the work of Paulo Freire through the thinking of Karl Marx (see Chapter 2), as critical pedagogy is underpinned by Marxist thinking and in many ways you could claim critical pedagogy is Marxism in action and education. I guess I have always had Karl and Paulo at my side, being a working-class girl from Plymouth. Through working with the 'privileged' (at an independent school) and researching with students, the homeless, refugees, asylum seekers and disabled children, young people and their families, Karl and Paulo helped me to make sense of these experiences and think more about the role of education in society.

The work of Paulo Freire and Karl Marx has had a profound effect on my life and I finally acknowledged this more formally through my doctoral studies (Parker, 2011). In this work I acknowledged both Marx's meticulous and urgent analysis of capitalism as having an illuminating, provoking and liberating effect upon me; and Freire's critical pedagogy for transformative change, which I will be sharing with you in this chapter, as having a profound impact upon the way I thought about education. After Anyon's (2011) reading of Marx, I have come to see 'capitalism as a primary source of systematic, social, economic and educational inequality' (Anyon, 2011: 5). Marx has shown me that this has come about through living in a society that is structured around the production of economic goods. In other words, what is produced, who produces it, how it is produced, and how it is exchanged determines the lives and sort of society that we have. Take a modern-day example, like an employee of Sports Direct on a zero-hour contract (you get called into work when you are needed, receive no sick or holiday pay, and at the time of writing there is no sign of government moves to draw up legislation to stop such exploitative practices). Your condition/life and the opportunities open to you are shaped by this relationship you have to your employment. After all, how can you plan to go on holiday? Purchase goods? It will certainly be difficult to secure a home without a regular income. Now imagine you are a shareholder of the same Sports Direct, whom according to the *Guardian* (2013) are enjoying record profits (www.theguardian.com/business/2013/jul/28/sports-direct-staff-zero-hour-contracts). How different your life and opportunities are through your relationship to your employment. But it is not only Sports Direct; Buckingham Palace also use zero-hour contracts for some of their part-time staff – Marx would say this is an example of economic exploitation by the wealthy. So capitalism operates through production; and production creates commodities and consumerism. This is true whether it is factory-produced goods or items for sale in a shop. Commodities and consumerism also bear heavy consequences; for example, when we see an item of clothing (it could be anything – electrical goods, furniture, etc.), do we consider the human labour involved – do we think of how it was made? Who made it? What are the workers paid? What conditions do they operate under? Are they on zero-hour contracts and what difference does this make to people's lives? Or is it merely the price we see? Is the price alone an embodiment of the commodity? For more on this and the philosophy of Karl Marx, take a look at Chapter 2.

Furthermore, during this period now of late capitalism, public sector 'goods' such as health and education services are coming increasingly under attack through privatisation, as independent companies are deployed to run essential services from schools to catering services, which were once the singular domain of public services.

Giroux, examining the impact of the capitalist world upon education, wrote:

> Conscripting the university to serve as corporate power's apprentice, while reducing matters of governance to an extension of corporate logic and interests, substantially weakens the possibility for higher education to function as a democratic sphere, academics as engaged public intellectuals, and students as critical citizens. In a market driven and militarized university, questions regarding how education might enable students to develop a keen sense of prophetic justice, promote the analytic skills to hold power accountable . . . (have) become increasingly irrelevant. Public schools have fared even worse. They are subject to corporate modes of management, disciplinary measures, and commercial values that have stripped them of any semblance of democratic governance.
>
> (Giroux, 2011: 11)

ACTIVITY 1

Can you think of any examples that support and/or counter the points that Giroux (2011) is making?

Paulo Freire

The work of Paulo Freire shows us that education can be at the heart of any change. We turn to his capacity for hope and a critical pedagogy that is *daring to dream* (Freire, 2007) of educational and social change. Therefore, this chapter provides an insight into Freire's critical pedagogy and the subsequent critical revolutionary pedagogy that has developed from both Freire's critical pedagogy and the philosophy of Karl Marx.

The work of Paulo Freire reflects both his compassionate and intellectual response to the poverty and hunger of those around him. Born in 1921 in economically depressed Recife in Brazil to middle-class parents, he found himself sharing the plight of the poor, which led him to realise the impact of the 'culture of silence of the dispossessed' (Shaull, 1996, in Freire, 1996: 12) for himself. He came to realise that the 'silence' of the poor was as a direct result of their position and oppression in society. Instead of being educated to become critically aware and empowered, this group of people remained immersed in an educational, social and political situation that maintained the ongoing 'culture of silence'. Therefore, Freire turned to education as a means to end the oppression that came from this 'silence' and the experience, practice and philosophy that emerged from this educational process was to shape his critical pedagogy.

Dialogic approach

At the heart of this educational process was a dialogic approach, in which the educator engages to understand students' expectations and experiences, which we will be exploring later in the chapter. This was first articulated in 1959 in his doctoral thesis at the University of Recife and was later to inform his teaching at the same university where he worked as a Professor of History and Philosophy of Education. The dialogic approaches that he developed from this underpinned the approach he deployed in his role as Secretary of Education and General Coordinator of the national plan of adult literacy in literacy campaigns across the northeast of Brazil, but wasn't without notoriety. This led to Paulo Freire being arrested and persuaded to leave the country. He fled to Chile where he worked for five years on adult literacy programmes with UNESCO and the Chilean Institute for Agrarian Reform. In 1969 he was appointed visiting Professor of Studies in Education and Development at Harvard University; and from 1970–80 he spent ten years as a special educational advisor to the World Congress of Churches. In 1980 Freire returned once more to Brazil and played a significant role in shaping the country's educational policies until his death in 1997. In 1991, as a testament to the iconic work and his steadfast commitment to social justice, the Paulo Freire Institute was created (www.paulofreire.org). Since then, Freirean institutes/centres have sprung up across the world committed to the legacy of his life and work.

> Paulo's epistemology convinces and invites us – especially those of us who are educators – to think and choose, to join in and take action in continually projecting the concretization of *possible dreams* whose nature is as ethical as it is political. We must believe that we can make *apparently impossible dreams* possible, so long as we live out that *existing*, truly. It is *dreaming and existing* that 'allows' us to keep making ourselves into beings who fight for liberation, *Being More*.
>
> (Ana Maria Araujo Freire, 2001, in Freire, 2007: xi)

Pedagogy of the Oppressed

There is no such thing as a neutral educational process. Education either functions as an instrument that is used to facilitate the integration of the younger generation into the logic of the present system and bring about conformity to it, or it becomes 'the practice of freedom', the means by which men and women deal critically and creatively with reality and discover how to participate in the transformation of their world.

(Shaull, 1996, in Freire, 1996: 16)

Pedagogy of the Oppressed was first published in 1968 in Portuguese, and in 1970 it was translated and published in English, which extended its circulation considerably (at the time of writing, it is freely available online at: www.users.humboldt.edu/jwpow ell/edreformFriere_pedagogy.pdf).

   Pedagogy of the Oppressed has subsequently become one of the classic texts of critical pedagogy, influencing educators, community developers and students across the world. This section will primarily focus on *Pedagogy of the Oppressed*, but will inevitably touch on concepts and ideas that were to emerge later in Freire's writing to give you a broader insight into the critical pedagogy that he continually engaged in throughout his life. Reflecting on his later work, *Pedagogy of Hope* (2004), Freire felt its 'threads and the fabrics whose essence, as it were, was *Pedagogy of the Oppressed*' (Freire, 2004: 4); and I would argue that the same claim could be made about much of his subsequent work; it all germinates from and towards *Pedagogy of the Oppressed*.

Banking

Giroux claims there has been no intellectual to match Paulo Freire's 'theoretical rigour or his moral courage' (Giroux, 2013, in Lake and Tress, 2013: ix) in standing up against the dominant forces of neoliberal capitalism. Increasingly, sites of education, schools, colleges and universities are deployed to either serve or reproduce the interests of capitalism. Pedagogy, once an engaged progressive practice (Dewey, 1997, and Rousseau, 1762/2003), has become an instrument colonised by administrators seeking to standardise, measure and assess its effectiveness through narrow market-driven outcomes, like SATs and league tables. Giroux (2011) identifies the consequences of this as a 'stripped down version of education' (Giroux, 2011: 8) with reductionist goals promoting 'economic growth and global competitiveness' (Giroux, 2011: 8), which has seen teachers being increasingly deskilled and disempowered; and teaching and learning practice reshaped to reincorporate memory, rote and reproductive assessment. Freire (1996) identified this educational practice as the 'banking' concept of education:

> Education thus becomes an act of depositing, in which the students are the depositories and the teacher is the depositor. Instead of communicating, the teacher issues communiqués and makes deposits which the students patiently receive, memorize and repeat.
>
> (Freire, 1996: 53)

The consequences of the banking approach are that it reduces learners to 'adaptable manageable beings' (Freire, 1996: 54), indoctrinating them to accept the world, serving the interests of capitalism and the minority, as it is.

> The banking concept of education, which serves the interests of oppression, is also necrophilic. Based on a mechanistic, static, naturalistic, spatialized view of consciousness, it transforms students into receiving objects. It attempts to control

thinking and action, leads men and women to adjust to the world and inhibits their creative power.

(Freire, 1996: 58)

ACTIVITY 2

How helpful is the metaphor of 'banking' to describe the processes of schooling?

To what extent does this make sense in the context of your experience of education?

Through discussion with a colleague, find some examples from practice to illustrate the idea of banking education. Can you find any counter examples?

Antidote to conformity

Pedagogy of the Oppressed provides an antidote to the domestication and conformity that comes from the 'banking concept of education'. It seeks instead to liberate us through pedagogical practices that will dispel the 'culture of silence' which has inhibited both the educator's and learner's space and practice.

> We need to say no to the neoliberal fatalism that we are witnessing at the end of this century, informed by the ethics of the market, an ethics in which a minority makes most profits against the lives of the majority. In other words, those who cannot compete die. This is a perverse ethics that, in fact, lacks ethics. I insist that I continue to be human ... I would then remain the last educator in the world to say no: I do not accept history as determinism. I embrace history as possibility (where) we can demystify the evil in this perverse fatalism that characterizes the neoliberal discourse in the end of this century.
>
> (Freire, 2002: 27)

To counter the teacher-to-student transmission model of the domesticating banking approach, Freire (1996) advocates a dialogical approach to education (see Chapter 11 for more information on dialogical approaches), because 'only through communication can human life hold meaning' (Freire, 1996: 58). Unlocking the relevance of students' everyday reality is the key to creating an authentic dialogical approach to learning, where the teacher and student learn from each other's knowledge and experience, which provides the basis for claims of validity rather than relying on a socially and politically constructed curriculum. Instead, students and teachers are engaged dialectically in creating new knowledge. The concept of dialectics in a Freirean sense is based upon the Marxist notion that political and historical events are due to a conflict of social forces caused by materialism, which provides the basis of our social reality and understanding, which in turn provides the foundation for Freire's dialogical approach to education.

Problem-posing education

At the heart of this process is problem-posing education, which breaks with the 'vertical' (Freire, 1996: 51) patterns of the banking approach to education, as knowledge is transformed from being static and possessed singly by the educator to something far more collaborative, emerging, fluid and dynamic, transforming both the roles of student and educator:

> The teacher is no longer merely the one-who-teaches, but one who is him/herself taught in dialogue with the students, who in turn while being taught also teach. They become jointly responsible for a process in which all grow.
>
> (Freire, 1996: 61)

Whereas the banking approach to education is inconsistent with creating new knowledge, problem-posing education, which is distinctive to the emergence of problem-based learning in universities (which has become increasingly popular but not necessarily critical), involves a constant unveiling of new knowledge. Whereas 'the former attempts to maintain the submersion of consciousness; the latter strives for the emergence of consciousness and critical intervention in reality' (Freire, 1996: 62). Therefore, the potential for new knowledge is limitless and impossible to reproduce in narrow insular curricula. At the heart of this process is praxis, which simply means critical reflection and action, and in some ways pays homage to Marx's observation: 'Philosophers have only interpreted the world in various ways; the point is to change it' (Marx, 1845: 173).

Conscientisation

There are dominant and prevailing ideologies that exist in society and mould our thinking. It is therefore useful to understand our thinking as being culturally shaped and formed in particular ways and it is important that we remain constantly aware of this to ensure that we do not bring this 'cultural invasion' (Freire, 1996: 133) of historically and socially constructed 'thinking' to our interpretations and understandings, particularly as it is often constructed from notions of superiority and inferiority i.e. disabled/non-disabled; male/female; white/black; rich/poor. Praxis requires us to critically reflect upon these dominant ideologies and recreate knowledge and understanding in new, alternative and liberating ways. It is at this point that we would have achieved Freire's notion of 'conscientizacao'. 'Conscientizacao' translates rather poorly in English to *conscientisation*, which means a process of raising awareness to a new level of critical consciousness. This translation is 'poor' as it does not capture the notion of both developing a conscience and consciousness, which is at the heart of Freire's pedagogical campaign for learning to be truly transformative for both the individual and society. The original and untranslated term, 'conscientizacao', means 'joint knowledge, consciousness, feeling or sense' (Cruz, 2013: 171) and represents the successful fusion of the combined processes of dialogue, problem-posing education and praxis. Furthermore, Freire (1996) was clear that it is necessary for the process of 'conscientizacao' to be contextualised contemporarily to ensure that it addresses the current social, political and ideological forces.

ACTIVITY 3

The Paulo Freire Project (www.freireproject.org) is a truly excellent initiative dedicated to the life and work of Paulo Freire. There are many different resources available on the website written by leading scholars in this field. Please watch the film 'Why Critical Pedagogy?' available at: www.freireproject.org/freire-project-tv and respond to the following questions:

- What dominant/prevailing ideologies emerge in the film?
- What problem-posing approaches to education are asserted?
- How do the pedagogies deployed differ from your own experiences of education?

Transformative learning and action

It is from this conceptual basis that Freire's notion of transformative learning and action is understood. Educator and student would be engaged in the joint and collaborative process of reconstructing knowledge and education to transform themselves and the world they live in.

> The radical committed to human liberation does not become the prisoner of a 'circle of certainty' within which reality is also imprisoned. On the contrary, the more radical the person is, the more fully he or she enters into reality so that, knowing it better, he or she can better transform it. This individual is not afraid to confront, listen, to see the world unveiled. This person is not afraid to meet the people or to enter into dialogue with them. This person does not consider himself or herself the proprietor of history or of all people, or the liberator of the oppressed; but he or she does commit himself or herself within history to fight at their side.
>
> (Freire, 1996: 21)

Cultural circles

I am going to leave this section with an outline of Paulo Freire's cultural circles, which I think neatly encapsulates his critical pedagogy. Cultural circles were developed from the work Freire was undertaking with the poor in Brazil and are very much a reflection of Marxism in action by developing community learning in which individuals become aware of the exploitative forces that shape their educational, social and political circumstances. Cultural circles operate as dialogical groups, which discuss topics that have significance in people's lives. These topics are then developed into illuminative themes, which are then generally related to nature, culture, politics, work and relationships – whatever shapes individuals' lives. The themes generally expressed the contemporary contradictions and challenges that faced Paulo's students in their daily lives. Often the groups Freire worked with were unable to read and write, as there was no free public schooling system, so visual images were used instead. These were used to gather stories and information to create complete pictures (codifications) of individuals' day-to-day lives and experiences. The group achieved levels of critical consciousness by comparing the pictures with their own realities and connecting their experiences with the historical, political and cultural circumstances of the day. This was often followed by a desire for literacy to further extend personal and social expression. To think about this in terms of the ideas we have considered so far in this chapter regarding Freire's critical pedagogy, there is dialogue, concientisation (consciousness raising/developing conscience) and praxis – the philosophy of critical pedagogy and Marxism in action.

Critical revolutionary pedagogy

The collaborative and transformative nature of critical pedagogy has made it a dynamic rather than static pedagogic process, which has enabled it to adapt and develop into further pedagogic forms, like critical revolutionary pedagogy. Critical revolutionary pedagogy has primarily emerged through the work of the internationally acclaimed educator and critical pedagogue, Peter McLaren, Professor of Education at the Graduate School of Education and Information Studies at the University of California.

ACTIVITY 4

For a real taste of the work of Peter McLaren, watch 'Critical Pedagogy and Revolutionary Praxis in the Age of Imperialism' (www.youtube.com/watch?v=NJYoEZaCkYY) in which McLaren discusses critical revolutionary pedagogy and praxis, paying particular attention to social class and the current crisis of capitalism.

- Summarise the points that Peter McLaren is making.
- What role do you see for education, as a result of watching the film?

McLaren's work has emerged against claims that Freire's original concept of critical pedagogy has become 'conceptually impoverished and politically domesticated' (McLaren and Farahmandpur, 2001: 136) and reduced to a type of theory-empty student-centred learning devoid of any social analysis or ambition for revolutionary change. This is because 'capitalism has been naturalized as commonsense reality' (McLaren, 1998: 435), which has made any form of educational challenge redundant, a further example of neoliberal capitalism in action. A further attack on critical pedagogy has come from postmodern critical theory that McLaren terms the currently 'most fashionable form of educational criticism' (Sardo, 2001: 412). McLaren (1998) claims that postmodern critical theory reproduces capitalism's inequalities and cites Rikowksi (1995):

> the insertion of postmodernism within educational discourses lets in some of the most unwelcome guests – nihilism, relativism, educational marketisation, to name but a few – which makes thinking about human emancipation futile. Left postmodernism, in denying the possibility of human emancipation, merely succeeds in providing complacent cocktail bar academic gloss for the New Right Project of marketising education and deepening the rule of capital within the realm of education and training.
>
> (Rikowksi, 1995, in McLaren, 1995: 443)

Connections with Marx

Cotter et al. (2001) would claim that this is another example of how increasingly different forms of radical pedagogy have been colonised by the 'bourgeois left' (Cotter et al., 2001: 420), which seeks to replace the once fundamental aspect of Marxism with a form of liberalism that 'humanises capitalism' (Cotter et al., 2001: 420). This replaces the historical Marxist struggle for empowerment and emancipation in critical pedagogy with 'local tactics involving undecidability, hope, friendship, faith and various forms of conjectural micro activisms' (Cotter et al., 2001: 420).

The effect of this colonisation of critical pedagogy has been the disappearance of the issue and function of social class, which has been disregarded and 'reduced to an effect rather than understood as a cause' (McLaren and Farahmandpur, 2001: 136) of inequality and oppression. Yet it remains at the heart of understanding how the capitalist reproductive function operates through structures like the education system. With this in mind, a re-centring (McLaren and Farahmandpur, 2002: 239) of social class remains at the core of McLaren's critical revolutionary working-class pedagogy, which aims to:

> create the conditions of pedagogical possibility that enable students to see how, through the exercise of power, the dominant structures of class rule protect their practices from being publicly scrutinised as the appropriate resources to serve the interests of the few at the expense of the many.
>
> (Ebert and Zavarzadeh, 2008, in McLaren, 2010: 5)

We can understand this in terms of our earlier discussion of zero-hour contracts, which McLaren would interpret in the context of the following:

> New mechanisms of accumulation have spurred the development of a model in which transnational fractions of capital have become dominant. They include a cheapening of labour and the growth of flexible, deregulated and deunionized labour where women always experience super-exploitation in relation to men ... The role of the nation state has changed to meet globally uniform laws that protect capital against the interests of the international working class.
>
> (McLaren, 2010: 5)

This inflicts a 'culture of silence' (Shaull, 1996, in Freire, 1996: 12) upon these modern-day (exploited) workers, reflecting the earlier observation of Hayat Imam (1997): 'Today ... creation of wealth has become the fundamental value at the centre of global society and analyses of economics are devoid of issues of morality, human needs and social conscience' (Imam, 1997, in McLaren and Farahmandpur, 2001: 137).

Critical literacy

Critical revolutionary pedagogy seeks to expose and end such practices through an interventionist approach to teaching and learning, which requires the return to the classical Marxism that influenced and underpinned the work of Paulo Freire. It raises important questions for education in terms of its ongoing role as a vehicle to facilitate the aims of capitalism and its possible future role in achieving social goals, like the eradication of poverty and increasing paid employment. At the heart of moving towards this aim and critical revolutionary pedagogy is critical literacy, 'where literacy is defined as a practice of reflecting, analyzing, and making critical judgements in relation to social, economic and political issues' (McLaren and Farahmandpur, 2001: 144). Critical literacy is practised through the classroom dialogue and interactions of students, as they share their lived beliefs and experiences, which in turn are analysed and explored in terms of what they reveal in terms of individual (students') position within the existing capitalist structure and their role (if any) in reproducing the aims and functions of capitalism. Drawing upon Freire's process of 'conscientizacao', teachers 'as revolutionary intellectuals' (McLaren and Farahmandpur, 2001: 144) will invite students to analyse their own narratives to expose and dispel prevailing dominant discourses that may have featured in constructing their own identities and in the telling and understanding of their own stories. This will include examining and exposing the function of culture and language, which has been constructed from capitalist agendas that set 'high culture apart from popular culture and that privilege the former over the latter' (McLaren and Farahmandpur, 2001: 146), and working instead towards:

> empowering the working class and marginalized social groups . . . to interrogate theoretically forms of both high culture and popular culture so that they can analyze, articulate, express, and construct meaning from multiple positionalities located in their lived experiences dealing with racism, sexism and class exploitation.
>
> (McLaren and Farahmandpur, 2001: 146)

The focus will be upon developing alternative student and subject positions that generate class consciousness and illuminate issues relating to exploitation and oppression as a means of transforming the existing social arrangements.

ACTIVITY 5

How does the Burke and McManus report (2009) Art For a Few (available from the Freire Institute. (University of Roehampton) at: http://blueprintfiles.S3.amazonaws.com/1321362562-AFAF_finalcopy.pdf) help to illuminate the points McLaren is making?

Reflexive emancipatory practice

> On whose side are we when we teach and act?
>
> (Mayo, 2013: 9)

Adopting a clear position can lead to a transformation in the educational space to a politicised site of critical engagement and reflexive emancipatory practice, redefining the role of educator from Giroux's (2003) notion of the 'de-skilled corporate drone' to McLaren's and Farahmandpur's (2001) vision of 'teachers as activists', committed to educational and social change.

ACTIVITY 6

Think about your own story/narrative. How has it been shaped by the forces of capitalism? How are you and 'others' positioned as a result? What type of knowledge has been created? How can we use this in the classroom?

Through my work I have been most privileged to work with some truly inspiring people and groups; most recently, the wonderful adult literacy group, Shout It Out (http://suetorrmbe.co.uk/#/sue-torr-mbe/4561865952), run by the remarkable Sue

Torr. Last Tuesday evening, as part of a community project between the University of Plymouth and Shout It Out, a group of students and myself volunteered at the group to help support their learners' developing literacy and numeracy skills. Our welcome was overwhelming, as was our learning. We were shown how to turn a pack of cards, a jigsaw puzzle and numerous cups of tea into effective pedagogical tools for the development of literacy and numeracy skills – great teaching from a community learning group that attracts little if any funding. We met students at different stages in their educational journey into literacy, and listened to stories full of energy, possibility and transformation. It made me think of Freire's cultural circles and consider how dialogue and a *Pedagogy of the Heart* (Freire, 2006) can open up possibilities and opportunities for transformation to ensure that people who have previously struggled to learn to read and write can begin a new journey in the world. I would agree with Freire and McLaren: this transformative practice should not be left to the mercy of capitalist thinking and neoliberal funding.

> Daring to dream is also a pedagogy of conscientization (the building of awareness and conscience).
>
> (Ana Lucia Souza de Freitas, 2007, in Freire, 2007: xxvii)

References

Anyon, J. (2011) *Marx and Education*, London: Routledge.

Burke and McManus (2009) Art For a Few. Available at http://blueprintfiles.s3.amazonaws.com/1321362562-AFAF_finalcopy.pdf [Accessed on 15 July 2014].

Cotter, J., DeFazio, K., Ganter, B., Kelsh, D., Sahay, A., Torrant, J., Tumino, S. and Wilkie, R. (2001) The 'Radical' in 'Radical Teaching': Pedagogy Now, *Textual Practice* 15 (3): 419–29.

Cruz, A. L. (2013) Paulo Freire's Concept of Conscientizacao, in Lake, R. and Tress, T. (2013) (eds) *Paulo Freire's Intellectual Roots: Towards Historicity in Praxis*, London: Bloomsbury.

Dewey, J. (1997) *Experience and Education*. London: Simon and Schuster.

Freire, P. (1996) *Pedagogy of the Oppressed*, London: Penguin Books.

Freire, P. (2002) *Pedagogy of the Oppressed*, New York: Continuum.

Freire, P. (2004) *Pedagogy of Hope*, New York: Continuum.

Freire, P. (2006) *Pedagogy of the Heart*, New York: Continuum.

Freire, P. (2007) *Daring to Dream: Toward a Pedagogy of the Unfinished*, Boulder, CO: Paradigm.

Giroux, H. (2003) Public Pedagogy and the Politics of Resistance: Notes on a Critical Theory of Educational Struggle, *Educational Philosophy and Theory*, 35 (1): 5–16.

Giroux, H. (2011) *On Critical Pedagogy*, New York: Continuum.

The Guardian (28 July 2013) Sports Direct: 90% of Staff on Zero-Hour Contracts. Available at: www.theguardian.com/business/2013/jul/28/sports-direct-staff-zero-hour-contracts [Accessed on 20 July 2014].

hooks, b. (1994) *Teaching to Transgress*, London: Routledge.

Irwin, J. (2012) *Paulo Freire's Philosophy of Education: Origins, Developments, Impacts and Legacies*, New York: Continuum.

Lake, R. and Tress, T. (2013) (eds) *Paulo Freire's Intellectual Roots: Towards Historicity in Praxis*, London: Bloomsbury.

Marx, K. (1845) Theses on Feuerbach, in McLellan, D. (2004) (ed.) *Karl Marx Selected Writings*, Oxford: Oxford University Press.

Mayo, P. (2013) *Echoes from Freire for a Critically Engaged Pedagogy*, London: Bloomsbury.

McLaren, P. (1998) Revolutionary Pedagogy in Post-Revolutionary Times: Rethinking the Political Economy of Critical Education, *Educational Theory*, 48 (4): 431–462.

McLaren, P. (2010) Revolutionary Critical Pedagogy, *Journal of Education and Information Studies*, 6 (2), Article 7.

McLaren, P. and Farahmandpur, R. (2001) Teaching Against Globalization and the New Imperialism: Toward a Revolutionary Pedagogy, *Journal of Teacher Education*, 52: 136–50.

McLaren, P. and Farahmandpur, R. (2002) Critical Pedagogy, Postmodernism, and the Retreat From Class: Toward a Contraband Pedagogy, in Hill, D., McLaren, P., Cole, M. and Rikowski, G. (2002) (eds) *Marxism Against Postmodernism in Educational Theory*, Lanham, MD: Lexington Books.

Parker, M. (2011) *Utopias of Education*. Doctoral thesis, University of Sheffield.

Rousseau, J-J. (1762/2003) *Emile*, London: Everyman.

Sardo, M. (2001) Rage and Hope: The Revolutionary Pedagogy of Peter McLaren: An Interview with Peter McLaren, *Educational Philosophy and Theory*, 33 (3–4): 411–25.

4

Being in education
Phenomenology and existentialism
Ken Gale

Overview

Phenomenology and existentialism are philosophical approaches that concern themselves with the study of things as they appear in our experience and with structures of our consciousness. This chapter is designed to encourage students to open up and explore the concerns that these two approaches to philosophy have in relation to experience and to begin to apply them in education settings. Two widely acclaimed twentieth-century German phenomenologists, Husserl and Heidegger, engaged in an inquiry into human existence and in particular looked closely at individual subjectivity in terms of consciousness, awareness and the experience of the external world.

A particular focus of this chapter will therefore be upon Heidegger's use of the notion of 'dasein', literally to do with being-there or being-in-the-world, and the way in which Heidegger's thinking encouraged an inquiry into the authenticity of self or being in relation to the environment, the community and the immediate world of experience. Heidegger was particularly concerned with challenging both the inadequacy and the necessity of identifications of the self, for example as 'teacher' or 'student', because as significations these identifications were always shifting and changing in the light of new experiences.

The chapter will also therefore explore some of the tenets of existentialism that emerged; first, in France directly after the Second World War. This followed a period of study on phenomenological thought carried out in Germany by the French philosopher and writer Jean-Paul Sartre. In particular, the chapter will engage in an inquiry into the works of Sartre, Maurice Merleau-Ponty, Simone de Beauvoir and others, and how these might be seen to apply to contemporary education settings.

A major starting point for existentialist thinking is that existence is always prior to essence or determined, ordered systems of rational thought. So, for Sartre, as we are 'surging up in the world' we are always having new encounters with the world, and our introspections and reflections upon these will serve to challenge and problematise previous constructions of the self in relation to the world. The chapter will therefore encourage readers to apply phenomenological and existentialist thought to subjectivity and the self within the context of change in education in the twenty-first century.

QUESTIONS

- How might a phenomenological or existentialist view of being be conceptualised and how might such a view be contextualised in contemporary education settings?
- How is the potentiality of self and subjectivity changed and influenced by changing experiences of teaching and learning?
- What is the significance for the theory and practice of education of the phenomenological and existentialist view that existence is always prior to essence?

Introduction

We can begin our inquiry into phenomenology, phenomenological thought and its relevance to our understanding of education in contemporary settings by briefly looking at the highly influential philosophy of Prussian philosopher Immanuel Kant, widely considered to be a central figure of modern philosophy. In his most famous book, *The Critique of Pure Reason*, Kant described and distinguished between objects as *phenomena* and objects as *noumena*. The former he described as objects that are shaped by and comprehended through perception and the action of the senses, and the latter as objects as things-in-themselves or as objects that do not present themselves to us in space and time and about which we are unable to make judgments. The distinction that Kant offered here has provided the basis for much philosophical discussion and analysis in terms of what is famously known as the question of appearance and reality. This can be framed in terms of the intriguing and fascinating question: when things appear to us as the objects of our senses, is that how they really are? This also leads us to the equally challenging and controversial binary distinction that has troubled social scientists and educationalists for decades between *subjectivity* and *objectivity*.

ACTIVITY 1

What do you understand by the distinction between subjectivity and objectivity? Write down what it currently means to you and as you work through this chapter try to revise and evaluate this meaning.

The legacy of Kant

In many respects, phenomenology and phenomenological thought emerged as a reaction to what many see as the problematic nature of these established and fundamental binary distinctions. According to Kant, what he referred to as transcendental objects are objects we can only comprehend through our senses and are merely representations of objects we ultimately cannot know. These noumenal objects, given to us through *a priori* thought and deductive reasoning, can only be partially known through perception of our senses and therefore we are never able to fully know what he referred to as the 'thing-in-itself'. Therefore, Kant's *rationalism* and the problematic nature of this binary is best understood in relation to philosophical *empiricism*, whereby we use *a posteriori* or inductive reasoning as a means of providing us with some certainty about the world and the objects in it.

So, for example, our 'knowledge' that tomorrow the sun will rise in the east and will set in the west is premised upon *a posteriori* thought, or upon the 'evidence' of our senses, that, in the past, this is what it has always done and that, therefore, this is what it will do today and in the future. According to Kant, therefore, we can only infer the extent to which our thinking corresponds with these noumena, or things-in-themselves, through our experience of the world and our observations of the influence and effects of that which we perceive through the use of our senses; that is, of phenomena.

ACTIVITY 2

'Some bachelors I know are lonely' is an example of a statement that we might make following the use of inductive or *a posteriori* reasoning. It has this status because the knowledge claim that it makes is dependent upon experience or empirical evidence for verification. By contrast, the statement 'All bachelors are unmarried' is an example of deductive or *a priori* reasoning where no such proof is required.

Write out examples of some similar statements through the use of deductive and inductive reasoning using the words 'teacher' and 'student' instead of the above: when you have done this, share your examples and discuss them with a colleague or friend.

The rationalist nature of Kant's transcendental philosophy was developed further in the work of Descartes, who also saw thinking as prior to experience in terms of our understanding of the world. So, for Descartes, thought exists and thought cannot be separated from me; therefore, I exist – I think, therefore I am. Descartes claimed that the deductive certainty provided by the rationality of *a priori* thought meant that even if there is doubt about existence then something or someone must be doing the doubting, therefore the very fact that doubting is taking place is a proof of (my) exist-ence. By contrast, phenomenology, according to Edmund Husserl, primarily involves reflection on and study of consciousness and of the phenomena that appear in acts of consciousness. So, where for Descartes essence, rationality and the noumena are prior to experience and our perception of the world, Husserl's approach and that of other phenomenologists is therefore a clear attempt to place experience and existence as prior to any rationalist attempts to categorise, define and essentialise the world and the objects in it. Husserl attempted to engage in a reflective study of individual conscious-ness and to take the experience of what appears to us in the world – phenomena – and to try to extract meaning from these experiences as a way of gaining understanding of those experiences and of the world in which we live.

Hegel's phenomenology

The nineteenth-century German philosopher Georg Friedrich Hegel is accredited with introducing to philosophy what can be simply referred to as a dialectical approach to the study and practice of phenomenology. In his life and work, Hegel was con-cerned with challenging some of the religious orthodoxies to be found in Kant and those who followed his writing. Influenced by the work of Baruch Spinoza, Hegel wanted to offer a view of the world that shifted away from what he saw as one in which God was some form of abstract construction, an artifice, that could only be understood through the application of high-minded thought and abstract reasoning. Hegel was therefore concerned with taking Spinoza's concerns with the relationship between (imperfect) man and (perfect) God and providing a religious view of the world that offered some form of humanistic accessibility.

While Hegel's work is challenging to read, he does offer a form of phenomenology, sometimes referred to as utopian in ambition and form, that, while condemned in his time as atheistic, offers a methodological approach to phenomenology that is grounded in what might be referred to as a rational approach to experience. Hegel's dialectics are known for setting up an exchange in what he referred to *dialectical triads*, between the *thesis, antithesis* and *synthesis* of thought that is based upon experience. In simple terms, each triad involves an engagement between a *thesis* which is then challenged in opposition by its *antithesis*, which after due reflection and exchange produces a new *synthesis*. The production of this new synthesis is seen as always moving thought and experience forward in rational, albeit linear ways. The synthesis becomes the new thesis which then has the potential to be challenged and opposed by a new antithesis, and in the completion of the next new triad a new synthesis is formed, and so on.

The dialectical idealism of Hegel's philosophy has been described by some observers as an early example of a 'March of Progress' theory in which, because of its rational approach based upon experience of the world, each dialectical triad takes human thought and action forward in positive and beneficial ways. Hegel's approach to philosophy is sometimes referred to as 'dialectical phenomenology'. We can take this to mean that each 'thesis' actively provides an example of an experience of the world, of a phenomenon; of something that presents itself to our consciousness through the operation of our senses. This 'thesis' is then confronted by another similarly constructed but oppositionally different 'antithesis' which then, through reflection, argument and rational engagement, produces the final thesis in the triad, the 'synthesis'. Hegel's thought has been criticised for being both idealist and utopian because it also argues that it will finally enable an understanding of the absolute, ontological and metaphysical 'Spirit' that is behind all experience of the world.

ACTIVITY 3

Consider the way in which Hegel's dialectical approach might be applied in education.

Imagine a discussion taking place in a classroom. Imagine the students all offering different points of view on an educational topic (inclusion, assessment, discipline etc.) and trying to represent their different points of view in an argument.

If a 'thesis' can be considered to be a body of knowledge, based upon experience and from a particular point of view, describe an example of a process whereby this body of knowledge could, first of all, be challenged and opposed by an 'antithesis' and how, secondly, this exchange might produce a third thesis, the 'synthesis', as a consequence.

Try to demonstrate in your example how the argument can be seen to move through the three stages of the dialectical triad and to evolve into an improved or more rational or logical (final) position.

ACTIVITY 4

Consider the way in which Hegel's dialectical approach was adopted and applied by Marxist thought.

The historian A. J. P. Taylor said that Marx turned the philosophy of Hegel on its head. With some guidance from your tutor, look again at the chapter in this book on Marx and Marxist thinking and try to think of ways of explaining Taylor's point of view.

How do you think this approach might be applied to our understanding of education today?

Twentieth-century phenomenology – the influence of Husserl

As previously mentioned, it was the philosophical approach of Edmund Husserl that helped to instigate the emergence of phenomenology as an influential approach to philosophical thinking in the twentieth century and it was his adoption of the term, around the turn of the century, that was highly influential in it becoming a recognisable and respected philosophical school.

Husserl's approach established phenomenology as a method of philosophical inquiry as a direct counterpoint to the previously dominant rationalist philosophies that emerged directly out of the thinking of Kant, and which promulgated the dualist thinking that had preoccupied philosophical discussion since the publication of the work of Descartes. The attention paid by Husserl and those phenomenological thinkers who followed him to the significance of experience and of one's reflection upon it served to severely destabilise the kinds of thinking and practice that saw a separation between rationalism and empiricism, mind and body, subjectivity and objectivity and so on. It is also reasonable to argue that the emergence of phenomenology as a major body of knowledge and method of inquiry also led to the emergence of such significant modes of philosophical thinking as Existentialism and Experiential Learning, and such important modes of inquiry as action research and reflective practice. By turning the rationalist dictum that essence precedes existence on its head, the emergence of phenomenology, as a method of both thought and action, led the way for a whole new approach based upon the lived experience of the self and of conscious reflection upon that lived experience.

ACTIVITY 4

Look at the chapter in this book on John Dewey and experiential learning (Chapter 9); spend some time making notes that help you to illustrate some of the potential links between what Husserl and other phenomenologists have said about existence preceding essence and the work of Dewey, Kolb and others working in the field of experiential learning. What influence do you think this has upon the emergence of action research and Stenhouse's (1975) notion of the 'teacher-as-researcher'?

Husserl and intentionality

Up until this point, the kinds of rationalist philosophy described here put forward the view that 'reality' cannot be grasped or directly understood because we are conscious of it only as a representation or an 'appearance' that is only available to us through our perceptions of reality. In short, our minds carry with them representations of reality. Husserl offered a challenge to this view which he based largely on the philosophical thinking of Brentano. For Husserl, the central concept in his phenomenological thought is 'intentionality'. Intentionality emphasises that consciousness does not simply exist, it is always *of something* or, put another way, consciousness is never empty or directionless; it is always there *for something*. For Husserl, 'intentionality' involves a focusing on something that has multiple shapes and forms, which could be both subjective or objective and could be of reason, emotion, intuition and so on: in whatever way it is described, it is there *for* consciousness. What is there for consciousness is to do with intentionality. So, for example, if one looks at a landscape painting, the focus might be on the stream flowing in the foreground; it might then shift to the cows grazing in the meadow and then again to the clouds in the blue sky above and so on. According to Husserl, our intentionality not only brings the experience of the world alive within our consciousness, it also helps to subvert the mind/body dualism that rationalist philosophy has prevailed upon thought for many years. He argues that it does this through a realisation that consciousness is always directed toward or is *of* something so, therefore, that which it is *of* is also of the mind and hence not separate from it. Phenomenology argues that intentionality, therefore, subverts mind/body dualism through the notion of lived experience; the *experience* of the object, upon which intentionality focuses consciousness, is also of the mind: mind and body are conflated through intentionality.

This view of intentionality within phenomenology also presents the thinking subject engaging with experience as also having had previous experiences. These previous experiences will influence intentionality in that they will form certain points of view, ways of 'looking' or perspectives. So we not only perceive the sea, we might also perceive it as 'dangerous' or 'welcoming' or 'rough'. In this way, Husserl suggests that we give it 'intentional content' which provides our description and gives details that are in some way indicative of the 'intentional objects' of our thought. This further works to trouble and diminish the problematic effects of mind/body dualism.

ACTIVITY 5

Husserl and intentionality:

Take a look at a composite scene. This might be a view from your window onto a busy street, it might be a picture in a book, or it might be some images that you have displayed on your computer screen. Allow yourself to look at this for a while and try to be alert to the way in which your focus shifts from one object to another or from one part of the scene to another. Can you reflect upon what is happening here? In what ways are your thoughts and reflections about the scene as a whole shifting and changing in focus and in emphasis? In what sense is your 'intentional content' having an influence upon the 'intentional objects' of the scene you are observing?

The view of intentionality that is to be found in phenomenological thought is not about the more everyday use of intentionality which involves offering an expression of deliberate intent to do something or to act in a particular way. Rather, the phenomenological view of intentionality is something that is part of everyday lived experience; it is with us all the time and, while it is always changing with experience, it is something we cannot avoid. Phenomenological thought and the philosophical methods that emerge from it are dependent on the description of phenomena as they are presented to consciousness, in their immediacy.

Heidegger

While Heidegger was a student of Husserl's, it is evident in his work that the former made great attempts in his philosophical approach to distance himself from Husserl's generally, and more particularly in his attempt to offer a phenomenological and humanist view of the world that was substantively different to that of his predecessor. In his most important and influential work, *Being and Time*, Heidegger poses what he considers to be the essential philosophical question of human existence: what is it to be? The influence of Descartes on his position is clear when he posits that to even ask the question implies that the answer is already provided and understood. The humanist inflection in Heidegger's work is substantial and provides a clear basis for distinguishing and placing his philosophical approach at a distance from that of the transcendentalist and theistic work of Husserl.

The title of *Being and Time* itself gives a clue to the main phenomenological concerns of Heidegger's philosophy. By moving the subject and the concerns with being away from the theistic relations with God, Heidegger argued for the need to pay attention to our own contemplations as being both temporally within language and spatially within the world and, therefore, providing a conflated conceptualisation of being and time. In taking this approach the philosophical shift that Heidegger provided moved the emphasis of contemporary philosophical thought away from epistemological concerns with meaning toward an interest in existence and with being. In *Being and Time*, Heidegger is at pains to offer an understanding of what it is that makes beings possible and, in this respect, he places a substantive and substantial emphasis on being as the subject of discourse or self-reflection. In many respects his work laid the ground for the later concerns with discourse and text in the poststructural philosophies of Foucault and Derrida, by suggesting that language serves not only to reveal truth about the world but also to conceal it. Interpretation is always possible and ontological positioning becomes unstable and unpredictable through the changing situatedness of human existence. For Heidegger, being cannot be contained by the signs and representations that are used to identify it; in fact, being transcends language because it is always prior to language. Heidegger often crossed out the word 'being' and allowed the deletion to remain, in an attempt to show that the word is synonymously necessary and inadequate. It is of interest to note that a fundamental feature of the deconstructive method developed and used by Derrida employed a similar strategy. Derrida did this by placing words and concepts *sous rature* or 'under erasure' to demonstrate the fragility and potential breakdown between text and what it is used to represent.

ACTIVITY 6

Think about the strategy of placing being and/or language 'under erasure': how could you use this strategy in a classroom to help learners begin to understand the idea that meaning is situated in a particular time and within a particular space?

Heidegger and Dasein

So, for Heidegger, the nature of existence is predicated upon the temporal and spatial shifts of uncertainty that are an unavoidable part of living in an always changing world that is continually in need of interpretation. Our existence is always situated; it is always in the world. Heidegger describes the quality of being through the use of the concept of *dasein*. This term can be translated as being-there or being-in-the-world and provides a fundamentally significant basis for understanding the phenomenological and, indeed, the main humanist orientation of Heidegger's work.

As subjects we are constantly involved in encounters with the world which place us in crucially significant relation to the past and the future in relation to our existence in the present. Our ability to both understand and interpret the world and the objects that exist within it and in relation to us is therefore significantly bound up with our humanity and with time. In a world of potentially useful things, of objects that are infused with all kinds of social, cultural and natural influences, the authenticity of our existence is always imbued with being there, of being in relation to these objects in the world. *Dasein* has the potential to offer an awareness of our own consciousness, in that every time we experience a new encounter with the world, our existence is questioned and requires some kind of reflective interpretation as a means of gaining a sense of understanding of our positioning in the world and of our own humanity.

In the phenomenology of Heidegger, *dasein*, while having a central and pivotal role, also offers great challenges to the way in which followers of a phenomenological approach might lead their lives. *Dasein* brings sharply into focus features of the paradox of living in close relationship with other humans while at the same time nurturing an experience of being and a sense of self that is ultimately individual, alone and deeply aware of the limits of one's own mortality and proximity to death. Phenomenologists and existentialists such as Kierkegaard focused upon these challenges in their philosophical writings and concerned themselves with the angst and the feelings of dread that such abandonment could bring to existence.

Existentialism – the influence of Sartre

The concerns with personhood, authenticity, abandonment and mortality generated a great deal of interest in Europe in the years immediately following the Second World War. Within this context, the philosophy of Heidegger is widely regarded as having a major influence on the emergence of existentialism throughout Europe and particularly in France during the post-war years.

Heidegger's work had a substantial and significant influence on the emergent existentialist thought of French philosopher Jean-Paul Sartre. Sartre's arguably most well-known philosophical work, *Being and Nothingness*, not only pays a substantial debt to the thinking of Heidegger but also is often read alongside *Being and Time* by those wishing to gain deeper insights into the principles and practices of phenomenological and existential thought. Sartre studied philosophy in Berlin in the 1930s and developed a substantive and committed interest in the work of Husserl, Heidegger and others. Many observers point to the highly pragmatic nature of the existentialist philosophy that Sartre developed as a consequence of reading these phenomenological works.

Sartre never abandoned his commitment to the Cartesian certainties of the self, but in holding onto the importance of subjectivity, he also worked to develop from Heidegger a philosophical stance on human reality, of being in the world, that focuses on the practical or existential concerns of life in preference to a consideration of epistemological views on the meaning of social relationships.

Sartre's arguably most accessible work is a transcript of a lecture that he gave in Paris at the end of 1945 titled 'Existentialism is a Humanism', which was eventually published as a book titled *Existentialism and Humanism* (1973). This book probably provides the clearest account of the emergence of existentialist philosophy from its phenomenological roots and in so doing was responsible for a substantial shift in late twentieth-century thought and political action. A useful starting point for engaging with Sartre's existential thought can be gained through the following activity taken from *Existentialism and Humanism*.

ACTIVITY 7

Read this quotation from Sartre and answer his question at the end:

> If we draw, for example, a black maltese cross upon a white square, we can perceive either the cross itself, or the spaces between its limbs, as the statement that is being made, but we cannot perceive it in both ways at once. In the latter case – taking the black as spaces between – we see the figure as a conventionalized four-petalled flower in white upon a black ground. What makes us perceive it as one or the other?' A gardener would perhaps be more likely to see it as the flower, and the military man as the cross.
>
> (Sartre, 1973: 13)

Write down your answers to Sartre's question: what do you understand by the final statement in the quotation? Now make some notes as to how you reached your conclusions (you could use an image of a Maltese cross from Google Images to assist you in this activity).
On the same page, Sartre says of our reaction to the preceding figure:

> Perception depends upon this pre-existent element of choice, which determines the form in which we perceive not only all the varieties of geometrical figures but every phenomenon of which we become aware . . . There is therefore no objectivity.
>
> (ibid.)

What do you think of the argument that Sartre makes here? Is it logical? Do you agree with his conclusion?

In the opening section of this chapter, we examined some aspects of the philosophical approach of Kant and considered his view that all things have certain noumenal qualities or essences that enable us to identify them as distinct categories of difference with certain transcendent or universal qualities of being. However, in arguing from the basis of experience, Sartre and the existentialists assert that our existence in the world must precede any ability or means that we might have of defining ourselves or the essential features we might possess. Sartre himself describes this fundamental position in the following way:

> What do we mean by saying that existence precedes essence? We mean that man first of all exists, encounters himself, surges up in the world – and defines himself afterwards . . . he will not be anything until later, and then he will be what he makes of himself.
>
> (ibid.: 28)

For Sartre and the existentialists, therefore, man is 'condemned to be free' (ibid.: 34). Man is always abandoned because there is no God and no pre-existing definition of man by which to determine what decision or what course of action should be taken in any place or at any particular time. Existentialism is premised upon there being no reference point or fixed datum by which human action can be designed or judged; the free will offered by existential thought is not bound by any form of determinism that might attempt to provide orders, commands or even recommendations for action.

What the existentialists refer to as the authenticity of human existence is based upon the fundamental responsibility that such a position entails. This is because human action has no preceding set of values or procedures which can provide a direction, a justification or an excuse that can be used to guide that action in any way.

ACTIVITY 8

On pages 35 to 36 of *Existentialism and Humanism*, Sartre provides us with an example that might help us in coming to understand the nature of freedom, abandonment and responsibility that plays a fundamental part in producing the existentialist position that 'existence precedes' essence. Read this passage carefully and then consider:

a   What course of action you might take if you were in this position.
b   What thoughts, principles or values influenced you in your decision making.
c   If you might be able to influence others who might be faced with a similar issue to deal with.

On completion of this activity, write down some of your thoughts and reflections that engaging in this activity has prompted: do you think the position of the existentialists is a tenable one? Do you think that existence precedes essence?

As a humanistic form of thought, the philosophy of existentialism provided by Sartre, de Beauvoir, Camus and others also makes an argument for existence that is not wholly or exclusively individual or independent of others. The kinds of rationalist thinking that informed so much Continental philosophy of the twentieth century were based upon the *a priori* principle of Descartes that argues deductively that 'I think, therefore I am'. The logic of this argument is used to confirm the existence of 'I' but it gives no certainty to the existence of others. The proof for the existence of others is based upon and derived from the *a posteriori* principles and practices of empiricism, which argues that we can know of human existence and of the world generally by arguing inductively. So, for example, I can claim to *know* that the sun rises in the east because it has always done so and that, therefore, it will do so in the future. Empiricism provides us with a form of certainty because as we observe the sun rising in the east again and again, our record of this substantiates the truth of the claim for its existence.

Sartre's existentialism argues differently and makes a claim for the certainty of human existence that also establishes the conditions of its own existence. Rather than saying that when we assert 'I think, therefore I am' we provide certainty for the existence of 'I', he argues that 'when we say "I think" we are attaining to ourselves in the presence of the other, and we are just as certain of the other as we are of ourselves' (ibid.: 45). According to this view, human existence is inextricably linked to others and therefore it is not possible to gain any knowledge or formulate any truth about the self except in relation to those with whom existence is shared. In making this argument, Sartre also posits the term 'inter-subjectivity' to define this relationality of self and other: 'It is in this world that man has to decide what he is and what others are' (op. cit.).

The posthuman critique – a coda

When Rosi Braidotti points out that 'Existentialism stressed Humanist conscience as the source of both moral responsibility and political freedom' (2013: 19), the legacy that phenomenology and existentialism leaves with twenty-first-century thought is essentially and clearly a humanist one. By fundamentally placing existence before essence and engaging in an inquiry about what it means to have being in the world, both philosophies take as their starting point – their initial premise – human existence in the world. In the words of Sartre, 'There is no other universe except the human universe, the universe of human subjectivity' (1973: 55). When Nietzsche famously and notoriously proclaimed 'God is dead', he raised the need for interpretation in philosophy, encouraging us to begin to think around and beyond the theological insistence that belief in humanity and human existence was somehow self-evident and based upon the undoubted existence of God. The stability and metaphysical certainty provided by a belief in the existence of God and the claims for the universal validity for human existence that are based upon it are challenged when we begin to pay close attention to the secular claims of Nietzsche's attack upon the implementation of natural laws and values.

The current emergence of posthuman forms of thought offer a fundamental challenge to the domination of the human subject and the very existence of the academic discipline of the humanities. Posthuman thinking works to de-centre 'Man' from his central position as the master and measure of all things, and in so doing encourages an examination of nature and culture, not in oppositional and dualistic terms, but rather as part of an always changing continuum in which the material and the discursive are continually being blurred and are always in play with one another.

References

Braidotti, R. (2013) *The Posthuman*, Cambridge: Polity.

Heidegger, M. (1962) *Being and Time*, Oxford: Blackwell.

Husserl, E. (1997) *Psychological and Transcendental Phenomenology and the Confrontation with Heidegger* (1927–1931), trans. T. Sheehan and R. Palmer, Dordrecht: Kluwer.

Sartre, J.-P. (1973) *Existentialism and Humanism*, trans. P. Mairet, London: Methuen.

Stenhouse, L. (1975) *An Introduction to Curriculum Research and Development*, London: Heinemann.

Welton, D. (ed.) (1999) *The Essential Husserl*, Bloomington: Indiana University Press.

CHAPTER

5

Foucault and the construction of knowledge, meaning, identity and practices

Ken Gale

Overview

The work of Michel Foucault is particularly relevant to those who are interested in the ways in which knowledge, meaning, identity and practices are influenced by the settings in which they are found. So, for example, in some of his early works, such as *Madness and Civilization* and *Discipline and Punish*, he attempted to show how institutions such as the asylum and the prison contained, controlled and constructed certain members of society in particular ways. This chapter is designed to encourage the reader to consider the ways in which Foucault's thought can be applied within educational institutions such as the school, the college and the university.

Foucault's thinking offers a challenge to rational, linear and dialectically progressive thought by arguing that what we say and what we do – quite simply, how we behave – in all walks of life or situations is produced by these situations; in short, all knowledge, meaning, identity and practices are social or cultural products. He argues that language, or discourses, what he refers to as 'technologies of self', serve to construct us in particular ways and that over time this becomes a form of control. First, the chapter will use examples, case studies and 'critical incidents' to explore and inquire into the way in which such processes might be seen to be at work in a variety of education settings. Second, the chapter will encourage readers to employ Foucault's thinking as a means of inquiring into the social, historical and cultural conditions that might have made these educational practices and ways of thought possible and in so doing to investigate their socialising and disciplinary effects. So, for example, Foucault's metaphorical appropriation of Bentham's Panopticon will be used to explore how the uses of power, influence and control might be exercised though formal and informal curriculum models and practices. The chapter will therefore encourage readers to apply Foucault's thought to the exercise of power in contemporary education settings.

QUESTIONS

■ How does Foucault's view that social institutions contain, control and construct members of society in particular ways influence our thinking about the current role of educational institutions?

- How can Foucault's argument that knowledge, meaning, identity and practices are social or cultural products be applied to teaching and learning in contemporary education settings?
- How might an inquiry into the social, historical and cultural conditions that influence the theory and practice of education help to reveal and explain the possible socialising and disciplinary effects of schools, colleges and universities?
- How are education practices, according to Foucault, linked to the exercise of power?

Introduction

> A critique is not a matter of saying that things are not right as they are. It is a matter of pointing out on what kinds of assumptions, what kinds of familiar, unchallenged, unconsidered modes of thought, the practices that we accept rest ... Criticism is a matter of flushing out that thought and trying to change it: to show that things are not as self-evident as we believed, to see that what is accepted as self-evident will no longer be accepted as such. Practicing criticism is a matter of making facile gestures difficult.
>
> (Foucault, 1988: 154)

In this quotation we can find the basis of the fundamental contribution that the thinking of Foucault makes to the theories and practices of education in contemporary societies. In essence what this quotation is saying for those who are interested in studying education is that at the heart of any theory and practice of teaching and learning is the practice of critique. As an applied philosophical practice, Foucault always encourages those who read and make use of his writings to engage in the practical task of making the familiar strange. He encourages us to take up the philosophical practice of inquiring into those taken-for-granted, everyday assertions, points of view and customary practices as a means of considering the conditions that might have might have made their acceptance and use possible. So the value of Foucault's thinking within the theory and practice of education is that it encourages us to work critically with what we say and what we do and to provide us with both a methodology and a range of methods for carrying this out. In this respect, we can begin by asserting that Foucault's philosophy could be considered to be constructivist in both content and style, prompting us to look at how we go about representing and constructing the world around us.

Biographical details

Providing biographical details of Foucault and his life is not a straightforward activity and it is possible that Foucault himself would offer a challenge to those who decide to embark upon the enterprise. In response to a question about his identity, Foucault once famously said:

> I don't feel it is necessary to know exactly what I am. The main interest in life and work is to become someone else you were not in the beginning. If you knew

when you began a book what you would say at the end, do you think you would have the courage to write it?

(Martin et al., 1988: 9)

So in many of his writings Foucault challenged the notion of the author and in so doing offered a dismissal of the idea of a biographical text or study. As the thinking involved in carrying out this study into the contribution of Foucault's thought to the study of education begins to emerge, we shall see that such a view is based upon the radical idea that notions of reality always have to be questioned and that we should always consider the critical possibility that the world around us is not simply made but made up. So when we identify someone as, say, an author, Foucault would also have us consider that this is our identification and it is one which might be challenged by others. The logic of Foucault's argument, therefore, is based upon the view that identity, but also meaning, knowledge and so on, is constructed, is not generalisable and is very specific to the social and cultural settings in which they are found. Therefore, according to this view, identity, meaning, knowledge and so on are situated and are, in large part, constructed by the language and interactions that operate within these cultural settings or situations.

However, for our purposes here we can assert with a reasonable degree of validity and rigour that Foucault was an author, that also in his public life he was a scholar, an intellectual, a critical historian, a philosopher and so on. Talking about how he was identified and positioned in his public life, he once said:

I think I have in fact been situated in most of the squares on the political check-erboard, one after another and sometimes simultaneously: as anarchist, leftist, ostentatious or disguised Marxist, nihilist, explicit or secret anti-Marxist, techno-crat in the service of Gaullism, new liberal etc.

(Foucault, 1984: 383)

It is clear that in presenting himself in these constantly changing, elusive and mercurial ways, Foucault not only tells us something about the complexities of his own colourful and often troubled life but also through these multifaceted illustrations and quotations reveals a great deal about his approach to philosophy. In so doing he provides us with a way forward in looking at the important role his approach offers in bringing philosophy to education studies in society today.

Foucault was born in Poitiers in France in 1926, the son of a doctor. After an early Catholic boarding school education, Foucault entered the highly prestigious École Normale Supérieure in Paris to study philosophy. Throughout his life he wrote extensively about history, historical change and the way in which historical accounts provide us with very particular views of the world. He was interested in the way in which modern social institutions such as prisons, hospitals, schools and so on construct us in particular ways. This interest inevitably led him to consider the ways in which we gain knowledge of people and the world from living in these institutions and how this knowledge is linked to power. The publication of his early work *The Order of Things* (1966) led to gaining a teaching position at the University of Paris (Vincennes) during which time he was actively involved in the student unrest that took place in May 1968. In 1970 he was appointed to the chair of history of systems of thought at the Collège de France where he continued to write, publish and campaign for the remainder of his life until his death in 1984. There are many biographical texts of Foucault which can expand upon these details; these include and can be found in: Miller (1994), Matthews (1996) and Eribon (1993).

The construction of identity, meaning and action in education settings

Towards the end of the nineteenth century, John Stuart Mill (1962, 1985) claimed to have provided the philosophical grounding for our understanding of liberty; a form of thinking that was to have a major influence on the development of education in the twentieth century. Grounding his principles for thought, expression and action upon notions of rationality and utility, Mill claimed to have provided the basis upon which the individual and the State could live in rational, harmonious and ultimately functional ways to promote a democratic and libertarian society. The logic of Mill's approach was premised upon the belief that all individuals potentially are able to exercise a freedom of thought; they are free to think what they like. Next, as social beings, they then have to consider how to express themselves freely and acceptably to others and, finally, how to act in the social worlds they inhabit.

At a similar time in history, Marx (1974) described how what he referred to as the ideological superstructure of capitalist society serves to support the inequalities of its economic infrastructure by demonstrating how institutions such as the church, the family, schools etc. pass on, through largely covert means of socialisation, the ideas and thinking of the dominant economic class to individuals in society and how, in turn, these processes work to support and control these inequalities by translating their economic power into social, political, cultural and other forms of power.

While his writing bears clear post-Marxist qualities (for a brief while, he was a member of the Communist Party), Foucault was at pains not to produce a grand narrative or macro-theory characteristic of so many of the nineteenth-century philosophers such as Mill, Marx and others. So, greatly influenced by the philosophical writings of Nietzsche, Foucault's discourse theory offers a micro-political analysis of the acquisition of knowledge and the operation of power in modern societies which qualifies and troubles the kind of binary thinking that is offered and is central to the conflicting political philosophies outlined above and which dominated thinking up to this point. The social and cultural constructivism that Foucault's philosophical thinking both proposed and engendered was therefore in stark contrast to the major philosophical traditions that had preceded its emergence.

Since the writing of Descartes, the positioning of philosophical thought and practice in western societies has been established in terms of a dualism that was entailed by his famous and well-known a priori principle, *cogito ergo sum*: I think, therefore I am. This idealist principle asserts that thinking is taking place, I am doing the thinking, and therefore I exist. So the philosophical tradition of *idealism* asserts that all we can know with any certainty is the content, the ideas, of the mind and from this we can infer the existence of the world around us.

It has been argued that taking such a position offers us a *subjective* view of the world. In contrast, what is sometimes referred to as a common-sense view of the world argues that the world around us, the world out there, beyond the workings of our mind, must have an existence of its own. The realist tradition is based upon the view that we can know the material world directly through the operation of our senses and that this is a world that has a factual, concrete reality that can be observed, tested and understood in a way that is scientific, empirical and independent of our judgment. *Realism* claims to offer an *objective* view of the world. While *constructivism* offers a number of different possible forms and interpretations, for our purposes we can describe it as a philosophical tradition that while there might be a world of existence that exists beyond the workings of our mind, it is one that we give meaning to through our own processes of knowing. Constructivism takes the view that the world cannot be known in objective terms but that it is possible for us to reflexively engage with various interpretations and meanings that might be offered about it.

The emergence of Foucault's discourse theory

We have initially and somewhat generally characterised Foucault's approach as being constructivist by suggesting that he presents identity, meaning and action as being in some way produced or created by the social and cultural settings within which they are situated. According to this thinking, therefore, the 'site' of the classroom, the micro-settings of the playground, the street, the bar and so on, become, in Foucault's approach, crucially important in the formation of identity, thought and action. Within these sites, as within any cultural context, language can be seen to play a key role and, for Foucault, is instrumentally significant in producing meaning within any given historical period. Along with other post-structural theorists of the twentieth century such as Deleuze, Derrida, Lyotard, Irigaray and others, Foucault is often seen as being responsible for the 'linguistic turn' that has come to characterise a great deal of contemporary philosophical thinking.

So if we think of the many different kinds of discussions or various linguistic exchanges that we might participate in within classrooms, playgrounds and other social settings, then we can begin to explore what was important for Foucault when he began to first formulate what has become known as his 'discourse theory'. In terms of the construction of knowledge and power, 'discourse' or 'discursive practices' are the cornerstones of Foucault's thinking and are, for him, normally represented by the fundamentally important elision, greatly influenced by the philosophy of Nietzsche, of 'power/knowledge'.

According to this view, discourses are sets of culturally and historically situated norm or rule-governed statements which are constructed and used by groups of people in particular settings, such as schools, colleges or universities, which embody knowledge and give meaning to identity and action in these settings. In Foucault's own words: '(A) body of anonymous, historical rules, always determined in the time and space that have defined a given period, and for a given social, economic, geographical, or linguistic area, the conditions of operation of the enunciative function' (1972: 117). One of the important aspects of this quotation is to do with the anonymity of what he refers to as the 'rules' of the discourse. Participants in the discourse may not be consciously aware of these rules but the rules are, nevertheless, shared by all those who are part of the group to which they apply.

It is at this point, Foucault suggests, that we find the conflation of knowledge and power; somehow we 'know' the rule, we are unaware of its origin, yet we are prepared to conform to its requirements. So at the heart of the inquiry that Foucault encourages us to undertake as we analyse the influence of discourse in all aspects of society are some important questions. How is it that one particular statement or utterance appears at a given time and in a given place rather than another? What are the social and cultural conditions that made this statement possible? How does this statement gain legitimacy in society rather than another?

ACTIVITY 1

Consider the way in which practice identities are produced and regulated.

Consider the following questions in relation to your family, classroom, workplace and peer group(s):

1   Write down some examples of what you think is 'say-able' and 'do-able' in these social and cultural settings. Then do the same for what might be 'unsay-able' and 'undo-able'.
2   How do you consider what is 'say-able' and 'do-able' and 'unsay-able' and 'undo-able' come into being in these settings?
3   How is the line between the 'say-able' and 'do-able' and the 'unsay-able' and 'undo-able' policed or regulated?
4   How might this line be altered or resistances to it put in place?

Foucault and discourse in education

We have seen that the constructivist flavour of Foucault's thinking is based upon the idea that material things, the behaviours and all the constituent elements of the world around us exist but they only take on meaning and become objects of knowledge within the operation of discourses. According to Foucault, discourses systematically order, arrange and represent the world. Therefore, objects existing in the world do not have meaning of themselves; it is the various systems of representation that operate in different 'sites' that work to give meaning to those objects and in so doing objectify them. In this way, we gain knowledge of those objects but also because they are represented in particular ways we are in a power relation with them.

Identity is for Foucault a way of representing a person, so if, for example, we are engaging in a discussion about someone, we can say that the person we are talking about is the subject *of* our discussion. However, in this discussion we are engaged in making various representations of this person so this person becomes subject *to* the discussion and as such becomes the object of the discussion. For Foucault this would be an example of a discursive practice; a technology of self in which the person is constructed as an object by the operation of the discourse. For Foucault, such a process is also linked to the emergence of disciplinary effects in which subjects begin to engage in practices of self-regulation. Therefore, being subject *to* the discourse has the effect of situating, constituting and hence regulating the self in ways that Foucault describes as producing 'docile bodies'.

Foucault used the model of the Panopticon, designed by the nineteenth-century Liberal thinker and reformer Jeremy Bentham, as a basis for describing the ways in which the organisation of surveillance of institutional practices in prisons, hospitals, schools and so on can discipline and create 'docile bodies' through the implementation of systems of self-regulation. Over a period of time the inmates within the 'all-seeing' institution begin to behave as if they are constantly being watched, and thus their behaviour is regulated according to the requirements of the institution.

ACTIVITY 2

Try to find and copy an image of the Panopticon in a book or on the Internet.
   In what ways do you think systems of regulation of this kind might influence socialisation in schools or the operation of a hidden curriculum?

The influence of discourse

Discourses, as systems of representation, will operate differently in different 'sites' and therefore, according to the logic of Foucault's thinking, as we are represented differently in these 'sites' it will be possible for us to have different situated selves. So, for example, if we attend the doctors or go to the hospital for an appointment, this view would argue that certain medical discourses would operate to identify or represent us in certain ways. We might be seen as being a particular kind of person with a certain kind of illness or condition that requires a specific kind of treatment. If we attend a party or a wedding, certain social, ethnic or gender discourses might be seen to operate and the way in which we are dressed or how we speak or act would have an influence upon how we are identified by the systems of representation that operate there.

A more explicit example can be taken from the history of education in Britain to illustrate this point. Particular attention was given to what became known as working-class underachievement during the 1960s and 1970s following the publication of survey data that showed that levels of achievement among working-class children fell some way behind those of children from other class backgrounds. Concerns about these results led to the emergence of a range of research-based interpretations that pointed to deficiencies and deprivations in the social and cultural nature of working-class life at the time. So, for example, Sugarman's (1966) study into child-rearing practices among families of different class backgrounds claimed to show that middle-class parents preferred to use a system of 'deferred gratification' when bringing up their children, whereas parents in working-class homes were more likely to use 'immediate gratification' to punish or reward the actions of their children.

Sugarman claimed that the practices of deferred gratification were much more likely to nurture in middle-class children motivation, ambition and enthusiasm to study and work for a future as they moved through the different stages of the education system. The pathologising of children's behaviour in this way also led to providing teachers with a technical vocabulary of underachievement which encapsulated the inevitability of class-based differences in ability and provided a justification for classroom practices based upon the use of levels and standards and different methods of classification within the structural configuration of schools according to class-based typifications.

This provides an example of a form of schooling that, through the operation of a particular educational discourse, constructs children in certain ways and plays a significant part in the way in which their educational experiences are formed. According to Foucault's thinking, systems of representation of this kind work to transform individual pupils into objects of knowledge; it is discourse, not the individuals themselves, that produce knowledge.

Constructing a pedagogical approach?

A study of the philosophy of Foucault that would promote an examination of the use of discourse in education would therefore need to take into consideration a number of important points of analysis which will assist in a study of education.

Points of analysis could be based on the following questions:

What kinds of statements provide us with knowledge of education?

First of all, this study would need to be able to recognise and indicate a range of *statements* which provide knowledge about education.

E.g. 'Vocational education helps to provide for the economic well-being of society.'

E.g. 'Attitudes are caught, not taught.'

These statements would be illustrative of the substantive content of the discourse and as such would provide the basis for further consideration. Statements that provide us with knowledge about education are therefore likely to reflect and vary across time and space so that taking a historical perspective and a cross-cultural perspective would enable us to compare and contrast how knowledge about education, according to Foucault, is produced.

What are the rules which prescribe certain ways of talking about education?

Having examined a number of statements that provide us with knowledge about education, an evaluation of the role of discourse in education would need to take into consideration the *rules* which prescribe certain ways of talking about education. These would be both inclusive and exclusive in their ways of dealing with education matters. As we have already seen, discourses tend to provide a basis for what might be 'say-able', 'do-able' or 'think-able' at a given time and place.

E.g. 'Food is not to be eaten in classrooms.'

E.g. 'Children should be seen and not heard.'

Again, the use of historical and cross-cultural perspectives will enable us to compare and contrast how knowledge about education and the rules associated with it are, according to Foucault, produced.

How can we identify the subjects that are identified within a particular education discourse?

We have seen that, according to Foucault, discourses work to transform *subjects* into *objects*, so it is therefore important to identify the *subjects* that are identified within a particular education discourse. In this respect it would also be important for us to be able to recognise and indicate the different characteristics, attributes and features that are discursively associated with a particular identified subject as these would help us to come to 'know' about more about the educational 'site' at this time.

E.g. 'a good teacher', 'a bad student', 'an interfering parent', 'a caring classroom assistant', 'an old-fashioned head teacher'.

How do the everyday, the normative and the customary come to acquire legitimacy and authority within a particular educational setting?

An important aspect of the knowledge about education in society at a given time and how the bringing together of power and knowledge comes about is based upon the way in which the everyday, the normative and the customary come to acquire *legitimacy* and *authority* within a particular setting. How does a sense of embodying the 'truth of the matter' at a certain time or in a certain place come about? Foucault would encourage us to try to establish the conditions that allow an individual to become identified as 'a subject who knows'. Foucault uses the term 'technologies of self' to describe the means by which subjects are identified in particular ways. So, in contemporary education, discourses of gender, age, ethnicity and class can all be seen as conferring authority, or its lack, upon a particular subject or subject position.

What are the practices *within education institutions that gain legitimacy and enforce authority?*

Ball (1990) has argued that management acts as a 'moral technology' in establishing legitimacy and authority in education settings. By this term he is referring to the *practices* within schools, colleges and universities that gain legitimacy for dealing with the subjects whose conduct is being regulated and organised according to the dominant ideas within a given discourse. So, for example, we might identify the practice of classroom observation and inspection systems for teachers, classroom assistants and so on as a practice which regulates in this way by helping ideas of good or bad practice to be established and accepted.

What are *discourse formations* and how do they operate?

Foucault argues that within any given space or time certain *discourse formations* will exist and might help us to characterise, identify and give meaning to the nature of the social and cultural conditions of that space and time. So with the ever-shifting movement of these *discourse formations*, he argues that different discourses will arise in particular historical moments or in different places and supplant the existing ones. This process will work to produce new conceptions of management, teaching, gender relations and so on and will also serve to establish relationships between different discourses. So, for example, discourses of gender and sexuality might form together to impact upon practices of inclusion in a particular education institution. It might be observed, for example, that changes in religious beliefs and practices produce discourses that connect with discourses that are informed by ethnic origin or affiliation and go to make up a particular *discourse formation*. Foucault noted that every discourse potentially contains the seeds of its own downfall and that often resistances to a particular discourse can lead to the creation of a new discourse.

ACTIVITY 3

In considering how we might use the work of Foucault in helping us to construct a pedagogical approach, the preceding passage raises a number of questions that need to be addressed. These are as follows:

What kinds of *statements* provide us with knowledge of education?

What are the *rules* which prescribe certain ways of talking about education?

How can we identify the *subjects* that are identified within a particular education discourse?

> How do the everyday, the normative and the customary come to acquire *legitimacy* and *authority* within a particular educational setting?
>
> What are the *practices* within education institutions that gain legitimacy and enforce authority?
>
> What are *discourse formations* and how do they operate?
>
> Using the italicised words to guide you, try to answer these questions in relation to your experience of education, perhaps in a school you have attended, work experience placement you have carried out or in relation to your university studies at the present time.

Education and discourse theory: a conclusion

From the above it has become clear that for Foucault, discourses are synonymous with systems of social relations, organisation and control. This chapter argues that we can begin to theorise discourses in ways that help to provide a practical basis for developing the systems of social relations that are of interest in our education studies. In arguing that knowledge, action and identity are all objects of *discourse* and in this respect what they mean depends upon this, Foucault also provides us with a means of looking critically at the social organisation of education in schools, colleges and universities in the UK in the twenty-first century. We are provided with an intriguing basis of inquiry and research into education if, according to this view, the systems of identification and representation that are part of discursive practices serve to construct these objects and in so doing remain concealed. From a Foucauldian perspective, therefore, it is clear that meaning, knowledge, identities and practices are *discursively constructed* and as such are highly situated and are products of historically and culturally specific systems of rules. The question for the purposes of this chapter is to consider what applications to education can be made from this perspective and the line of reasoning that it proposes. In arguing for a theory and practice of *discourse analysis and evaluation*, Foucault proposed what he referred to as archaeological and genealogical methods which could be used to inquire into the social, cultural and historical conditions that have made the theory and practice of education possible in any place and at any particular time.

References

Eribon, D. (1993) *Michel Foucault*, trans. Betsy Wing, London: Faber and Faber.

Foucault, M. (1961) *Madness and Civilization*, London: Tavistock.

Foucault, M. (1970) *The Order of Things*, New York: Random House.

Foucault, M. (1972) *The Archaeology of Knowledge*, trans. A. M. Sheridan Smith, New York: Pantheon.

Foucault, M. (1976) *Discipline and Punish*, Harmondsworth: Penguin.

Foucault, M. (1984) Polemics, Politics and Problematisations, in P. Rabinow (ed.) *Foucault Reader*, New York: Pantheon.

Foucault, M. (1988) Practising Criticism, trans. A. Sheridan et al., in L. D. Kritzman (ed.) *Politics, Philosophy Culture: Interviews and Other Writings, 1977–1984* (pp. 152–8), New York: Routledge.

Kant, I. (1968) *The Critique of Pure Reason*, trans. Norman Kemp Smith, London: Macmillan.

Kendall, G. and Wickham, G. (1999) *Using Foucault's Methods*, London: Sage.

Martin, L., Guttman, H. and Hutton, P. (1988) (eds) *Technologies of the Self*, London: Tavistock.

Marx, K. and Engels, F. (1974) *The German Ideology*, London: Lawrence and Wishart.

Matthews, E. (1996) *Twentieth Century French Philosophy*, Oxford: Oxford University Press.

Mill, J. S. (1962) *Utilitarianism*, London: Fontana.

Mill, J. S. (1985) *On Liberty*, London: Penguin.

Miller, J. (1994) *The Passion of Michel Foucault*, London: Flamingo.

Popkewitz, T. and Brennan, M. (1998) (eds) *Foucault's Challenge: Discourse, Knowledge, and Power in Education*, New York: Teachers College Press.

Sugarman, B. (1966) Social Class and Values as Related to Achievement and Conduct in Schools, *The Sociological Review*, 14 (3): 287–301.

Willig, C. (ed.) (1999) *Applied Discourse Analysis: Social and Psychological Interventions*, Buckingham: Open University Press.

Deleuze
The pedagogic potential of always creating concepts
Ken Gale

Overview

In response to the question, 'What is philosophy?', Deleuze and Guattari claim that 'philosophy is the discipline that involves creating concepts' and that the 'object of philosophy is to create concepts that are always new' (1994: 5). This chapter is therefore designed to take this philosophical practice and to encourage an application of the approach within education settings. This approach will apply a Deleuzian notion of creativity which will not promote a pedagogic existence in which concepts are allowed to rest on the dusty shelves of the academy, becoming fixed and congealed; rather, it will involve readers in creating them as part of a continuous process of inquiry and expression. In this chapter, therefore, the philosophy of Deleuze will be used, first of all, to encourage readers to engage in the practice of conceptualisation, in working out and forming ideas about education matters, and then once this has been done to follow this up with the practice of contextualisation, encouraging them to apply and use these ideas in different backgrounds and settings. In encouraging the use of these processes, the chapter is also designed to introduce the reader to some of the important concepts and approaches to be found in the philosophy of Deleuze. So, for example, in following Deleuze, we find that the formal, institutional spaces in which teaching and learning take place can be referred to as territories. Potentially, these spaces are not fixed, stable and unchanging and can be actively and creatively engaged with through processes of territorialisation. As these territories are conceptualised and re-conceptualised by teachers, learners and others in different ways, they gain different meanings within the context of a creative evolution that forms and re-forms in a constantly shifting frisson of energetic life. Therefore, this chapter will suggest a means of using the philosophy of Deleuze to think and act creatively in a range of different contemporary education settings.

UNIVERSITY OF WINCHESTER
LIBRARY

QUESTIONS

■ How does Deleuze's view that 'philosophy is the discipline that involves creating concepts' influence the theory and practice of education?
■ How might Deleuzian philosophical practice be designed to encourage creative approaches within contemporary education settings?
■ How might education institutions be seen to exercise power through Deleuze's notion of territorialisation?
■ How might the practices of conceptualisation and contextualisation be used to facilitate teaching and learning practices?

Introduction

> That is, philosophy is not the simple art of forming, inventing and fabricating concepts, because concepts are not necessarily forms, discoveries, or products. More rigorously, philosophy is the discipline that involves creating concepts . . . the object of philosophy is to create concepts that are always new . . . Concepts are not waiting for us ready-made, like heavenly bodies. There is no heaven for concepts.
>
> (Deleuze and Guattari, 1994: 5)

This quotation, taken from Deleuze and Guattari's (1994) last collaborative book, *What Is Philosophy?*, provides a central tenet, a *modus vivendi* and a practical basis for actually *doing* philosophy. Deleuze and Guattari were consistent in their claims about what philosophy should be and what it could do, and this quotation exemplifies their position clearly. Philosophy is active, it is something that is done, and in this respect it is always a creative practice. In this respect, therefore, this chapter will argue that a philosophical approach of this kind is essential to the theory and practice of education studies.

So in taking this approach it is important to work with behaviours and activities and to express these in terms of verbs. In doing this it is possible to begin with the quotation above and argue that 'creating concepts' involves an active process of conceptualisation. Inherent in this process are questions such as 'What do you think it is?', 'How do feel we should proceed?', 'What is your idea of this?', 'How do you conceptualise this (or that)?'. Further, it could be argued that in promoting this philosophy of use, these processes of conceptualisation can also lead to processes of contextualisation. St. Pierre talks of her reading of Deleuze and her application of his philosophy to education and says:

> I had plugged into his circuits and, without thinking too much about it, found myself plugging his concepts into everything in my life so that it has become different than it was before. I expect the pleasure of reading great philosophy is the thrill that even a non-philosopher can find in events (a life) that were once impossible.
>
> (2004: 284)

Within the context of the pedagogical intent of this book, such an approach has the potential to promote in education and other settings a form of student-centred learning where the emphasis is shifted away from the teacher teaching to the learner learning.

ACTIVITY 1

Look up the following reference: Jastrow, J. (1899) The Mind's Eye, *Popular Science Monthly* 54, pp. 299–312. In the reference you will find that Jastrow uses an image to make a point about the mind. Can you see this image differently? Does it become ambiguous? Can you see it in a number of ways? Why do you think you see one aspect of the image before another?
    Show the image to some friends and colleagues: what is their reaction to the image?

Conceptualisation as a process

It is clear from the preceding activity that there are different ways in which we can see this figure operating. Originally, Jastrow (1899) tried to use the figure to illustrate the workings of the mind, to demonstrate how the brain 'switches' between seeing a rabbit and a duck or a duck and a rabbit. Wittgenstein famously used the image in his philosophy lectures at Cambridge in the late 1940s and, as Monk points out, '(t)he point about the figure is that it can be seen under more than one aspect: the same drawing can be seen as a duck and as a rabbit. And it is this aspect of *seeing-as* that interested Wittgenstein' (1991: 508). *Seeing-as* can be used to suggest agency, so that, based upon our experience of the world, we can make decisions about how we see the image and whether, for us, it is a duck or a rabbit. Wittgenstein was also interested in what we might describe as the creative or representational nature of this process of *seeing-as*. The image represents something to us and through this representation we have a sense of reality. The so-called linguistic turn that occurred in the post-structural movements of the late twentieth century were greatly influenced by Wittgenstein's (2001) thinking at this time. As an example of this, the chapter on Foucault in this book is designed to demonstrate the way in which language, specifically through the various operations of discourse, works to represent and construct the world in particular ways. Foucault argued that discourses serve to construct knowledge, meaning, identity and so on in a form of *seeing-as*; we see the world according to the influence of discourse.

In applying the philosophy and the thinking of Deleuze to education, the duck/rabbit image can be used to encourage students and learners to be actively involved in the creation of concepts and to involve themselves and others in the processes and practices of conceptualisation. In such a process they are encouraged to exercise agency and realise, to actually *make real*, their own experiences. By promoting a form of agency of this kind, learners are encouraged to be involved in *meaning-making* rather than being constrained to conform to pedagogical practices which involve *teaching meaning*. Therefore, for Deleuze, conceptualisation of this kind emphasises not so much the processes and practices of representation or illustration, but the importance of an active and realist involvement in creativity and invention.

Conceptualisation and becoming

For Deleuze, then, creating concepts and the active process of conceptualisation is also a practice of *becoming* which not only involves using ideas and concepts in practices of meaning-making but also acknowledging their inevitable connection with affects and percepts in the complexities of relational space. By offering my view of the world, I am active in situating this view in relation to a multiple world of feeling, value, instinct, intuition and so on that not only involves my self but the selves of others. In this respect, therefore, it makes sense not to talk about something that can be essentialised or fixed into a category of difference. Such a view resists talking about my *being* or my *identity*, as some *thing* that can be placed in a category or a classification. So rather than talking about my *species*, my identification as a 'human', a 'man', heterosexual and so on, it makes more sense to talk of a constantly individuating process of what Deleuze refers to as *becoming*. According to such a view, self always has the potential to change, it is always differentiating, it is always seeing and being seen differently. 'We can be thrown into a becoming by anything at all, by the most unexpected, most insignificant of things' (Deleuze and Guattari, 1988: 292). Deleuze's philosophy encourages us, therefore, not to think in terms of closed systems and structures, but rather to think of the changing, the flowing, the always mutating ways in which selves, languages, organisms, cultures and so on are always becoming. As Colebrook points out, this is a cause for optimism, creating a space for opportunity and recognising that the

> [i]mpossibility of organising life into closed structures was not a failure or loss but a cause for celebration and liberation. The fact that we cannot secure a foundation for knowledge means that we are given the opportunity to invent, create and experiment. Deleuze asks us to grasp this opportunity, to accept the challenge to transform life.
>
> (Colebrook, 2002: 2)

Such an approach involves taking lines of flight, not resting with the fixity of particular structures, forms and contents, and always shifting thought in its fluid relationality with affect and percept. It is in this sense that subjectivity and notions of the self are always in play. By working with becoming, Deleuze encourages us not to simply accept that one or other exists in a particular category of difference such as 'woman', 'heterosexual', 'Scottish' and so on and to live creatively in emerging relational spaces in which differentiating selves are always working, transmutating and living with processes of knowing and not yet known. In this way, knowing, learning and meaning are always about becoming with selves and others, in actively working to dissolve the rigidity of binary distinctions between right and wrong, inside and outside, teaching and learning and so on. This involves always working with complexity, always being engaged in differentiating and always acknowledging the possibility of the multiple. In terms of specific educational practices, Richardson talks of 'writing as a method of inquiry' (Richardson and St. Pierre, 2005) where to write is to act, to explore and possibly to find something out.

ACTIVITY 2

In this activity we can consider how Deleuze's notion of 'becoming' might be contextualised and put into practice within a classroom setting to promote equality and inclusion. So, how might the teaching and learning practice of 'differentiation' that is often recommended in the planning and running of classes be used to promote 'becoming'? How might the practice of 'differentiation' be employed to challenge the fixed binary classifications of 'boys/girls', 'old/young', 'ability/disability' etc.? How could such an approach be used as a way of taking a 'line of flight' in relation to the way in which different kinds of learners might be seen and engaged with in classrooms?

Also, and with substantial pedagogical intent, Deleuze talks of the use of writing in a similar way:

> How else can one write but of those things which one doesn't know, or knows badly? It is precisely there that we imagine having something to say. We write only at the frontiers of our knowledge, at the border which separates our knowledge from our ignorance and transforms the one into the other. Only in this manner are we resolved to write. To satisfy ignorance is to put off writing until tomorrow – or rather, to make it impossible.
>
> (2004: xx)

Creating concepts and using them

So, clearly, what is central to the philosophy of Deleuze and Guattari and its relevance to education studies is a sense of *becoming*, where talk is of the process of creating concepts in ways that are fluid and open, where closure and working with a fixed approach to meaning and knowledge are to be avoided. From this it is clear that their approach to research, pedagogic practices and education generally would always encourage reflexivity about any established or foundational representations that might precede or hamper a creative process of becoming. So there is an emphasis in their work upon engaging in processes of active, fluid, experimental and transgressive conceptualisation. Having an idea of something, raising questions, taking nothing for granted means working with the not yet known, linking such ideas with affect and percept in an ongoing creative method of inquiry. Within such a mode of inquiry, processes of *contextualisation* are also very important; using the curious and troubling query 'What if . . . ?', it is always innovative and invigorating to work to place such ideas within spatial and temporal settings. This involves a formative approach which always emphasises process over product, which promotes an ethical and aesthetic sensitivity over a technical rational formalism and which always encourages putting ideas into use, doing something with them, and as Deleuze says, 'plugging them in'.

Nomadic thought and inquiry

There is a pedagogical intent that can be drawn up from a recognition of what Deleuze and Guattari refer to as 'nomad thought' or 'nomadism' (1988), where nomadic inquiry involves a movement in space, smoothing out existing patterns and opening up a new trajectory or pathway. This creation of 'smooth space' offers an entry into the not yet known, perhaps digressing or going off the rails, following what they sometimes refer to as a 'line of flight'. The line of flight has the potential to open up both the possibilities of an escape from the constraints of existing 'striated space' and in taking perhaps a radically new direction in thought, feeling or value. In this way the geographies, the emotionalities and the tensions of a particular space are always being re-drawn. Each new line of flight works to both smooth and striate space. In this respect we might imagine the nomad travelling across the desert in search of an oasis. The movement of the nomad, the footprints of the camel in the sand leave marks that striate the space and in doing so smooth out those marks that might already have been there. Each 'striation' is then there to be followed by other travellers or to be smoothed over by different and subsequent engagements with that space.

ACTIVITY 3

1   Give an example that could be used to illustrate how space can be:
   a   Social
   b   Cultural
   c   Emotional
   d   Material
   e   Ethical
   f   Gendered
   g   Other.

2   In groups, discuss ways in which Deleuze's and Guattari's views of smooth and striated space could be applied to these examples.

3   In groups, discuss ways in which the notions of smooth and striated space could be used:
   a   As a form of learner-centred education
   b   As a transformative learning experience
   c   As an illustration of training.

Territorialisation and power

In relation to the above point, Deleuze also talks about 'nomad thought', 'nomadism' and 'nomadic inquiry' in relation to 'territorial' rhythms, movements and changes. So when he talks of 'territory', it is to do with boundary and distance and is set in fields and terrains. In a literal sense we can think of the spaces we inhabit in education as territories; so the classrooms, laboratories and workshops to be found in any education institution could be considered in this way. Therefore, thinking of these spaces as territories also opens up the possibilities of considering them in relation to power. So, for example and according to this view, in offering a point of view in a classroom discussion we can say that a student is territorialising the classroom space in particular ways; in offering her view, she is working to 'smooth out' existing views, or striations, and replace or modify them with her own. In this sense territorialisation can be about marking a boundary or promoting a particular sense of self. In the relational space of the classroom and the discussion that is being held there, 'territorialisation' can be seen to be part of rhythmic and interactive processes also involving both 're-territorialisation' and 'de-territorialisation' as others in the discussion engage with the topic and offer other points of view. Deleuze and Guattari talk about territory as being 'first of all the critical distance between two beings of the same species' (1988: 319) and describe how this is established and re-established in the following way:

> If need be, I'll put my territory on my own body, I'll territorialise my body: the house of the tortoise, the hermitage of the crab, but also tattoos that make the body a territory. Critical distance is not a meter, it is a rhythm. But the rhythm, precisely, is caught up in a becoming that sweeps up the distances between characters that are themselves more or less distant, more or less combinable.
>
> (Deleuze and Guattari, 1988: 320)

Negotiation, play, discussion, the dialogics of language and so on can all be seen to contribute to and be constitutive of this rhythmic territorialisation. Through the use of language, both verbal and non-verbal, we say who we are, what we like and where we are going. Rhythmically, we 'stake out' a territory in relation to the territories of others, establishing harmonies and incompatibilities, resonances and dissonances. This approach also offers a radically different view of subjectivity and self and other in relational spaces such as schools, colleges and universities.

In a traditional sense we tend to talk about subjectivity and self in terms of what might be considered recognisable *categorical differences of extensive bodies*, perhaps in terms of specifications of age, race, class and gender. Using these specifications, we construct and then identity, for example, an elderly, Asian, middle-class man or a young, white, working-class girl. In this way we create categories of difference and specification which give us a sense of being or of who someone is. We might then go on to attribute other features to these general classifications which are all used to build up and characterise that person in particular ways. Post-structural philosophies and approaches suggest that this process is one of *essentialising*, of working to create *being* in a foundational and established sense.

In a more radically creative sense, Deleuze encourages us to think of becoming rather than being, where rather than talking about the *categorical difference of extensive bodies* it makes sense to talk about the complex *differentiation of intensities* that can be found to work between them. This might be seen in terms of affect, value, intuition and so on. So the space between bodies or selves is always something that is being territorialised, changing, being negotiated or emerging in different ways. We can gain a sense of the complexities of territorialisation in the following:

> Two animals of the same sex and species confront each other: the rhythm of the first one 'expands' when it approaches its territory or the centre of its territory: the rhythm of the second contracts when it moves away from its territory. Between the two, at the boundaries, an oscillational constant is established: an active rhythm, a passively endured rhythm and a witness rhythm.
>
> (Deleuze and Guattari, 1988: 320)

In talking about working in his writing relationship with Guattari, Deleuze offers the following description which also describes the complexities of processes of differentiation and territorialisation rather than the acceptance of and reliance upon categories of difference:

> We were only two, but what was important for us was less our working together than this strange fact of working between the two of us. We stopped being 'author'. And these 'between-the-two's' referred back to other people, who were different on one side from on the other. The desert expanded, but in so doing became more populous. This had nothing to do with a school, with processes of recognition, but much to do with encounters. And all of these stories of becomings, of nuptials against nature, of a-parallel evolution, of bilingualism, of theft of thoughts, were what I had with Felix. I stole Felix and I hope he did the same for me. You know how we work – I repeat it because it seems to be important – we do not work together, we work between the two.
>
> (2002: 17)

Rhizomes

These sometimes harmonious, sometimes challenging and always recombinant and rhythmic moments of *territorialisation* and *re/de-territorialisation* are represented in the work of Deleuze in 'rhizomatic' forms: with Guattari he uses the figure of the rhizome as a way of trying to explain the intensely complex nature of these territorialisations and between-the-two's. So within education, where we are involved in learning and research, we can be seen to engage in forms of dialogic inquiry, as we use processes of conceptualisation and contextualisation to inquire into the not yet known. Also, as these continuing processes of differentiation influence our becomings when we nomadically circle and engage with texts, theories, studies and the many narratives of others, we both create and are created by *rhizomatic* patterns and flows.

As our thoughts, feelings and values, expressed in utterances, are folded in to establish *territorial* distances, the thoughts, feelings and values of others interact, combine and exchange with them in rhythmic response, allowing new utterances to emerge and new meanings to unfold. Deleuze and Guattari use the figure of the 'rhizome' as a means of describing the complex, ever-changing nature of 'becoming' in 'nomad thought' and inquiry. The following quotation gives a sense of how they see the rhizome operating:

> A rhizome ceaselessly establishes connections between semiotic chains, organisations of power, and circumstances relative to the arts, sciences and social struggles. A semiotic chain is like a tuber agglomerating very diverse acts, not only linguistic, but also perceptive, mimetic, gestural, and cognitive: there is no language in itself, nor are there any linguistic universals, only a throng of dialects, patois, slangs, and specialised languages. There is no ideal speaker-listener, any more than there is a homogenous linguistic community. Language is . . . 'an essentially heterogeneous reality'. There is no mother tongue, only a power takeover by a dominant language within a political multiplicity. Language stabilises around a parish, a bishopric, and a capital. It forms a bulb. It evolves by subterranean stems and flows, along river valleys or train tracks; it spreads like a patch of oil. It is always possible to break a language down into internal structural elements, an undertaking not fundamentally different from a search for roots . . . a method of the rhizome type . . . can analyse language only by decentering it onto other dimensions and other registers. A language is never closed upon itself, except as a function of impotence.

(1988: 7–8)

> **ACTIVITY 4**
>
> Think of an educational institution with which you are familiar – your old school or the university where you are studying now – and then try to use some of the examples and explanations from the quotation above as a means of putting Deleuze's and Guattari's description of the rhizome into use.
>
> When you have done this, share and discuss your example with your colleagues/friends.

Education and the fold

Deleuze uses the imagery of the figure of the *fold* (2003) to provide an 'image of thought' in which the complexities and contradictions within rhizomatic forms can be seen to emerge through processes of folding in and unfolding. In a classroom discussion perhaps, as participants express their views and structure their arguments, ideas might be folded in, and through the process of the discussion other ideas might be seen to emerge or to unfold.

> I share a memory of my mother with her mixing bowl, her sleeves rolled up and her arms bare, gradually adding flour, butter, water and other ingredients in a growing and sweet smelling cake mixture; I remember that she used to talk about 'folding in the butter' and it is this image of folding in that begins to allow the idea of the fold to unfold for me. As the butter is folded in, from the outside so to speak, some richness, some new quality begins to emerge in the mix, something is unfolding.
>
> (Gale, 2007: 475)

Within this complex rhizomatic mapping of creativity and exchange, we can discover in Deleuze a view of education and of the self that is full of complexity and change but which has the potential of creativity, of new ways of thinking and doing, always at its centre. The fold can be related to the folding in of ideas and concepts and the unfolding of new ones as discussion and negotiation animate the exchanges between groups of students and their teachers. In this respect, education is full of events; each new conceptualisation, each new concept that is created, marks a new event in the constant folding in and unfolding that its potential always offers. The 'process of folding in adds richness, multiple layers and intensification, the process of unfolding opens out, reveals and makes the familiar strange' (ibid.).

The use of discussion in education can be a valuable and creative pedagogical method; its subtle, nuanced and always eventful energies can facilitate and help to construct learning of diverse kinds and qualities. The discussion as a teaching and learning method can therefore be a powerful and influential means of developing new lines of flight in terms of knowledge and skills but also in terms of affect and percept: the discussion can help to build confidence, enhance motivation and allow agency to flourish within and against the constraining effects of institutional, curricular and policy-based structures. The Deleuzian creative practice of conceptualisation is therefore not simply about the creation of new ideas in a learner-centred domain of education practice; it has tendencies and leanings which pay attention to realist ontology and a holism of the self.

A holistic attitude and approach of this kind uses 'discussion' both in literal and metaphorical senses. Its foldings and unfoldings can be challenging and discomforting as well as constructive and accommodating; they provide a useful basis for looking at and being aware of the constant shifting of *intensities and* the fluid interplay between concept, affect and percept. In this respect, Deleuze draws upon the thinking of Bergson (1998), which in turn enables us to think of educational practice as a matter of 'creative evolution' in which learning is not simply about knowledge and skills but rather can be seen within an embodied, holistic and ultimately transformative body of thought and action. The *moments* that populate a particular discussion can be seen as conceptual, affective and perceptual events in which *movements* in terms of holistic learning take place. The possible transformations that can occur within these ethically sensitive spaces of learning can therefore be seen to contribute to this Deleuzian or Bergsonian process of 'creative evolution'.

ACTIVITY 5

You are with a group of students on your education studies programme and in the process of a module you are involved in having discussions about different learning matters. These could include assessment, the hidden curriculum, motivation, inclusion, discipline and so on. Using your understanding of Deleuze's (2003) conceptualisation of the fold, try to describe what might fold into and unfold from such discussions; how might such processes and exchanges help to promote understandings of these learning matters?

Philosophy as action

In conjunction with this thinking about and with Deleuze in terms of teaching and learning practices, it is also possible to envisage forms of research that emanate from these ways of thinking. Deleuze always claimed that his was a philosophy of use and action: he encourages those who take up his ideas to 'plug them in', to see what they do to encourage us to work with the transitive 'what if'. So we have here a possible educational methodology which can be employed in active experimental and creative ways, and which can be seen also to contribute to the confidence and the well-being of the learner: 'It's your turn, go on, why not give it a go, see what happens!'. We can link the research-based ethos of such an approach with the work of Laurel Richardson (2000) who argues that writing can be seen and used as 'a method of inquiry'. In her work Richardson encourages us to work from and as a challenge to those discourses and traditions that say that writing should be done in particular ways and with particular outcomes in mind. So in thinking and working against such constraining influences, she encourages that we write to inquire and to find out, and through the writing be prepared to take a journey into the not yet known.

It seems that the resonances with the possibly educative applications of Deleuzian philosophy are many. So we can, for example, take Deleuze's work with the 'fold' and relate it to processes of individuation, and of using writing as a means of becoming something other than what we might have been before we started writing. In such writing practices, the endogamous 'folding in' adds richness, multiple layers and intensification, while the exogamous unfolding opens out, reveals and leads to new and exciting fields of play and investigation. In this respect, the unfolding can be seen not only as an emergence but also as a synthesis or a synthetical moment, part of a process where as new elements are added or folded in, new relationships and connections are made or folded out.

The potentiality of such an approach can be likened to Deleuze's figure of the 'rhizome' referred to earlier, in which there are a multiplicity of interconnected shoots going off in all directions; as it grows, folding in and unfolding occurs, an assemblage of ideas, data, impressions, interpretations and notes connect in pluralistic ways that defy totalising exposition. Using the philosophy of Deleuze as the basis for both a pedagogical and research-based theory and practice within these rhizomatic flows and lines of flight informs a sense of always becoming in the relationality of a diverse range of educational spaces, of experimenting and encouraging critical and qualitative flexing, where the processes of teaching, learning and inquiry not only provide insights and critical judgments but also moments of evocation, excitement, exhilaration and drama.

References

Bergson, H. (1998) *Creative Evolution*, trans. A. Mitchel, New York: Dover.

Colebrook, C. (2002) *Gilles Deleuze*, London: Routledge.

Deleuze G. (2003) *The Fold: Leibniz and the Baroque*, London: Athlone Press.

Deleuze, G. (2004) *Difference and Repetition*, trans. P. Patton, London: Continuum.

Deleuze, G. and Guattari, F. (1988) *A Thousand Plateaus: Capitalism and Schizophrenia*, trans. B. Massumi, London: Athlone Press.

Deleuze, G. and Guattari, F. (1994) *What Is Philosophy?* London: Verso.

Deleuze, G. and Parnet, C. (2002) *Dialogues II*, London: Continuum.

Gale. K. (2007) Teacher Education in the University: Working with Policy, Practice and Deleuze, *Teaching in Higher Education* 12 (4): 471–83.

Jastrow, J. (1899) The Mind's Eye, *Popular Science Monthly* 54, 299–312.

Monk, R. (1991) *Ludwig Wittgenstein: The Logic of Genius*, London: Vintage.

Richardson, L. (2000) Writing: A Method of Inquiry, in N. Denzin and Y. Lincoln (eds), *Handbook of Qualitative Inquiry* (Second edition), London: Sage, pp. 923–48.

Richardson, L. and St. Pierre, E. (2005) Writing: A Method of Inquiry, N. Denzin and Y. Lincoln (eds), *The Sage Handbook of Qualitative Research* (Third edition), Thousand Oaks, CA: Sage pp. 959–78.

St. Pierre, E. A. (2004) Deleuzian Concepts for Education: The Subject Undone, *Educational Philosophy and Theory*, 36 (3): 283–96.

Wittgenstein, L. (2001) *Philosophical Investigations* (Third edition), trans. G. E. M. Anscombe, Oxford: Blackwell.

7

Feminisms, philosophy and education

Ken Gale

Overview

Feminist thinking is most commonly associated with different forms of direct action and political thought. It can be argued and demonstrated that the philosophical character and practice of feminism, or, more accurately, feminisms, are linked to philosophies of politics, ethics and rights. In this respect an understanding of the relationship between philosophy, feminisms and education will be enhanced by close related reading of other chapters in this book. The current and more common practice of talking with and about 'feminisms' rather than the singular 'feminism' allows for an inquiry into and a practice of a variety of different forms and analyses of the position of women in society. Such an approach also opens up the possibility of examining 'masculinisms' within the broader context of an inquiry into the philosophies of gender and the relationship that these might have with current educational thinking and practice.

Feminist thinkers have enriched exploration of issues of identity and sexuality by questioning the idea of detached and disembodied rationality and narrow, traditional ways of representing ideas. They have challenged inequalities between the sexes and critiqued the lack of reference of women's achievements in school and university curricula. Therefore, in working to engender a philosophically informed approach to feminisms and education, a perspectives-based approach will be used in this chapter as a means of opening up differentiated analyses of the possible relational spaces that might be seen to exist between these terms or bodies of thought. In this respect, a philosophically informed and critical approach to feminisms and education can also be nurtured and facilitated by taking both historical and cross-cultural perspectives in building up such an analysis.

From a historical perspective, the emergence of feminist thinking has been widely characterised and understood through the recognition of at least three 'waves' of thought that also identify particular movements and forms of action. While these can be seen as originating within particular and quite specific historical contexts, the thinking and practices they might be seen to entail can be examined, thought about and engaged with within numerous settings. By also looking at these perspectives outside of their historical origins, this chapter will therefore also offer the opportunity of critically examining their relevance in different cultural and institutional settings at the present time. Such an approach is designed to offer a philosophical approach to feminisms which will encourage and promote their application and use within a range of current education settings.

QUESTIONS

- How does the philosophical approach to thinking about feminisms help to promote critical practices within teaching and learning?
- How have feminist ways of thinking promoted exploration of issues to do with identity, gender, sexuality and knowledge construction in contemporary education settings?
- What is the educational value of taking historical and cross-cultural perspectives of feminist thought and gendered practices in social institutions?

Introduction

An analysis of the influence of feminist philosophy and thought on the theory and practice of education can initially be promoted through the lens of an historical perspective. While such an approach is neither exhaustive nor fully explanatory, it will provide this chapter with the basis for organising and then considering how feminist ways of thinking and doing have had an effect upon education institutions at the present time.

First-wave feminism: liberalism and reform

While Mary Wollstonecraft's (1982) *A Vindication of the Rights of Women*, written in 1789, is regarded as a landmark text in liberal feminist thought, what we now know as first–wave feminism became intellectually, socially and politically visible at the end of the nineteenth century and the beginning of the twentieth century and was most famously manifest in the Women's Suffrage movement of that time. First–wave feminism was based upon a philosophy of equality and human rights and from a philosophical point of view was connected to and emerged out of the philosophies of libertarianism and utilitarianism espoused initially by Jeremy Bentham and activated and promoted by John Stuart Mill (1962, 1974).

As a philosopher and a parliamentarian, Mill always worked toward what he considered to be right and in the late nineteenth century was one of the earliest (male) advocates of women's rights. In 1869 he published an essay entitled *The Subjection of Women* in which he argued for institutional reforms and the equality of women in social, economic and domestic life. At the time of publication, this essay was an affront to European conventional norms for the status of men and women. Mill credited his wife, Harriet Taylor Mill, with co-writing the essay and some similarity exists between this essay and that published earlier by his wife in 1851, *The Enfranchisement of Women*.

In his famous book, *On Liberty*, Mill constructed a logical argument, grounded initially upon the freedom of thought, wherein individuals are free to think what they like. Then, acting rationally and with social utility in mind, they begin to think about how they can express these thoughts to others with whom they co-exist in the social world. Using a persuasive rhetorical approach they then, according to Mill, consider the question: how can I exercise freedom of expression; how can I say this or that? The final stage of Mill's logical argument brings the solitary, rationally thinking individual into direct contact with others in the community by asking: how can I, as an individual, free-thinking person, act in relation to others? How I can gain freedom of action in the community? The logic of Mill's argument is both detailed and laboriously crafted in his book and it exposes for us the difficulty that we might experience when, for example, we consider the person who might hold a prejudicial thought or attitude in the mind, so to speak, and then has to consider how putting that thought or attitude into action might constitute a practice of discrimination in the wider community. With the emergence of neo-liberal policies and practices in the early twenty-first century, this remains a powerfully relevant question to address in both education and the conduct of the wider community.

Philosophy of reform

So, first-wave feminism, and the changes it advocated to improve the position of women in society, were essentially based not upon revolutionary change, but upon a philosophy of reform, of working within the institutions of society, employment, the church, the family and the school to bring about equality and a set of social, economic and legal conditions that would help to promote equality between different groups in society. In terms of power and the *agency* of women to bring about change in relation to these conditions, the philosophies of liberalism advocate working within the existing *structure* of society to bring about the changes that are necessary to create a more just, fair and egalitarian society.

This involves, as Giddens describes, 'an active constituting process, accomplished by, and consisting in, the doings of active subjects' (1993: 121). Giddens has used the term 'structuration' as a way of describing the operation of such processes and the action of individuals in relation to these structures. The relational space that can be seen to exist between agency and structure also reflects the powerful and energising dynamic that works between free will and determinism which has interested and tasked philosophers for many centuries and which is at the heart of Mill's philosophical approach outlined above. In this respect, the reformist tendencies of this first wave of feminist thought and action can best be described as *liberal feminism*, in which those who were active in the movement sought, as agents, to promote change in relation to the existing structures of society. Numerous examples of the kinds of reforms that were achieved in this way include, most notably, the extension of franchise and women achieving full voting rights gained through the passing of the Representation of the People Act 1928, and later with the enactment of such legislation as the Equal Pay Act 1970 and the Sex Discrimination Acts of 1975 and 1986.

Second-wave feminism: gender and power

As we open our exposition of and inquiry into what is known as second-wave feminism, it is probably timely to point out that the wave metaphor in use here is helpful in suggesting that these waves do not simply break on a single shore at one time in history and then ebb away and have no tide to bring them to break on some future shore. As such, the liberal and reformist influences of first-wave feminist can still be found to have effects in social, political and education fields today. The second wave of feminist theory and practice initially created considerable social upheaval both in terms of the main tenets of radical philosophical thought that it proposed and in terms of its activist approach to gender politics.

At the heart of the radicalism of the second-wave feminism that emerged mainly in the USA and the UK in the early 1970s was a 'sexual politics' (Millett, 1970) that identified men as the main reason for sexual and gendered inequalities in society. The theory and practice of radical feminism focused upon the patriarchal nature of social relationships and highlighted this as being the centrally divisive force upon which all other forms of power, inequality and oppression in society were based. For Kate Millett and other radical feminists, 'the personal is political' became a ubiquitous activating slogan and the heartbeat of their philosophical thought. If male domination could be eradicated from all aspects of personal relations, this would lead, in turn, to a radical transformation of all the controlling inequalities to be found in education, law, politics and all aspects of institutional life.

Consciousness raising

So if, for radical feminism, 'the personal is political', how does this become an activating philosophical principle? Drawing upon the thinking of critical theory, radical feminists concerned with the effects of male domination in patriarchal society began to promote 'consciousness raising' among women deemed to be subject to the unequal distribution of power in society. Critical theory has its origins in the philosophy of a neo-Marxist group of theorists that emerged in the 1930s in Germany and became known as the Frankfurt School. Influenced by the work of Marx and Gramsci (see Chapter 2), these philosophers focused upon the way in which the ideologies of capitalist society, through the influence of schools, the church, the legal system, the mass media and so on, become internalised by the mass of society and in so doing create a stable system of inequality in society.

Gramsci's hegemonic approach to the use of power and the maintenance of oppression in capitalist society demonstrates how cultural influence and control, in terms of establishing the norms, values and beliefs of society, leads in turn to the domination of the controlling economic class. Gramsci, in combining aspects of Marxist and Freudian thought, argued that influence, through different social and cultural media, works on the level of internalisation, so that the social and cultural normative establishes the individual and the personal. Radical feminists worked to highlight the political in the personal by forming 'consciousness-raising' groups in an attempt to nurture an understanding of women's oppression brought about by what they perceived to be the hegemonic influence of capitalist and patriarchal media. By raising awareness of inequalities that persist within the personal relations of society such as marriage, child rearing and education, radical feminism consciously worked to dismantle the patriarchal institutions that had established these inequalities in the first place.

At this time, a number of radical feminists focused upon the role played by language in the internalisation of patriarchal norms and values. When Adrienne Rich proclaimed 'This is the oppressor's language/Yet I need it to speak to you' (1975), the rhetorical persuasiveness of the quotation serves to demonstrate the powerful hegemony asserted over women simply through the use of what were perceived to be masculine or masculinised forms of language. In this quotation, Rich is referring to what Gibbon referred to as 'generic masculinism' (1999: 24) whereby a male-as-norm bias is present in, for example, the inclusive use of male personal pronouns, such as 'he' or 'his' or the deployment of nouns such as 'man' or 'mankind' to refer to all members of the human species. Gibbon offers further support for Rich's claim when she refers to what Schultz calls the 'semantic derogation of women':

> Schultz argues that it is men who have 'created English' and especially slang. Analysing the language used by men in describing women is, she claims, revealing. What appears is a catalogue of pejorated, demeaning terms reflecting men's fear, contempt or hatred of women.

> (ibid.: 72)

ACTIVITY 1

Gender and language:

Gibbon (1999: 73) cites Schultz in suggesting that pairs of masculine and feminine terms have over time tended to privilege the former over the latter. Examine the following list of pairs of words and see if you can detect any preferences in terms of negative or sexual connotations.

bachelor	spinster, old maid
wizard	witch
lord	lady
baronet	dame
governor	governess
courtier	courtesan
master	mistress
sir	madam
king	queen
Mr	Mrs

1   When you have finished annotating your list, discuss your responses with a colleague/ friend.
2   When you complete your undergraduate study, you will gain a bachelor's degree. It is possible that you might continue with your educational career and study for a master's degree. In these cases, would it seem odd for you to graduate with a spinster's or a mistress's degree? If so, why? Why might this seem to be unusual? Discuss your responses with a colleague/friend.

The relationship between language and gender will be discussed in further detail in the following section, where the emphasis on gender shifts toward the way in which gender difference and gender identity is represented in particular ways in society. In what has been generally referred to as the postmodern era, many feminists have concerned themselves with examining the way in which gender is actually created and constructed by social and cultural forces and influences. The following section examines these changes in relation to the role and function of education in contemporary settings.

Third-wave feminism: postmodern perspectives

> One is not born, but becomes a woman. No biological, psychological, or economic fate determines the figure that the human female presents in society: it is civilisation as a whole that produces this creature, intermediate between male and eunuch, which is described as feminine.
>
> (De Beauvoir, 1952: 249)

In offering this view in her book *The Second Sex*, feminist, existentialist scholar, historian and lifelong activist Simone de Beauvoir in many ways heralded the way in which gender and feminist thought would be carried forward in the so-called postmodern era. In the third wave of feminist theory and practice, the stability and uniformity of the wave metaphor become more and more troubled as the flows and currents of postmodern thinking twist and turn in multiple directions and the vagaries of tide flows become less and less predictable. We might ask the initial question in relation to the quotation above: in what ways does education contribute to the way in which one 'becomes a woman'?

In suggesting that 'feminist theory more properly belongs in the terrain of postmodern philosophy', Flax (1995: 145) offers a *via negativa* in which some unification of identification seems to be possible. In other words, in providing us with a means of coming to know what feminism and postmodernism are *not*, we can provide ourselves with an entry point into a possible way of knowing what they are or might be. So, Flax argues, 'postmodern philosophers', which include, in her view, feminist thinkers, would be highly sceptical about the following:

1   The existence of a stable coherent self . . .
2   Reason . . . can provide an objective, reliable, and uniform foundation for knowledge.
3   The knowledge acquired from the right use of reason will be 'true' . . .
4   Reason itself has transcendental and universal qualities . . .
5   All claims to truth and rightful authority are to be submitted to the tribunal of reason . . .
6   By grounding claims to authority in reason, the conflicts between truth, knowledge, and power can be overcome . . .
7   Science . . . is also the paradigm for all true knowledge . . .
8   Language is in some sense transparent . . . (and) merely the medium in and through which . . . representation occurs . . .

(ibid.: 144–5)

So, postmodern and poststructural feminist approaches, in taking a lead from the earlier quotation from de Beauvoir, see gender not as something that is fixed in the person, perhaps in genetically or biologically determined ways; rather, they prescribe to the view that gender is somehow constructed through the cultural influences that impact upon and help to establish social relations. Existentialist and phenomenological thought would argue that selves are established through processes of having encounters, experiencing and being in the world. So Heidegger, for example, does not simply talk about the common-sense reality of *being* but qualifies it by referring to *being there* or *dasein*. Our living experience of *being there* situates us both in terms of our embodiment and our consciousness.

According to this view, our being changes according to each new encounter with the world and as a consequence is changed in some way by that experience. Humanist and phenomenological thought therefore posits a *realist* view of the world in which the self, *being there*, as described by Heidegger, is formed through experience of that world. The quotation from de Beauvoir talks about the way in which all individuals can be seen to be 'produced' through the dynamics of social relations, so the emphasis in the quotation is upon the gendered self being made or created rather than being born. We can refer to this as a *constructivist* view of the world.

ACTIVITY 2

Consider the following quotation in relation to Heidegger's notion of *dasein* or *being there* and in how it might apply to the experience of education:

I first became interested in emotion's absence-presence as a student of philosophy . . . it began to dawn on me that emotion's exclusion from philosophy and science was not a coincidence . . . the division between 'truth' and reason on the one side and 'subjective bias' and emotion on the other – was not neutral division . . . Emotion had been positioned on the 'negative' side of the binary division. And emotion was not alone on the 'bad' side of the fence – women were there too . . . as a woman, I was already marginalised . . . I did not qualify as a man of reason . . . by raising the spectre of emotion publicly, I confirmed my disqualification from their club.

(Boler, 1999: xvi)

Write a few lines in response to the following questions:

- What does this quotation tell you about 'philosophy and science' in relation to gender and education?
- In Boler's experience, what does it mean to say that 'emotion had been placed upon the negative side of the binary division'?
- Why do you think Boler saw herself as marginalised in terms of a) gender and b) education?
- In terms of gender and education, what do you think it means to be disqualified from 'their club'?

Share your writings with a colleague.

Poststructuralism, Foucault and gender

Foucault was not well known for his work on gender, but there is a great deal in his philosophical and historical writings that can help to illuminate our understanding of gender, particularly within the context of educational institutions like schools, colleges and universities (see Chapter 5). There is a highly visible and important constructivist dimension to Foucault's work, in that he wrote extensively about the way in which culture and in particular language work to produce meaning, knowledge and, significantly for this chapter, identity. Where in the work of Heidegger and phenomenology we saw an argument for the way in which individuals might be formed through experience, in the work of Foucault we see the way in which identities are formed through processes of representation.

The influence of language

The significance of language in these processes of identification, representation and reification cannot be understated. Central to Foucault's writing on language is his theory of discourse. In talking about the micro-politics of gender, we can examine what he referred to as 'technologies of self', the means by which identities are discursively constructed or produced through processes of subjectification. Discourses are:

> practices that systematically form the objects of which they speak ... Discourses are not about objects; they do not identify objects, they constitute them and in the process of doing so conceal their own invention.
>
> (Foucault, 1974: 49)

ACTIVITY 3

Return to and examine Activity 1 in this chapter in which you engaged in thinking about gender and language. Foucault would argue that (gendered) identities are actually *produced* by language in social, cultural and political settings or sites. He refers to this process as the discursive construction of identity. Foucault describes the language of discourse as 'technologies of self', arguing that processes of identification, how we are *seen* and how others *see us* are culturally specific and occur in specific ways in different spaces and at different times.

- Give some examples of gendered activities that might be acceptable for girls and not boys and vice versa.
- Give some examples of how these might change from one space (place) to another.
- Give some examples of how these might change from one time to another.
- What do your responses tell you about the social construction of gendered identity?
- How do the gendered word pairs in the earlier activity come to have meaning?

So, according to the thinking of Foucault and others, language, in the form of discourses, can be seen to create (gendered) selves as objects of knowledge and, at the same time, they obscure the origins of such processes. The power of discourse, therefore, is to do with the social and cultural forces that might be seen to contribute to this concealment. In educational terms, therefore, an important message can be learned from the thinking of Foucault in these respects. He argues that we need to examine the social, cultural, historical and political conditions that might be used to make these discursively constructed realities possible. Implicit in this is the role and practice of reflexivity. For Foucault, the power of discourse and the customary, habitual and traditional practices that are associated with it is that they *resist reflexivity*; they do not encourage us to think about why we do things in certain ways. So, in terms of gender and education, in any setting and at any particular time and in relation to anything that is said or done, the important reflexive questions that have to be asked are both simple and direct: Why is this say-able? Why is this do-able?

Irigaray and Cixous on gender and writing

Writing plays a key part in any educational practice. From the plethora of policies that work to construct and legitimate these practices, to the curricula, the lesson plans and the teaching activities designed by teachers, to the essays and assignments that are written by pupils and students in the assessment of their learning, writing is a central activity in the engagement of education theory and practice. Two significant contemporary feminist philosophers, Hélène Cixous and Luce Irigaray, have examined the role of writing in the construction of gendered identities. We will briefly consider the implications of their thought in relation to contemporary educational practices.

Cixous (1991) uses 'ecriture feminine' and Irigaray (1974) 'parler-femme' to challenge and disrupt what they recognise and claim to be the gendered hierarchical binaries that organise thought. By formulating and applying these approaches to writing, they offer a challenge to monological constructions of gender and sexuality that they see as inherently masculine and that are used to support patriarchal hierarchies of organisation in social institutions such as schools, colleges and universities. These philosophers argue that there are no selves other than those that have been created through systems of representation. These systems of representation animate identification and identity through the particularly gender-specific use of language.

So, for example, the use of reflective practices in education, which are predominantly based upon the view that when we reflect, in both thought and action, we somehow provide or discover a 'mirror' of reality, is actually, according to such thinking, subjecting the female body to a male gaze: the mirror reflects masculine values and identifies the female thus. In her examination of the role of film in the construction of identity, Laura Mulvey (1989) argues that patriarchal unconsciousness constructs women as passive objects through the power of the male gaze. In this respect, Mulvey argues, power is structured through the 'gaze' whereby man is the bearer of the look and woman is constructed through the image. So, according to this view, the gendered images we have of the world precede our experience of the world; they provide us with ready-made perspectives and mediate our ways of being in the world. Baudrillard has referred to this process as the 'precession of simulacra . . . it is the map that precedes the territory . . . it is the map that engenders the territory' (1983: 361).

ACTIVITY 4

Read the following chapter in the reference below and use the two examples to do with power and influence on page 160 to describe how what Mulvey refers to as the 'gaze' and what Althusser refers to in the chapter as 'interpellation' might work to provide us with a view of gender in education today. Do you think these examples provide us with a basis for understanding the influence of gender difference on levels of achievement in contemporary education?

Gale, K. (2009) Postmodernism and Cyberculture, in Wheeler, S (ed.) *Connected Minds, Emerging Cultures: The Rise of Cyberculture in Online Learning*, Charlotte, NC: Information Age Publishing, pp. 159–67.

In talking of 'parler-femme', Irigaray says the following:

> [They] are contradictory words, somewhat mad from the standpoint of reason, inaudible, for whoever listens with ready-made grids, with a fully elaborated code in hand. For in what she says too, at least when she dares, woman is constantly touching herself. She steps ever so slightly aside from herself with a murmur, an exclamation, a whisper, a sentence left unfinished . . . When she returns it is to set off again from elsewhere . . . One would have to listen with another ear, as if hearing an 'other meaning' always in the process of weaving itself, of embracing itself with words; but also of getting rid of words in order not to become fixed, congealed in them.
>
> (Irigaray, 1974: 29)

She also says that 'history cannot do without the existence of two human subjects, man and woman, if it is to get away from master–slave relationships' (1996: 5) and taken together it seems that these quotations talk about language as a colonising and territorialising force. Richardson (2005) argues that 'writing is a method of inquiry'. By using writing as a method of inquiry, she claims that there is a sense in which we are not only writing into the not yet known but that we are also offering a challenge to the ways in which conventional approaches to writing are often to do with the constitution of power and the construction of knowledge. In her terms, therefore, writing can act as what Tuhiwai Smith (1999) refers to as a 'decolonizing methodology': a means of challenging existing hierarchies and relational frameworks. As Derrida has pointed out, processes involving the construction of binary relations such as those of gender and sexuality engage in a textual and representational structuring of selves that usually involves the privileging of the former in the binary pair over the latter. For him it is necessary, therefore, to deconstruct, to 'practice an overturning of the classical opposition and a general displacement of the system' (1982: 329). For Derrida, the practical engagement of deconstructive approaches acknowledges that meaning as expressed in language, while always *necessary* as a mode of communication, is always *inadequate* as a universal signification of meaning or thought. Derrida therefore uses the term *sous rature* to describe the deconstructive strategy of always placing meaning, as represented by language, *under erasure*, always under the threat of being 'erased', changed or shifted in some way. He uses the following symbolic form to represent this deconstructive process: sous rature.

Reflexive approaches

So, by employing the discursively reflexive approaches of Foucault to establish the conditions of possibility for particular meanings, the deconstructive approaches of Derrida and so on, writing in these terms can be used in the way that Deleuze and Guattari suggest: to smooth out striated space, to de-territorialise, to show an 'incredulity toward metanarratives' (Lyotard, 1984: xxiv), to creatively exercise a tolerance of ambiguity and to work to make the familiar strange. In a vivid piece of poetic writing, Deleuze and Guattari argue that:

> there is no language in itself, nor are there any linguistic universals, only a throng of dialects, patois, slangs, and specialised languages. There is no . . . homogenous linguistic community. Language is . . . 'an essentially heterogeneous reality'. There is no mother tongue, only a power takeover by a dominant language within a

political multiplicity . . . (language) evolves by subterranean stems and flows, along river valleys or train tracks; it spreads like a patch of oil . . . A language is never closed upon itself, except as a function of impotence.

(1988: 7–8)

ACTIVITY 5

With direct reference to the quotations from Irigaray and Deleuze and Guattari, write a short piece, using whatever form you like (e.g. this could be in the form of poetry, dramatic writing, a poster, prose etc.), to illustrate how writing or language more generally can be used as a method to inquire into the gendered constructions of masculine and feminine identity in an education setting in contemporary Britain.

In this writing you might also want to try to illustrate how gendered inequalities might be seen to intersect with those of class, ethnicity, sexuality, etc.

When you have finished this work, share what you have produced, perhaps in a workshop or seminar setting, with your friends or colleagues on your current programme of study.

In acknowledging and working with what Barad (2007) refers to as the 'entanglements' and 'intra-actions' that exist and come into play between language, discourses and writing on the one hand, and the corporeal, cultural and materialist factors on the other, a number of philosophers and feminist thinkers have worked to try to disclose the ways in which language can actually be seen to inscribe and perpetuate gender difference. So, in actively engaging with a philosophy of education, it is important for teachers and students alike to consider the ways in which, in both formal and informal teaching and learning practices, in terms of both the pedagogic and the normative, the ways in which language can be seen to work to construct and advance difference in terms of gender. Therefore, by way of a conclusion that does not attempt to achieve closure or to engage in some kind of summative capturing, this chapter will end with two final activities and a number of important questions that can be addressed as a way of taking these issues forward.

ACTIVITY 6

Moments of being?

It was as if it became altogether intelligible; I had a feeling of transparency in words when they cease to be words and become so intensified that one seems to experience them; to foretell them as if they developed what one is already feeling . . . no one could have understood from what I said the queer feeling I had in the hot grass, that poetry was coming true. Nor does that give the feeling. It matches what I have sometimes felt when I write. The pen gets on the scent.

(Woolf, 1985: 93)

What does this quotation from Virginia Woolf tell you about the following:

a   Writing as gendered
b   Writing as a method of inquiry
c   Writing as placing meaning under erasure.

How is gender difference inscribed through the practices of writing?

How can this be engaged with through critical inquiry?

How can this be engaged with through the use of research practice?

How might the various inscriptions of gender that have been addressed in this chapter be seen and engaged with as a means of maximising successful approaches to teaching and learning and which are not disabled or impeded by unreasonable constructions of gender difference and practices of differentiation?

ACTIVITY 7

Feminism is a diverse, dynamic and changing field and movement. At the time of writing, there are new debates about feminism and a surge of feminist activism and gender equality work in schools and universities, as well as a number of high-profile public campaigns, often with a strong online presence.

1   To what extent are these debates taking place at your university?
2   Have a look at the following website and explore some of the issues being raised in the context of feminism and education: UK Feminista (http://ukfeminista.org.uk).
3   What questions about education policies and practices do these debates raise for you?

References

Atwood, M. (1984) *The Greenfield Review* 13 (3/4): 5.

Barad, K. (2007) *Meeting the Universe Halfway: Quantum Physics and the Entanglement of Matter and Meaning*, London: Duke University Press.

Baudrillard, J. (1983) *Simulations*, New York: Semiotext(e).

Boler, M. (1999) *Feeling Power: Emotions and Education*, London: Routledge.

Cixous, H. (1991) *Coming to Writing and Other Essays*, London: Harvard University Press.

De Beauvoir, S. (1952) *The Second Sex*, New York: Bantam.

Deleuze, G. and Guattari, F. (1988) *A Thousand Plateaus: Capitalism and Schizophrenia*, London: Athlone Press.

Derrida, J. (1982) *Margins of Philosophy*, Brighton: Harvester Press.

Flax, J. (1995) Postmodernism and Gender Relations in Feminist Theory, in M. Blair and J. Holland with S. Sheldon (eds) *Identity and Diversity: Gender and the Experience of Education*, Clevedon: Multilingual Matters, pp. 143–61.

Foucault, M. (1974) *The Archaeology of Knowledge*, London: Tavistock Publications.

Gibbon, M. (1999) *Feminist Perspectives on Language*, London: Longman.

Giddens, A. (1993) *New Rules of Sociological Method: A Positive Critique of Interpretative Sociologies*, Stanford, CA: Stanford University Press.

Irigaray, L. (1974) *Speculum of the Other Woman*, New York: Cornell University Press.

Irigaray, L. (1996) *I Love to You*, trans. A. Martin, London: Athlone Press.

Lyotard, J. -F. (1984) *The Postmodern Condition: A Report on Knowledge*, Manchester: Manchester University Press.

Mill, J. S. (1869) *The Subjection of Women*. Available at: www.constitution.org/jsm/women.htm [Accessed on 4 August 2014].

Mill, J. S. (1962) *Utilitarianism*, London: Fontana.

Mill, J. S. (1974) *On Liberty*, London: Penguin.

Millet, K. (1970) *Sexual Politics*, New York: Doubleday.

Mulvey, L. (1989) *Visual and Other Pleasures*, London: Macmillan.

Rich, A. (1975) *The Burning of Paper Instead of Children. Poems: Selected and New, 1950–1974,* New York: W. W. Norton.

Richardson, L. (2005) Writing: A Method of Inquiry, in Denzin, N. and Lincoln, Y. (eds) *The Sage Handbook of Qualitative Research,* 3rd edition, London: Sage.

Schultz, M. (1975) The Semantic Derogation of Women, in Barrie, T. and Henley, N. (eds) *Language and Sex: Difference and Dominance*, Rowley: Newbury House.

Tuhiwai Smith, L. (1999) *Decolonizing Methodologies: Research and Indigenous Peoples*, London: Zed Books.

Woolf, V. (1985) *Moments of Being,* 2nd edition, Schulkind, J. (ed.), London: Harcourt Brace.

8

Moral reasoning, ethics and education

Joanna Haynes

Overview

Ethics are concerned with the application of moral thinking to everyday life. Educational settings are widely held to be important sites for socialisation that provide particular opportunities to set standards of behaviour and develop moral understanding and ethical codes of practice. Most children attend school from the age of five or six until the age of eighteen. For many undergraduates, university life involves a move away from home to the independence of a new shared intellectual and social context with other young people, often in halls of residence. Such settings present educators and students with opportunities, choices and dilemmas in the day-to-day social experience of sharing public spaces, developing knowledge and learning together. They provide many points for moral enquiry and for developing ethical sensitivity through subjects of study, applied fields of practice and in everyday life. These aspects of education are contested and variously articulated in terms of, for example, virtue and character building, the inculcation of moral principles, teaching moral reasoning or developing an ethics of care (Noddings and Slote, 2003).

Notions of individual agency and autonomy are often central to discussion of moral reasoning and ethics. To be autonomous, it is argued, people require know-how to reflect on choices about how to live. They need to grow the capability to critically reflect and plan in an autonomous way, even if they later choose a non-autonomous life. Some recent thinkers have challenged the emphasis on individual autonomy, arguing that decisions and actions need to be based on an ethics of care and considered within the living context of ongoing and situated relations (Noddings, 2002). Across the spectrum of perspectives on ethics, there is broad agreement that education settings are important sites for moral education and for developing ethical sensitivity.

Philosopher Mary Warnock (1996) refers to schools as providing significant opportunities for moral learning because they often represent children's first experience of public life, of life beyond the intimate sphere of the family. Such intensive and extensive involvement in the public sphere is rarely repeated across the lifespan. In Power et al. (1989) psychologist Lawrence Kohlberg proposed that schools could use such involvement to teach moral reasoning by providing young people with carefully planned activities through which they could experience a 'just community'. Kohlberg is very well known for his presentation of stages of moral development and how they are evident in individual thinking and decision making (Kohlberg, 1981). By contrast, an ethics of care tends to emphasise the conditions and relations that support moral ways of life than the teaching of virtues in individuals (Noddings, 2002). This chapter sets out to illuminate these ideas. It discusses some of the ethical dimensions of teaching, learning and people's lives within educational settings and practices, drawing on the history of moral philosophy and contemporary discourses on ethics. It refers mostly to the context of schooling.

QUESTIONS

- How should we understand the relationship between moral philosophy and ethics?
- Why are educational settings regarded as places to develop moral imagination and moral reasoning?
- What are some approaches to teaching moral reasoning and ethics?
- What part do ethics play in the work of professionals in fields like education?

Introduction

This chapter begins by exploring some leading ideas used in discussing moral thinking and ethics. It provides a brief overview of influential philosophical perspectives that inform ideas about moral education policy and practice. There are three connected threads of exploration in this chapter.

One thread relates to ideas about the development of moral understanding in human beings. What's involved in learning moral reasoning? Does this understanding grow in a particular sequence or set of stages, according to age, and/or through opportunities to practise moral decision making in response to others, according to particular conditions and circumstances? Psychological theories of young people's cognitive development and related claims about their capacity for moral understanding have shaped education policy and practice. Some educationalists have suggested particular experiences and activities should take place in schools to reflect ideas not only on only how moral reasoning is learned, but also the social aims of education (see for example Lipman, 1993). Such ideas can profoundly influence how we understand the role of schools and education in shaping society.

A second line of enquiry relates to the moral dimensions of education in settings such as nurseries, schools and colleges. This involves thinking about the moral content and character of the curriculum; provision for active engagement with ethical aspects of learning and being together in educational settings; and different frameworks and approaches to *teaching* moral education. Schools promote moral and social values through both the official and the hidden curriculum.

The third line of enquiry is to do with the ethics of educational work: the roles and responsibilities of people such as teachers, tutors, support and other teaching-related staff. The chapter opens up questions such as 'What kind of moral authority should teachers have?' and 'What considerations govern the conduct of relationships between students and teachers?' Teaching is described as a profession and teachers as professionals. This leads to a fair amount of public contestation: teachers often talk about threats to their professionalism and politicians talk about the responsibilities of professionals.

In recent years, moral education in western societies has tended to be framed within the context of liberal values such as freedom and equality (Halstead and Taylor, 1996). Moral education has become increasingly linked to ideas about citizenship, human rights and the role of education in a democratic society. The moral, social and political are intertwined. The use of the term 'ethics' in educational practice increasingly reflects such connections.

ACTIVITY 1

In the introduction to his book *Education and Democracy: Principles and Practices*, A. V. Kelly states:

> Democracy [. . .] is a moral concept [. . .] Democracy is more than a form of political organisation or system of government; it is a way of life.
>
> (1995: xv)

To what extent do you agree with Kelly's position? Make a note of your reasons.

Talking about morality and ethics

Moral philosophy includes three different elements: first, abstract questions about the nature of morality and the language of morality; second, the exploration of different frameworks or sets of guidelines and rules for trying to work out what is good or bad, right or wrong; and third, the application of those moral theories to particular cases or issues.

Traditionally, moral frameworks tend to fall into three general categories:

- *Virtue ethics* focus on character and the development of qualities and dispositions in persons that enable them to choose good and right actions and to live good, worthwhile and happy lives. The origins of virtue ethics can be traced in both eastern and western traditions of ancient philosophy. In the western tradition, Plato and Aristotle are associated with virtue ethics, which are composed of three main elements, for which the Greek words are: *arête*, meaning virtue or excellence; *phronesis*, translated as practical wisdom; and *eudaimonia*, meaning happiness or flourishing.

- *Deontology* is an approach to ethics based on actions being governed by independently determined rules, duties and obligations. In Greek, *deon* = duty and *logos* = science. Such duties hold regardless of the consequences. As a theory it refers to choices that are morally required, forbidden or allowed. The influential philosopher Immanuel Kant (1724–1804) is strongly associated with deontological theory. The moral law, or categorical imperative (an absolute requirement), is regarded as a product of reason, through which we make free and autonomous decisions about how to act in any given situation. Moral acts are freely and autonomously chosen.

- *Consequentialist ethics* focus attention on the outcomes and consequences of human actions to determine whether they are good or right actions and promote general happiness. Utilitarianism has been very influential. John Stuart Mill, a leading exponent of utilitarianism, argued that actions are right in proportion to their tendency to promote happiness, and wrong in proportion to their tendency to produce the reverse of happiness. This is known as the principle of utility. The principle of utility involves an appraisal only of an action's consequences, rather than the character traits of the person who performs that action. Mill argues that the principle of utility should be seen as a means to generate secondary moral principles, such as 'don't steal', which help to promote general happiness. A keen advocate of freedom of thought and expression, Mill developed his ideas with his wife Harriet Taylor and his famous essay *On Liberty* was first published in 1859, just after her death.

ACTIVITY 2

Explore the following hypothetical scenario and reach an answer through discussion with other students of education.

One of your fellow students on the course, who is also a close friend, confides that he or she has cheated in an examination. Do you report the student in question to tutors in charge of the course or not?

Make a note of the main reasons for your decision and how you have gone about making it. What moral outlook has influenced your decision? Are you inclined to make moral choices through a desire to behave virtuously (for example, by being charitable or courageous), or on the basis of principles (for example, deception is wrong), and/or through consideration of the consequences (for example, if you tell the tutors, your friend may fail the exam)? What are the strengths and limitations of these perspectives? You might also consider what would be involved in applying an ethics of care.

Philosophical traditions

In his book *What is Good?* moral philosopher Anthony Grayling (2003) offers a very accessible introduction to the history of ideas in the western tradition on how we should live. He suggests that we can trace two main traditions of moral thinking about the good life:

- The humanist tradition: a broadly secular attitude rooted in ideas about human nature and the human condition in everyday lives.

- The religious tradition: a broadly transcendental view that locates the source of moral value outside the human realm, a source that places on the human realm a demand to realise aims and ends located beyond the world – usually in a life after death.

More recently we have seen the emergence of the posthuman (see for example Braidotti, 2013, and the previous chapter on feminism and education). Posthumanism is critical of the humanist tradition, for example in its hierarchical elevation of the human species above other species of animals, or in its tendency to speak without due reference to the sustainability of natural resources and the environment. Posthumanist thinking also expresses a range of new ideas in response to genetic, robotic, prosthetic, neuroscientific or digital technologies and their social and cultural implications.

Moral decisions in contemporary society are made in the context of the changes, dilemmas and choices created by such technologies and competing claims on the earth's resources and associated political debates.

Models of education

The position we adopt regarding the locus of moral authority and beliefs about moral judgement is critical when it comes to designing education systems and curricula. Some models of schooling are authoritarian: adults should instruct young people in the rules and model good behaviour, while young people should respect adult authority and be obedient. Other models allow for, and even encourage, the questioning of automatic obedience to authority, whether the authority of the teacher or the text. These deliberative models promote the early development of autonomous moral judgement and seek to create opportunities for such autonomy to be expressed in a meaningful way. Obedience and conformity are still perfectly possible, but have to be thoughtfully chosen: values of cooperation, mutual respect and collaboration tend to replace obedience. For those teachers and students whose beliefs arise from commitment to religious groups and are held as 'God given', participation in any form of open deliberation about moral 'truths' might be regarded as morally questionable, as a threat to faith and/or to belonging to a religious community. In such contexts, faith at the very least sits alongside reason, and sometimes takes its place.

In a pluralist society, we find a variety of models of educational practice: strict and liberal religious schools of different denominations; democratic schools; independent/ private schools; community schools; grammar schools and so on. Each school tends to be founded on a set of social rules and values. These values are both transmitted and experienced by those who work and learn in the schools. There is considerable common ground across such schools, at least in principle; but there can be significant points of difference, around such issues as, for example, whether creationism should be part of the science curriculum, whether religious worship should take place at school, or whether the curriculum should include sex and relationship education, and who makes these decisions.

Educational institutions also have to have a basis for the rules governing relationships among and between students, staff, parents and others. It's not unusual for schools to publish their behaviour and discipline policies. Examination of such documents reveals their underlying assumptions about children's social and moral development and the moral authority of the school to impose sanctions and punishments. Sometimes an institution's rules and aims can seem to be in contradiction with one another and this is often complicated by discussions about the *age* of reason and responsibility. It's worth pausing to consider these age–related ideas.

ACTIVITY 3

Were you aware that the age of criminal responsibility in England, Wales and Northern Ireland is currently 10 years old? In Belgium it is 18 and in Spain it is 16. In England, from the age of 10, the law says that children can be judged to understand their actions and the consequences of these actions and be held responsible for them. Read the guidelines on the government website: www.gov.uk/age-of-criminal-responsibility.

(continued)

(continued)

In 2014 a Private Member's Bill is under consideration that proposes to raise the age of responsibility from 10 to 12 years old. Have a look at this Bill and the stage it is at on: http://services.parliament.uk/bills/2013–14/ageofcriminalresponsibility.html.

Do you agree, or disagree, with the proposal to raise the age of criminal responsibility from 10 to 12 years old? What are your reasons?

According to a report, Professor Mackintosh and other neuroscientists claim that parts of the brain responsible for impulse control and decision making do not fully mature until at least the age of 20: www.bbc.co.uk/news/uk-16153045.

To what extent do you think the findings of the report from the Royal Society (royalsociety. org) should be taken into account in any review of the law governing the age of criminal responsibility?

Perspectives on the development of moral understanding and judgement

Colourful images of the brain in the context of neuroscientific research from authorities like the Royal Society constitute a very persuasive form of evidence in seeking to answer questions about young people's capacity to fully understand their actions. Thinking about the age of criminal responsibility might help to focus attention on questions of moral understanding but it is also a high-profile and emotive topic. One task for educationalists is to create conditions and opportunities for ethical understanding to develop while taking into account the risks of giving children either too little or too much responsibility for ethical decisions. Both the curriculum itself, and being with others at school, can instil conscience and help nurture the moral imagination along with values such as empathy, care and respect for others.

As an educator, I have had a career-long interest in the ethics of educational relationships and everyday interaction in classrooms, among teachers and students of all ages and in different settings. In my professional work in schools and with student teachers, I have often bumped into a very firmly held belief that young children are naturally self-centred. Confidently made assertions that children are unable to understand the perspectives of others are commonplace. Equally, the belief that they are developmentally incapable of engaging with abstract ideas, such as fairness, seems to persist. Influential theorists are sometimes cited in support of these views. Kohlberg (1981), for example, presented his 'pre-conventional' stage of moral development, in which young children are described as preoccupied with their immediate personal interests and concerned to ensure that their behaviour pleases the adults around them, or to avoid disapproval. These ideas have shaped the views of many of those who work with children. Other researchers challenge the idea of fixed stages (Tizard and Hughes, 2003). They tell a more complex and diverse story of children's lives and experiences instead, sometimes rejecting developmentalism altogether as a framework (see for example Burman, 1994; Dahlberg and Moss, 2005).

Meaningful opportunities for moral reflection

A critical factor in the development of moral reasoning is the extent to which we have opportunities to explore moral questions in contexts that are meaningful to us. For children, these might entail being encouraged to question and discuss fictional and real scenarios where ethical issues are raised; being allowed to participate in decision making; being sensitively included in dialogue about situations that crop up in their lives. Adults in turn make a choice about whether to skilfully mediate this process and whether to listen and take young children's perspectives seriously. Taking an active part in moral enquiry strengthens reasoning and empathy, whether in actual or imagined scenarios.

Piaget and Kohlberg

Piaget used stories to elicit children's ideas about honesty, property rights, punishment and fairness and he used games to uncover their ideas about rules. Piaget suggested that children moved from a morality of constraint, based on obedience of rigid rules imposed by adults, to a morality of autonomy, where rules can be modified and justice takes circumstances into account (Anning, 1997).

ACTIVITY 4

Fables, fairy tales and folk tales are often referred to as conveyors of moral 'messages'. From the following list of popular tales, choose one that you know well and consider any moral messages you think it reflects: *Little Red Riding Hood*; *Rapunzel*; *Snow White*; *Cinderella*; *The Three Little Pigs*. Which versions of the tale are you most familiar with?

Contemporary postmodern versions of such tales as *The Three Pigs* (Wiesner, 2001) tend to raise questions about the simplicity and certainty of the moral messages in traditional tales. They use humour and other devices to draw readers into thinking through the intentions and actions of the characters. Visit the children's section of your library and explore some examples of postmodern picture-books.

To what extent do you think either traditional or postmodern tales provide a good basis for moral education of children today?

Lawrence Kohlberg, whose doctoral studies published in 1958 focused on the development of moral thinking of 10–16-year-old boys, suggested that the process of moral development was more gradual. He suggested that young children begin at a pre-conventional level, in which they are concerned with their personal interests and avoiding punishment, then move to a conventional level, in which duty and laws are necessary to participate in and maintain a stable society. At this conventional stage, winning approval from one's immediate social group is most important (Kohlberg said that many young people and adults remain at this level). His mature level of moral development was the post-conventional, emphasising universal moral principles such as justice, rights, equality and human welfare (Kohlberg, 1981; Power et al., 1989).

Piaget argued that school should emphasise cooperative decision making and problem solving to nurture moral development, by requiring students to work out rules based on fairness (Anning, 1997). For Kohlberg, the goal of education was to encourage individuals to develop through the stages of moral reasoning to maturity. Moral dilemmas can be used as tools for such learning, requiring students to determine and justify a particular course of action. In dilemma-based activities, the role of the educator is to point out contradictions and challenge students to consider inconsistencies inherent in their 'level' of moral reasoning. Kohlberg also believed that young people need opportunities to operate as moral agents within what he and his colleagues termed a 'just community' (Power et al., 1989). The just community approach is regarded as Kohlberg's most mature theory of moral education and has been widely cited. Although Kohlberg initially recommended the discussion of moral dilemmas as a means of promoting moral development, he envisaged a more comprehensive and radical approach to the organisation of schooling to promote moral education (Power, 1988).

Care theories

Gilligan (1982) questioned Kohlberg's stages of moral development, arguing that his studies took a biased masculine perspective in characterising the 'highest' stage of moral development. Her moral stages comprised selfish, conventional and principled morality. She proposed that males are raised to think in terms of rules and justice, so moral decision making is straightforward, while females are raised to focus on caring for people. They tend to be more cautious in making moral judgements because of their perceptions of the complexity of relationships. Evidence suggests that most children use both an ethics of care and an ethics of justice in their moral reasoning, and that these two perspectives do not need to be counter-posed, but can work together. However, Gilligan's work helped to illustrate the situated nature of moral decision making and the influence of factors such as gender on a person's moral and social perspectives.

For philosopher Nell Noddings, models of moral education shaped by care ethics are process orientated, involving 'modeling, dialogue, practice and confirmation' (2002: 148). Care ethics are based on the view that every human being hopes for a positive response from other human beings. She writes:

> no one wants to be harmed by others or to live in fear of them. Everyone hopes for a helping hand in times of danger or more trouble than he or she can handle alone. Everyone wants enough respect to maintain at least minimal dignity.
>
> (Noddings, 2002: 148)

Care theorists seek to avoid a universalising care response and work for practice to recognise people's different needs, desired outcomes and values. They place a great deal of emphasis on listening and receptive attention and on the development of both self-understanding and empathy. In drawing attention to the relational sense of caring, the binary of altruism and egoism can be brought into question. Care theory suggests it might be less problematic to speak in terms of 'virtuous acts' rather than 'virtuous persons'.

An increasingly popular approach to conflict resolution that seeks to take such conditions and perspectives into account is known as restorative justice.

ACTIVITY 5

Restorative justice, based on humanistic values, is one of a range of approaches to conflict resolution in schools. It focuses on trying to repair the harm done to individuals involved in conflict, rather than on blame and punishment. It draws attention to the injury caused by conflict, rather than to the breaking of the rule (www.transformingconflict.org and www. restorativejustice.org.uk).

To find out more about the use of restorative justice in schools and youth settings, search the organisations' weblinks above.

■ To what extent do you agree with the principles and practice of restorative justice in schools?
■ What questions would you want to ask of those who support and practise this approach?

Communicative ethics

Historically, as outlined in the previous sections of this chapter, children and young people have often been regarded as lacking the experience and rationality to make moral judgements. Communicative ethics tend to favour participation and dialogue and to recognise the complex social dynamics of human interaction. They reflect a political understanding of factors that are known to constrain the deliberative process, such as distortions of power that prevent individuals or groups from expressing a voice or from being heard.

Philosopher Hannah Arendt (cited in Benhabib, 1992) describes as 'enlarged thinking' a reasoning process where the goal is not consensus or unanimity, but an anticipated communication with others, with whom we ultimately come to some agreement. This enlarged thinking does not function in isolation and requires the presence of others. Enlarged thinking cultivates moral reflexivity among children and adults alike. To be inclusive of all the 'Others' that constitute modern pluralist societies is also to recognise that moral thinking itself may be approached from different perspectives, dependent on one's position and experience in the world. Ideas that emphasise ongoing and dynamic communication to actively resolve moral questions have led to a move away from authoritarian models towards more participatory and deliberative systems of moral education, often based on values of active citizenship and human rights.

Human rights and children's rights

Citizenship and human rights in education scholars Audrey Osler and Hugh Starkey (2010) describe the Declaration of Universal Human Rights of 1948 as a cosmopolitan utopian vision. In recent times the human rights discourse has had a growing influence on law and policies governing the work of all public institutions and those they serve, including schools, but to what extent has this been taken up? This section of the chapter considers some of the issues in adopting a rights–based approach to school ethics.

ACTIVITY 6

What do you know about human rights history? Watch the 'potted history' of human rights: www.youtube.com/watch?v=nCQWwkERit4.

What struck you as significant in this film? What do you make of the concept of 'natural law' or 'natural rights'? Do you have any thoughts about the way human rights are presented in this film?

(continued)

(continued)

Watch the short film showing thirty Articles of the Declaration of Human Rights: www.youtube.com/watch?v=kJ2XMRJkyv4.

Which rights are you most actively concerned with currently? Are there any that you were unaware of?

Janusz Korczak

Polish educator, writer and paediatrician Janusz Korczak (1878–1942) was an early advocate of rights for children. The orphanage he ran in Warsaw had a children's parliament, court and newspaper. His charter of children's rights included a child's entitlement to love and respect, to errors and secrets, to being taken seriously and to living in the present. He included children's right to fail, to resist educational influences which enter into conflict with their beliefs and to protest against injustice. The charter referred to children's right to respect for their grief and the right to die prematurely (www.januszkorczak.ca). It's worth discussing the similarities and differences between Korczak's charter and the formulation of children's rights adopted by the United Nations in 1989 (UNICEF, 1995).

UNICEF

The 1989 United Nations Convention on the Rights of the Child (UNCRC) covers four broad categories including Survival Rights and Developmental Rights, such as the right to education, play and culture. It makes explicit reference to children's rights to information, freedom of thought, conscience and religion. Protection Rights involve keeping children safe from abuse and exploitation. Participation Rights make provision for children to take an active part in their communities. These include the freedom to express views, join groups and to assemble.

The Declaration of the Rights of the Child states that: 'the child, by reason of his physical and mental immaturity, needs special safeguards and care' (UNICEF, 1995: 3). One of the issues in respecting the rights of others, regardless of age, is our understanding and negotiation of 'special-ness' in any fellow human being and how it might be manifested from infancy through to adulthood and across the lifespan. In institutional settings such as schools, the balance of protection rights and participation rights needs to be worked out on the basis of active engagement with the children concerned, rather than on the basis of unspoken assumptions about their best interests and abilities.

As well as laying down Articles for the protection and care of children, the UNCRC recognises the child's right to autonomy, in keeping with development. This implies the goal of maintaining an 'open future' for the child, the awareness of choice and the means to make decisions. The Convention endorses children's rights to express their thoughts, views and feelings and to have these listened to and taken into account in decisions affecting them.

Children's rights in practice

Advocacy of children's rights has grown stronger over the last twenty years and with that much debate about its efficacy or value as an ethical framework for children's care and education. Much of the literature focuses on provision that makes it possible and more likely that children can express their views, regardless of age, and on the importance of adults actively removing obstacles to listening to children's voices, including the obstacles in their own hearts and minds (Clark and Moss, 2001). The focus of this advocacy in educational contexts tends to be concerned with children's participation in the organisation and management of administrative, servicing or more peripheral functions of establishments rather than with the central and everyday business of schools such as the content of the curriculum and pedagogy. There is generally more talk of consultation processes, rather than a positive drive to re-examine the ethical foundations of educational interactions and relationships.

Practitioners working in the early years of education and care are often at the cutting edge of thinking regarding children's participation. One model of communicative ethics, the Mosaic Approach (Clark and Moss, 2001), is concerned with enabling children to have a voice from the moment of their birth. Its framework is also multi-method, participatory and focused on children's lived experiences, family contexts and network of social connections. It aims to take the theory and practice of listening to children out of a form of occasional consultancy and into ongoing conversation and respectful mutual encounter in everyday life (Clark and Moss, 2001: 10).

UNICEF has established a UK-based initiative to encourage schools and other educational establishments to engage actively with children's rights, called the Rights Respecting Schools Award (RRSA) (www.unicef.org.uk/rrsa). Within a rights-based approach, rather than discussing and agreeing a set of classroom rules, children might be encouraged to develop a charter of rights and responsibilities. However, comparing displays of such work on classroom walls, an observer would be hard pressed to distinguish between the two sets of guidelines. The transition from traditional rule-based forms of discipline in compulsory schooling to a system based on recognition of children's rights has sometimes proved difficult. The RRSA has also been promoted by UNICEF in terms of its impact on school effectiveness, behaviour, attendance and academic standards, rather than solely on the grounds that such human rights should be recognised and acted upon. Marketing children's rights to schools in performative terms seems to be at odds with the spirit of the Convention.

Research on children's rights in schools

Lundy (2007) has undertaken research on Article 12 of the UNCRC, which legally gives children the right to have their views heard and taken into consideration in respect of all matters that concern them. Lundy suggests that there are considerable barriers to the implementation of Article 12 in schools and many are failing to fulfil their obligations. Article 12 is regarded as particularly significant in recognising children as full human beings with integrity who have the ability to participate freely in society. Lundy's research suggests that adult concerns about acting on Article 12 tend to fall into one of three groups: scepticism about children's capacity (or a belief that they lack capacity) to have a meaningful input into decision making; a worry that giving children more control will undermine authority and destabilise the school environment; and finally, concern that compliance with children's rights will require too much effort that would be better spent on education itself (Lundy, 2007: 929–30).

Lundy proposes a way of conceptualising Article 12 of the UNCRC which is intended to focus decision makers on four dimensions of the provision:

- Space: Children should be given the opportunity to express a view.
- Voice: Children should be facilitated to express their views.

- Audience: The view should be listened to.
- Influence: The view should be acted upon, as appropriate.

There is concern among some educationalists that the children's rights discourse reflects a particular cultural perspective on individual rights, sometimes creating a dichotomy between the rights of children and the rights of parents. It is criticised for an overemphasis on legal equality of all, regardless of age, and on education for the formation of certain kinds of subjects, with a limiting vision of social participation. Whether viewed from a legal or a sociopolitical perspective, rights–related policies and discourses shape the context in which teachers are expected to act as professionals.

The roles and responsibilities of teachers

Throughout this chapter I have tried to illustrate the ethical dimensions of educational theory and practice and its consequences for anyone working in the field. One of the characteristics of a 'profession' is the demands it makes on members to exercise complex judgements involving other human beings. Many professions have agreed standards to serve as detailed forms of guidance, relevant to their areas of practice. These legal standards govern teachers' roles and define the knowledge, understanding and skills required to exercise good judgement in the face of calls made on educators to act in accordance with such codes. A look at the final activity will provide you with a flavour of historical and contemporary influences on the ethics of teaching.

ACTIVITY 7

Education, the Law and You (NUT, 2012) provides advice for newly qualified teachers about the professional standards governing teachers' rights and duties. It provides background information on the 'duty of care'. The term 'in loco parentis' was used originally to denote the idea that teachers should take the same care as a parent would in similar circumstances. (www.teachers.org.uk/files/the-law-and-you--8251-.pdf)

- Read the first section of the document and note the distinctions between the common law, statutory and contractual aspects of teachers' duty of care (pp. 3–4).
- Read the sections on Physical Contact with Pupils (pp. 7–8). Read the sections on Teachers' Power to Discipline (pp. 10–11). To what extent do you think this guidance is consistent with a rights-based approach to relationships?
- Finally, read the sections on anti-discrimination, human rights and equality (pp. 11–13). How would you summarise the key responsibilities of teachers and the principles governing their relationships with students?

References

Anning, A. (1997) *The First Years at School*, Buckingham: Open University Press.

Benhabib, S. (1992) *Situating the Self: Gender, Community and Postmodernism in Contemporary Ethics*, Cambridge: Polity Press.

Braidotti, R. (2013) *The Posthuman*, Cambridge: Polity Press.

Burman, E. (1994) *Deconstructing Developmental Psychology*, London and New York: Routledge.

Clark, A. and Moss, P. (2001) *Listening to Young Children: The Mosaic Approach*, London: National Children's Bureau.

Dahlberg, G. and Moss, P. (2005) *Ethics and Politics in Early Childhood Education*, London: Routledge.

Donaldson, M. (1993) *Human Minds: An Exploration*, London: Penguin.

Gilligan, C. (1982) *In a Different Voice: Psychological Theory and Women's Development*, Cambridge, MA: Harvard University Press.

Grayling, A. C. (2003) *What Is Good? The Search for the Best Way to Live*, London: Weidenfeld & Nicholson.

Halstead, M. and Taylor, M. (1996) (eds) *Values in Education and Education in Values*, London: Falmer Press.

Kelly, A. V. (1995) *Education and Democracy: Principles and Practice*, London: Paul Chapman Publishing.

Kohlberg, L. (1981) *The Philosophy of Moral Development, vol. 1*, San Francisco: Harper & Row.

Lipman, M. (1993) *Thinking in Education*, Cambridge: Cambridge University Press.

Lundy, L. (2007) 'Voice' Is Not Enough: Conceptualising Article 12 of the United Nations Convention on the Rights of the Child, *British Educational Research Journal*, 33 (6): 927–42.

National Union of Teachers (2012) *Education, the Law and You*, London: The Strategy and Communications Department of the National Union of Teachers. Available at: www.teachers.org.uk/files/the-law-and-you--8251-.pdf [Accessed on 20 July 2014].

Noddings, N. (2002) *Educating Moral People: A Caring Alternative to Character Education*, New York and London: Teachers College Press.

Noddings, N. and Slote, M. (2003) Changing Notions of the Moral and of Moral Education, in N. Blake, P. Smeyers, R. Smith and P. Standish (eds) *The Blackwell Guide to the Philosophy of Education*, Oxford: Blackwell Publishing.

Osler, A. and Starkey, H. (2010) *Teachers and Human Rights Education*, Stoke-on-Trent: Trentham Books Ltd.

Power, C. (1988) The Just Community Approach to Moral Education, *The Journal of Moral Education*, 17 (3): 195–208.

Power, C., Higgins, A. and Kohlberg, L. (1989) *Lawrence Kohlberg's Approach to Moral Education*, New York: Columbia University Press.

Tizard, B. and Hughes, M. (2003) *Young Children Learning* (second edition), Wiley–Blackwell Publishing.

United Nations International Children's Emergency Fund (1995) *The Convention on the Rights of the Child*, London: UK Committee for UNICEF. Available at: www.unicef.org.uk/UNICEFs-Work/Our-mission/UN-Convention [Accessed on 19 July 2014].

Warnock, M. (1996) Moral Values, in M. Halstead and M. Taylor (1996) (eds) *Values in Education and Education in Values*, London: Falmer Press.

Wiesner, D. (2001) *The Three Pigs*, New York: Clarion Books.

9

Experience, education and democracy
The work of John Dewey
Joanna Haynes

Overview

One of the most well-known and influential theorists in the field of education is the American pragmatist philosopher John Dewey (1859–1952). He produced a large body of work on the philosophy and practice of education. This chapter sets out to examine a small selection of Dewey's liberal humanist ideas about education. Dewey's influence is extensive and sometimes his ideas are cited rather vaguely and uncritically. Dewey believed that the educational process should draw upon and enlarge the experiences of learners: using, testing and developing knowledge in the process of solving real problems. He experimented with both curriculum and pedagogy, proposing that education is about experience, but that not all experience is necessarily educative. He drew attention to the significance of engaged thinking and reflection, interaction between teachers and learners, and the learning environment. Dewey saw schools as places where students would learn how to live, as well as develop their knowledge and understanding. He suggested that schools could be sites for social reform and democratic progress. Throughout this chapter, you are invited to consider Dewey's influence on contemporary curricula and pedagogy.

QUESTIONS

- What were some of the influences on Dewey's thinking?
- How did Dewey understand the role of experience in developing knowledge?
- What were Dewey's ideas about the curriculum, teaching and learning?
- What role did Dewey envisage for schools in developing a democratic society?

Introduction

John Dewey was born in Burlington, Vermont, USA in 1859. As an undergraduate student he was exposed to Darwin's theory of evolution and its associated arguments regarding natural selection, at the time very new and radical ideas, first published around the time of Dewey's birth. These theories exerted a profound and lasting influence on his thinking and philosophical outlook. Reading Dewey's writing, we see how deeply notions regarding the human organism's interaction with the environment are rooted in his theories of learning and knowledge. Between the ages of twenty and twenty-two Dewey taught in high school and it was during this period that the idea of pursuing a career in philosophy took hold. Being a young person at university is often a time of heightened curiosity and openness to new ideas, and Dewey met some significant others who were to influence his intellectual development at Johns Hopkins University. From 1894 he worked at the University of Chicago and spent most of his academic career as a Professor of Philosophy at Columbia University.

Dewey's pragmatism

Dewey completely rejected the idea of philosophy as an abstract intellectual pursuit. He was influenced by the philosophy of pragmatism, which is based on the integration of theory and practice and holds that values, ideas and social institutions have their roots in the practical circumstances of everyday life. He took the view that philosophy has to be useful and make a difference to practice. He was wary of the tendency of educational theory to generalize and oversimplify things, preferring to carry out specific investigations (Thomas, 2007: 45). He was particularly taken with the thinking of his contemporary James Herbert Mead, a social psychologist who developed ideas on the self as a social and cognitive entity developing through the reflexivity of consciousness. Dewey and Mead were very close friends and influenced one another enormously.

In his talks to school students and parents, Dewey communicated his practical and experimental approach to education. He was not a detached armchair philosopher but a politically engaged person and a regular commentator on public concerns such as women's suffrage and the unionization of teachers. This sense of involvement is shown in his continuing to work and publish after retirement and right up until his death aged 92.

ACTIVITY 1

For a first taste of Dewey's work, you might like to watch the preview of an animated film about his life and work (www.davidsonfilms.com/giants-of-psychology/john-dewey-introduction-to-his-life-and-work) introduced by Professor Larry Hickman from the University of Illinois, a Dewey scholar and Director of the Dewey Center.

Dewey produced an enormous body of work during his lifetime and this chapter can only serve as a starting point to stir your interest in his ideas. The chapter begins with a look at the experimental school that Dewey founded in Chicago and some of his ideas about curriculum and pedagogy that emerged from that venture, drawing on online archives of the school's activities, *The Child and the Curriculum* (first published in 1902), and the scholarship of Laurel Tanner (1991). We consider the wider issue of how we can develop and try out new approaches to children's learning and the role of 'alternative' schools in stimulating thinking and action in education. We move from discussion of the curriculum to an exploration of the pedagogy of enquiry. We look at Dewey's ideas about experience as articulated in his *Experience and Education*, a series of lectures based on his critical reflection and experimentation, along with the deep

UNIVERSITY OF WINCHESTER
LIBRARY

debate it provoked about traditional and progressive forms of education, first published in 1938. We examine his educational philosophy in respect of the wider social aims of education and the role of the school in a democratic society, expounded in *Democracy and Education*, first published in 1916. Finally, we very briefly discuss some further critiques of his thinking by other educationalists.

The Chicago Laboratory School

ACTIVITY 2

Dewey and his colleagues founded an experimental school. Imagine you were given the resources and opportunity to create an experimental school:

- How would you design the buildings and environment?
- What background and expertise would you want the staff to have, both individually and collectively? Who else might be involved in the provision of education?
- What means would you use to evaluate the successes and failures of your experiment?
- Write down the three key aims of your experimental school, noting any influences from ideas and practices you have either read about or experienced yourself, and explain the thinking behind your aims to a colleague.
- What do you consider to be the risks of your experiment and how will you try to minimize their effects?

Compare and discuss your ideas with others in your classes. Collate these ideas and bring them to your reading of this and other chapters in this book.

Search online to find out about the educational philosophies of 'alternative' schools in the independent sector, such as Summerhill School, Suffolk (www.summerhillschool.co.uk), The Sands School, Ashburton (www.sands-school.co.uk), Brockwood Park School, Hampshire (www.brockwood.org.uk), and The Small School, Hartland (www.thesmallschool.org.uk).

Schooling is a highly contested issue. Dissatisfaction with existing provision or the desire to try out new approaches has often led educational dissenters and reformers to set up 'alternative' schools. You will have explored some current examples of such schools working in the UK today through your online research in the activity above. In the 1890s, when Dewey was at the University of Chicago, he founded and directed the Laboratory School with a group of close colleagues in his department, all of whom shared a very strong interest in education. The term 'laboratory school' conjures up images of controlled experimentation and scientific verification. It was called a Laboratory School because it was seen to be fulfilling certain knowledge creation functions for the University's Department of Philosophy, Psychology and Education, who managed and supervised the work of the school. It was regarded as a scientific project that would test and verify theoretical statements about education, experimenting and performing in the way that university department laboratories did for other subjects (Dewey, ca. 1890).

Many of those in and around the University of Chicago who were interested in the Laboratory School had children of their own and they were excited by the idea that their youngsters might experience a radical alternative to traditional forms of schooling, associated with the docility, receptivity and obedience required of children 'receiving' the subject matter to be taught (Dewey, 1938/1973: 18). The experimental University Elementary School grew quickly.

Focus on learning

Parents of students attending the school were drawn by a curriculum that encouraged children's curiosity and attended to the interaction *between* children and the subject matter to be taught, rather than focusing solely on subject content and its transmission. It was a place where the process of learning itself was recognized as worthy of serious observation and investigation. The experimental school lasted for eight years until 1904 and at its height involved around 140 children, aged between four and sixteen. Work at the Laboratory School is reflected in a collection of essays by Dewey called *The School and Society*, first published in 1899 (Dewey, 1956). The school enjoyed many successes and generated all kinds of new ideas that were tested out in practice in the school. Of course there were problems in running the school: problems associated with trying to break new ground. Perhaps the fact that the school was based in a university made it seem in some ways an artificial setting. There were ordinary differences of opinion over roles, administration, finance, its rapid growth, moving premises and the evolving curriculum. There was also a teaching practice school in the University, used for teacher training purposes, that was operating with progressive education principles, so departmental politics contributed to the struggles of the Laboratory School.

Other influences on Dewey's ideas

As well as the influence of pragmatist philosophy in his North-American context, Howlett (2013: 193) suggests that Dewey's ideas were also shaped by the ideas of the German educationalist Froebel (1782–1852), who is best known for founding the kindergarten system for young children, a gentle world of play based on games and songs, construction, 'gifts' and occupations. Froebel's philosophy of early childhood education consisted of four elements: self-activity, creativity, social participation and motor expression.

The kindergarten movement had taken off during the 1850s in the USA due to the pioneering enthusiasm of champions such as Alice Chapman (Encyclopedia of Chicago online source). Dewey's experimentation led him to challenge the kindergarten tradition whenever he regarded it as outdated or overly regimented. He found elements of Froebelian philosophy sentimental and its view of play too spiritual and symbolic in flavour. He preferred play at school to be associated with the immediate context of the social and economic environment, encouraging children's involvement in activities such as farming or cooking, for example. This rejection of the Romantic roots of the kindergarten movement is strongly connected to Dewey's view that the pursuit of individual development in education should not take place at the expense of the social development of citizens for future American society (Howlett, 2013: 194–5). Noddings argues that Dewey's view of children is practical, supported empirically: children differ in their interests and capacities; they have inclinations towards both good and evil; they are active, social creatures whose worthy interests should be identified, encouraged and guided (2010: 266).

ACTIVITY 3

In the preceding paragraphs you have read about some of the people who influenced Dewey's ideas, and you may have noted the dates of his birth and death and where he spent his life. Imagine how the times in which he lived, along with his interests, contributed to the development of Dewey's thinking.

Who and what has influenced your beliefs about education? To what extent are you conscious of these influences, such as where and when you grew up and went to school; your parents' beliefs, occupations and education; the people who may have inspired or discouraged you? How are these beliefs being reinforced or challenged by your current studies in education?

Create a visual map or diagram of these influences on your current thinking about education. Highlight areas of change in your thinking since beginning your studies.

Curriculum

In his book *The School and Society*, first published in 1899, Dewey outlined the principles of elementary education that grew out of his experimentation at the Laboratory School.

Dewey was critical of earlier work in psychology that tended to describe the mind in very individual terms. Dewey emphasized the importance of the social in every aspect of human learning. He argued that education had to be meaningful to the child and studies presented in terms of their relation to life in society, in order to be assimilated into the child's social needs and aims. He suggested that the failure to make good connections between school studies and children's wider lives was very wasteful:

> From the standpoint of the child, the great waste in the school comes from his inability to utilize the experiences he gets outside the school in any complete and free way within the school itself; while, on the other hand, he is unable to apply in daily life what he is learning at school. That is the isolation of the school – its isolation from life. When the child gets into the schoolroom he has to put out of his mind a large part of the ideas, interests, and activities that predominate in his home and neighborhood. So the school, being unable to utilize this everyday experience, sets painfully to work, on another tack and by a variety of means, to arouse in the child an interest in school studies.

> (Dewey, 1956: 90)

Dewey connected the origin and development of ideas in the human mind with the needs of social action. The notion of education as growth, for both individual and society, was entirely new and very much an idea of its time, associated with a view of the human being as a developing organism as well as with newly emerging perspectives on the self. Dewey felt that both the individual and society should evolve. In chapter 4 of his book *The School and Society* (1956), Dewey explains how the modern conception of mind as a process is in stark contrast with earlier ideas of the mind as static in terms of its capacity, varying through the lifespan only in terms of size or quantity, rather than quality of thought.

It's worth dwelling on this modernist idea of the mind for a moment as the metaphor associating the process of mind with 'growth' has been so powerful, often shaping language used to describe teaching and learning and to underpin educational proposals. Alexander (1995) examines the pervasive use of organic metaphors of gardening and the fulfilment of latent potentiality associated with progressive notions of primary education: 'children as plants and teacher as gardener, and the associated horticultural imagery [. . .] natural, ripening, unfolding, budding points, nurturing and so on' (1995: 13). While Dewey was critical of the Romantic flavour of such ideas, the language of developmentalism often tends towards very similar imagery and terminology of learning as growth. For Dewey, growth was not a movement towards a fixed goal, but an end in itself.

ACTIVITY 4

The term 'curriculum' is used in all kinds of ways and it is useful to pause and consider the various usages as we think about Dewey's experimental approach.

The term derives from the Latin word 'currere', meaning 'to run', and has been used to describe a course of study or a life course, as well as the content of a university or school programme of study.

In education circles it is often used to describe the activities and experiences that policy makers, theorists and practitioners believe to be desirable for children to grow into adults and to fully participate in public and social life and the world of work and community. The content of the curriculum is hotly contested, as you will realize from your reading of the educational press.

Further uses of the term include the formal or official curriculum, including the documented accounts of intended teaching and learning and hoped-for outcomes, and the informal or hidden curriculum, describing the complex matter of what students actually experience during their education, regardless of what is officially documented. The hidden curriculum sometimes includes experiences that are at odds with the formal programme of study.

For further discussion of curriculum, please read the section on Curriculum Theory and Practice at: http://infed.org/mobi/curriculum-theory-and-practice.

Dewey is often associated with the idea of an integrated, project-based curriculum, rather than one organized according to the logic of different subjects. During the seven-year lifespan of the Laboratory School at the University of Chicago, the curriculum, teaching approaches and grouping of children were all the focus of experimentation and evaluation. According to Dewey scholar Laurel Tanner (1991), many educational reformers have mistakenly believed they were following Dewey's thinking in conceiving of the curriculum as a programme made up mostly of integrated projects.

Drawing on the archives of the School's work, Tanner has written about what he describes as a relatively neglected aspect of Dewey's practical work in curriculum development. How should subject matter be organized at school? How do subjects relate to projects? Tanner explains that the curriculum at the Laboratory School was two-dimensional, consisting of:

> the child's side (activities) and the teacher's side (logically organized bodies of subject matter: chemistry, physics, biology, mathematics, history, language, music and physical culture).

> (Tanner, 1991: 102)

Experience and experimentation

Rather than the idea that the child was responsible for mastering the subjects entirely through his own efforts, Dewey saw each subject as a form of living personal experience, not just a body of facts. He drew a distinction between the logic of subject study and the psychology of learning it. The principle of his approach was to identify what of the subject was within the child's present and real experience and to develop learning from that meaningful baseline. For Dewey, the instructional challenge for teachers was how to discover and build on children's experiences while making sure that this would grow into systematized knowledge (Tanner, 1991: 102).

Tanner reports that the plan for the school included a list of subjects: arithmetic, botany, chemistry, physics, zoology, geography, history, geology and mineralogy, physiology and geometry. To begin with, teachers were generalists rather than specialists. Teachers started their planning from the subject matter and prepared activities that provided for progress in understanding. They did not start from the activities. The plan included activities like carpentry and cookery, which involved analysis of materials and processes, to provide contexts for learning. Children would also work together in mixed age groups to mediate between home and school and create community life. This plan was intended to provide a synthesis of the curriculum as a whole. Dewey argued for practical activities, citing children's seemingly natural impulses to investigate and make things. These were also outlets for the imagination. Dewey did not go along with a fanciful view of imagination, associated with fantasy and make-believe, but with a grounded sense that the imagination could be applied in everyday and familiar ways to bring about the 'thickening of experience' (Dewey, ca. 1890). The learning activities had both intellectual and social ends and called for communication and expression. Tanner points out that the idea that literature, for example, is a form of communication was at the time revolutionary. Subjects had been seen as existing for their own sake, rather than to enable communication in the world (Tanner, 1991: 105).

After two years, the curriculum plan for the Laboratory School was reviewed. First, specialist teaching was introduced. Second, while the school attempted to retain a family spirit through whole-school meetings and by older children sometimes helping younger ones, the policy of mixed-age grouping was mostly abandoned.

Learning about human occupations

Children in the school studied human occupations such as farming and these served as a means to address both the child and teacher dimensions of the curriculum. In keeping with developments at the time, they studied the impact of industry on family and community life through exploring, for example, the history of the textile industry, from its domestic to its industrial phases.

ACTIVITY 5

How would your list of subjects to be taught compare with those in Dewey's plan? Which would you include or remove? What subjects would you add?

Which human occupations do you think would be valuable to study in depth to support cross-curricular learning and to explore the relationship and mutual impact of work and production and home, family and community life? Choose an occupation and map out some initial ideas for a half-term programme of study appropriate for children aged seven to thirteen.

(continued)

(continued)

In Dewey's shoes, what would you have done to address the desire to avoid age compartmentalization and retain a sense of family life at school?

How do you think that coherence, relevance, synthesis and meaningfulness can be achieved in the school curriculum?

Through his experimentation, by the end of the life of the Laboratory School Dewey had identified three phases of children's educational development: four to eight years where subject matter is learned through the child's own constructive activities; eight to twelve years, a more purposeful and investigative phase; and finally from around thirteen onwards, Dewey felt children were ready to embark on distinctive intellectual studies (Tanner, 1991: 112). Dewey was to conclude that the two-dimensional curriculum was never resolved but always in the making.

Dewey was critical of progressive child-centred approaches, believing that the child and the curriculum must interact (see chapter 1 of *Experience and Education*, 1973). Concluding his review of the case regarding children's learning of subjects in *The Child and the Curriculum*, Dewey asserts that imposition or insertion of truth from without is not possible. He argues that 'all depends upon the activity which the mind itself undergoes in responding to what is presented from without' (1902: 39). For Dewey, the primary value of a formulated course of study is for the teacher, not the child. It enables the educator '*to determine the environment of the child*, and thus by indirection to direct' (1902: 39, original emphasis). For Dewey, this curriculum says to the teacher:

> Such and such are the capacities, the fulfilments, in truth and beauty and behavior, open to these children. Now to see to it that day by day the conditions are such that their own activities move inevitably in this direction, towards such culmination of themselves.
>
> (Dewey, 1902: 39)

Pedagogy of inquiry

So far we have discussed the curriculum explicitly and pedagogy only implicitly. The word 'pedagogy' has its origins in Ancient Greek language and philosophy, where paideia referred to the rearing and education of (selected) young people, towards an ideal of perfection. More recently, the term pedagogy has been used to refer to the art, or science, of instruction or to the practice, method or style of teaching. In some European countries a pedagogue is not necessarily a teacher, but someone involved in the broader care of children. The history of debates about pedagogy reflects these broad or narrow interpretations of the educator or pedagogue's role and responsibility: whether this refers to 'imparting' knowledge or to concern with the student's personal and social development, as well as their intellectual achievements.

Dewey criticized what he termed the 'spectator theory' of knowledge understood as a kind of detached seeing, and proposed an agentic theory of knowing. Dewey viewed knowledge as the outcome of active inquiry, a problem-solving process. Provisional but supported assertions about what we know can emerge through active experimentation. This is know-how that results from the intelligent pursuit of ends-in-view: a combination of reflective thinking and firsthand experiencing (Gregory and Granger, 2012).

Problem-solving thinking

Dewey regarded all learning as inquiry and inquiry as the means by which the growth of the mind and the self is maintained, via progressive problem solving: both a way to learn and a way to live. He regarded this process as inherently social. Inquiry describes two aspects of experience: external and internal. The external refers to experience in the world while the internal refers to the affective impact or meaning for the individual. Educational interaction between teachers and learners attends to both the external and internal dimensions of experience and creates habits of mind to enable further growth. Learning, for Dewey, describes the acquisition of useable knowledge, growth in the development of intellectual habits and more frequent and competent use of the tools of inquiry. Habit here is a dynamic construct, a predisposition rather than a series of repetitive acts (Noddings, 2010).

In *How We Think* (first published in 1910), Dewey developed a five-step model of thinking in inquiry characterized roughly as follows: i) a felt difficulty; (ii) its location and definition; (iii) suggestion of possible solution; (iv) development by reasoning of the bearings of the suggestion; (v) further observation and experiment leading to its acceptance or rejection; that is, the conclusion of belief or disbelief (Dewey, 1933: 37 cited in Noddings, 2010). Such a pedagogic model of rigorous investigation and reflection often underpins theories of experiential learning and you will find many examples of this cyclical framework for inquiry if you search online.

ACTIVITY 6

Read this extract on Dewey's account of his pedagogy below. What criticism do you think the current Education Minister would make of it?

As to methods, the aim is to keep alive and direct the active inquiring attitude of the child, and to subordinate the amassing of facts and principles to the development of intellectual self-control and of power to conceive and solve problems. Immense damage is done whenever the getting of a certain quantity of information or the covering of a certain amount of ground is made the end, at the expense of mastery by each child, of a method of inquiry and of reflection. If children can retain their natural investigating tendencies unimpaired, gradually organizing them into definite methods of work, when they reach the proper age, they can master the required amount of facts and generalizations easily and effectively. Whereas, when the latter are forced upon them at so early a period as to crush the natural interest in searching out new truths, acquiring tends to replace inquiring.

(The Dewey School, The Laboratory School Of The University Of Chicago 1896–1903, Part 1, Chapter 2: Experimental Basis of the Curriculum: www.archive.org/stream/ deweyschoolthela008095mbp/deweyschoolthela008095mbp_djvu.txt)

Educative experience

In *Experience and Education* (1973), Dewey famously wrote:

Experience and education cannot be directly equated to each other. Any experience is mis-educative that has the effect of arresting or distorting the growth of further experience. An experience may be such as to engender callousness; it may produce lack of sensitivity and of responsiveness. Then the possibilities of having richer experience in the future are restricted.

(Dewey, 1973: 25)

Dewey pointed out that both traditional and progressive forms of education offered experiences. It was the quality and *character* of educational experiences that concerned him, not only their immediate enjoyment but also their impact on later experiences: the experiential continuum (1973: 28). Educational experiences should arouse curiosity and strengthen initiative – he described experience as a moving force. In discussing freedom, he emphasized the freedom of intelligence and in discussing activity, he stressed intelligent activity:

> The teacher's business is to see that the occasion is taken advantage of. Since freedom resides in the operation of intelligent observation and judgment by which a purpose is developed, guidance given by the teacher to the exercise of the pupils' intelligence is an aid to freedom, not a restriction upon it.

(Dewey, 1973: 71)

Dewey was interested in the continuity and progression of learning. Instruction should begin from the experiences learners already have. A practical philosophy of experience, with its experimental approach to the curriculum, necessitates keeping track of activities, teacher reflection and review, highlighting the significant features of learners' developing experiences (1973: 87).

Education, community and democracy

Democracy is a moral as well as a political system, predicated on the view that society exists to promote the good life of all members. Dewey perceived democracy in three senses: as the protection of popular interests; as social inquiry; and as the expression of individuality. His concept of democracy, as a way of living and belonging, involves a vision of the relationships between groups and individuals, and the skills or processes they require for liberty and for growth. It is a democracy of ordinary people in communities, actively engaging in the process, and protection, of their own social evolution. Dewey's interests in social communities derived from his observations about the impact of the processes of industrialization on work patterns and family ways of life.

For Dewey, education is a social process and the school is a social community. Moral development and social development are completely intertwined. Moral education implies education that is morally justified as well as one that is designed to produce moral people. His theory of knowledge was a theory of active inquiry, deeply connected to real things and their uses, and this extended to life in the wider community – social life could also develop through processes of inquiry and experimentation. In *Democracy and Education*, he wrote: 'A democracy is more than a form of government; it is primarily a mode of associated living, of conjoint communicated experience' (from Dewey extract in Cahn, 2009: 418). Thus teachers in democratic societies must engage students in patterns of communication and interaction that will help to develop democratic habits of association as well as the requisite habits of mind. Democracy is always a work in progress.

Dewey suggested that education is vital to the sustenance of a deliberative democracy and 'the school must be a form of community life in all which that implies' (from Dewey extract in Cahn, 2009: 487). If you have investigated schools like The Sands and Summerhill, mentioned in the first activity in this chapter, you will have seen how some schools have taken up the idea of learning about and through democracy and schools being democratic communities. You can also look at Chapter 8 for discussion of Kohlberg's ideas of schools as just communities.

Critiques of Dewey

Dewey's influence has been considerable and his ideas have been widely debated. Nell Noddings (2010) has reviewed his key ideas from the perspective of care theory. She argues that care theorists put much greater emphasis than Dewey on teacher–student relationships and regard these as far more significant than the methods of teaching used. As far as democratic life is concerned, while Dewey outlined, for example, an integrated history curriculum that would teach about industrial history and the production of things, care theorists would also want to include the nature of domestic work, family and caring for and about things in the curriculum. Noddings also highlights Dewey's relative neglect of stories, poetry and imaginative dimensions of the curriculum.

Adopting a very different understanding of children's minds and their development as thinkers, Kieran Egan also critiques Deweyan conceptions of both pedagogy and curriculum design. He rejects the idea that teaching or learning activities should always move from the concrete to the abstract and always start from the familiar and move outwards to the unfamiliar. Egan rejects a curriculum based on movement from simple to complex, familiar to unfamiliar, concrete to abstract and empirical to rational. Instead he proposes that teaching itself should adopt a narrative framework to capitalize on young children's particular capacities for metaphorical and imaginative thinking (Egan, 1991) (see Chapter 10).

To begin your critical review of Dewey's thinking, read Egan's (2002) critique of his ideas in *Getting It Wrong from the Beginning: Our Progressivist Inheritance from Herbert Spencer, John Dewey, and Jean Piaget.*

References

Alexander, R. (1995) *Versions of Primary Education*, London and New York: Routledge.

Dewey, J. (ca. 1890) *The Dewey School, the Laboratory School at the University of Chicago*. Available at: www.archive.org/stream/deweyschoolthela008095mbp/deweyschoolthela008095mbp_djvu. txt [Accessed on 20 March 2014].

Dewey, J. (1902) *The Child and the Curriculum*, Chicago: University of Chicago Press.

Dewey, J. (1956) *The School and Society*, Chicago: University of Chicago Press. Available at: www.lib. uchicago.edu/e/spcl/centcat/fac/facch08_01.html [Accessed on 9 July 2013].

Dewey, J. (1973) *Experience and Education*, New York: Macmillan Press.

Dewey, J. (2009) Democracy and Education in *Philosophy of Education: The Essential Texts*, S. M. Cahn (ed.), London and New York: Routledge.

Egan, K. (1991) *Primary Understanding: Education in Early Childhood*, London: Routledge.

Egan, K. (2002) *Getting It Wrong from the Beginning: Our Progressivist Inheritance from Herbert Spencer, John Dewey, and Jean Piaget*, New Haven: Yale University Press.

Encyclopedia of Chicago. Available at: www.encyclopedia.chicagohistory.org [Accessed on 13 December 2013].

Froebel Web Online Resource, The Philosophy of Education. Available at: www.froebelweb.org/web2005.html [Accessed on 13 December 2013].

Gregory, M. and Granger, D. (2012) Introduction: John Dewey on Philosophy and Childhood, *Education and Culture*, 28 (2): 1–25.

Howlett, J. (2013) *Progressive Education: A Critical Introduction*, London: Bloomsbury.

Noddings, N. (2010) Dewey's Philosophy of Education: A Critique from the Perspective of Care Theory, *The Cambridge Companion to Dewey* (First edition), Cambridge: Cambridge University Press, pp. 265–287. Available at: http://dx.doi.org/10.1017/CCOL9780521874564.013 [Accessed 2 August 2014].

Tanner, L. N. (1991). The Meaning of Curriculum in Dewey's Laboratory School (1896–1904), *Journal of Curriculum Studies*, 23 (2), 101–117.

Thomas, G. (2007) *Education and Theory: Strangers in Paradigms*, Maidenhead: Open University Press.

10

Philosophy's children

Joanna Haynes

Overview

The history of western philosophy offers us several versions of childhood, of 'child' and of relations between adults and children. These perspectives on childhood have shaped educational policy and practice in particular historical eras, as well as being evident in professional training and development, schooling, parenting and childcare practised today. The chapter introduces some philosophical ideas pertaining to childhood and the key issues in contemporary debates regarding childhood. It concludes with a brief case study, philosophy for children, an educational approach that raises new questions about childhood and philosophy.

QUESTIONS

- What can we learn from the history of philosophy about ideas regarding children and childhood?
- In what ways have such ideas influenced educational theory and practice?
- What are some key questions and debates in the overlapping fields of childhood and education studies today?

Introduction

Many people who want to work in educational settings express a desire to make a positive difference to children and young people. They generally want to do their best, in respect of the lives of individuals they encounter, but also because of a belief in the power of education to lead to wider benefits: a public good. For those who aim to teach, it's not unusual for this quest to include a need to be equipped with some clear and definite knowledge and understanding – a wish to answer questions about how human beings develop and what they need to be able to learn. They want to know what kinds of approaches and interventions are the best. Gert Biesta states:

> Education, be it the education of children, the education of adults, or the education of other 'newcomers,' is after all always an intervention into someone's life – an intervention motivated by the idea that it will make this life somehow better: more complete, more rounded, more perfect – and maybe even more human.
>
> (Biesta, 2006: 2)

As education is such an important event and considerable public funding and interest is invested in it, these 'interventions' in the lives of children are highly contested. When it comes to the provision of formal education, the contestation arises from different beliefs about the nature of children and the value of childhood as well as competing ideas about the aims of education.

Ideas about children and childhood also appear in other chapters of this book. Chapter 9 explores Dewey's ideas about children as learners. Chapter 8 includes perspectives on children's moral education and rights for children. This chapter challenges the notion that childhood can be clearly defined and that we can pin down the essential characteristics of children. Childhood studies are multi- and interdisciplinary, drawing from a variety of subjects such as anthropology, psychoanalysis, history, sociology, psychology, literature and philosophy.

What childhood *is*, or what it *means*?

Broadly speaking, philosophical perspectives on childhood fall into two categories: those that give an account of how young human beings 'naturally' develop and what childhood *is*; and sociocultural accounts that argue that what childhood *means* and how it is *experienced* varies considerably, according to historical moment and place, as well as cultural, social and family context. Such binaries are not always constructive and educational and social practice with children tends to reflect movement along a continuum between these 'poles' of thinking. How can theories and individual stories be integrated so that good collective policies and practices of education and childcare can develop responsively in different locations?

In thinking about childhood, reading about the history of childhood is necessary, yet readings of history are disputed. This contestation keeps debates about childhood open. Philippe Ariès, for example, is widely cited for his argument that childhood is a post-seventeenth-century 'invention', a claim based on his historical analysis of visual arts, literary texts and dress styles (1965). Cunningham (1995) reports that Ariès succeeded in drawing attention to the problem of regarding childhood as a universal and natural phenomenon and to the significance of scholarly examination of historical images of childhood. Analysing the visual representation of children from different historical periods has become an established element of courses in education and childhood studies. Ariès' methods of analysis and his findings have been strongly disputed. Against Ariès' claim about the invention of childhood, Archard (1993) writes that to have a concept of childhood merely entails the view that children differ in some way from adults. He argues that in the medieval period a clear language *did* exist to distinguish infancy as a stage of human life. Archard believes that distinctive ideas about childhood go much further back in history than Ariès suggests.

Childhood as a changing construct

Hendrick (1992: 1) explains that Ariès 'focused on the social significance of children within the family, on the meaning of "the family", and most controversially, on the nature of the parent–child relationship' and that we have Ariès to thank for the idea that childhood is a changing construct. He notes the emergence of competing conceptions of childhood and the fact that conflicting views of childhood co-exist. Hendrick (1992: 1) argues that 'as women have been "hidden from history", so children have been "kept from history"'. This analysis is suggestive of an ideology of childism comparable with sexism, classism or racism: ideologies that justify and maintain the oppression of groups of human beings such as women and people of colour. Childism might be considered alongside ageism: unfair judgement or treatment of others justified solely on the grounds of age. When we consider the concept of child, we tend to draw a comparison with the concept of adult. Characteristics of children are contrasted with those of 'grown-ups' and these qualities invoked to explain or justify relations between them.

This chapter introduces enduring philosophical ideas about children and childhood that influence thinking and practice today. We trace the origins of these beliefs and identify ways in which childhood is being reconceptualised. We examine different accounts of childism and adultism and how they open up thinking about the positions of children and relationships between adults and children. The final section of the chapter examines the view of childhood of one educational approach: philosophy for children embodies a radical position on children's capacities as thinkers and learners (Haynes, 2008).

Enduring ideas about child, childhood and education

ACTIVITY 1

In his book *Childhood and the Philosophy of Education* (2011: 4), Andrew Stables proposes three ways in which the term 'child' is used today in everyday language:

- Child 1 is the child of one or more parents and anyone with living parents is such a child, regardless of age. Stables suggests that ancestor worship is a practice that rests on this sense of child and is associated with duty, respect and gratitude towards parent figures, including deities. Ritualised demonstrations of reverence for our forebears are common in many cultures. Child 1 also expresses relational, generational and biographical features of childhood. In countries and times where people live well into their seventies and eighties, many have the experience of living as the children of parents for a good proportion of their lives, and these relationships continue to shape our experiences long after our parents die. Psychoanalytic discourses have underlined the lasting impact of being the child of this father and that mother, and the enduring life narratives formed through these relationships.
- Child 2 refers to the section of the population between birth and eighteen and 'bestows protection at the cost of individual freedom [...] implies lack of readiness and a period of constrained preparation with few responsibilities'. There are many contemporary examples of social policy or practice that confirm this view, such as the school-leaving age, the age of consent, the age of criminal responsibility and laws regarding the sale of tobacco or alcohol and employment of minors.
- Child 3 refers to the state of being a novice: unready, under prepared. It is context rather than age dependent. Anyone can be described as naïve and 'childlike' in certain

situations, and positioned – perhaps diminished, elevated or patronised – by such a description. Some human behaviours and dispositions are ascribed mainly to Child 3 – innocence, irrationality, playfulness and wildness, for example. Bachelard offers us the term 'premature man' (1971: 107).

To what extent do you recognise these three accounts of the use of the term 'child'? Think of examples of where you have come across these usages. Do you think there are further categories of use that can be developed to enrich this discussion?

(Categories of child developed from Stables, 2011)

Plato

In western society, philosophical perspectives on childhood have strong roots in the works of Plato and Aristotle. Plato's interest was in forms of education that would lead to the ideal society rather than in childhood per se. Stables (2011) explains that Plato was concerned with the not–yet–competent aspect of childhood, associated with Child 3 above. Plato referred to the natural and variable potentiality of children and believed that their education should be based upon qualities he regarded as innate in the child. Plato tended to talk about the young in terms of their future usefulness to the state and Stables traces this theme within recent educational discourses (2011: 27). Plato is described by Gutek (1997: 22–3) as the founder of western idealism, whose educational objectives are: assisting learners to realise the potentialities inherent in their human nature; and enabling students, through the institutions of schools, to be exposed to the wisdom of their heritage. Such ideas about the realisation of individual 'potentiality' and the transmission of an enduring body of knowledge and traditions continue to be articulated in contemporary debates about schooling and the curriculum.

Plato's educational ideals were an integral part of his broader political vision for society, outlined in *The Republic*. He argued that children should be removed from their parents for the purposes of their education, and placed under the guidance of guardians, so that training could be strictly controlled and access to arts and literature carefully censored (see Chapter 1 for further discussion of Plato's ideas on education). Parents could not be fully trusted with such an important job as education and the inadequacy of parents to educate their children for the full responsibilities of citizenship creates the need for schools to be established and run by the state. This position helped to generate distinctions between child–rearing and education, private and public, and the segregation of experience and knowledge.

Aristotle

A student of Plato's, Aristotle argued that a truly educated person uses reason to guide their ethical conduct and political behaviour. According to Aristotle, who founded his own school in Athens (The Lyceum), education should enable the cultivation of reason in the interests of good moral character, happiness and well-being, and schooling should conform to what he described as the natural pattern of human growth and development. His educational ideas, outlined in Books VII and VIII of his *Politics*, are based on such a pattern: the first five years are about physical growth, movement, games, protection from exposure to bad language and listening to carefully selected stories, followed by two years of watching others at work on lessons which they will later learn themselves. He proposes two periods of education, from age seven to puberty and from puberty to age twenty-one, based on what he calls the divisions of nature. Aristotle writes: 'The purpose of education, like that of every kind of art, is to make good nature's deficiencies' (Book VII, Chapter 17 from excerpts selected for Cahn, 2009: 139).

As for Plato, education was central to Aristotle's philosophy. His ethics and politics were intertwined. Aristotle did not see children in isolation: what is good for the individual is also good for society. As generations reach maturity, they become responsible for the formation of future generations. Aristotle's recommendations for children, resting on the idea that the reasonable life is the way to happiness, indicate that the best approach to curriculum planning is that 'reasonable adults know what is best for their merely wilful charges' (Stables, 2011: 37).

In terms of the cultivation of reason, Curren (2009) explains how Aristotle distinguishes between moral and intellectual virtues:

> Moral virtues are defined as dispositions to feel and be moved by our desires or emotions neither too weakly nor too strongly, but in a way that moves us to act as reason would dictate, and to take pleasure in doing so. Intellectual virtues are defined as capacities or powers of understanding, judgments and reasoning that enable the rational soul to attain truth.
>
> (Curren, 2009: 150)

For a person to have good judgement, all virtues should be cultivated through education: moral virtues as a result of habit, thoughtfully developed under supervision and coaching, and intellectual virtues as a result of teaching. Aristotle's ideas arose in the context of a society in which very few enjoyed free citizenship and cannot simply be transposed to contemporary society. However, Curren claims that there is still value in the belief that experiencing the development and self-directed use of our abilities is strongly associated with living a fulfilling life. He concludes:

> If reasonableness is a human quality that needs assistance to develop, and an ethic of respect for people as rational human beings requires dealing with people as much as possible through truthful and reasoned instruction and persuasion and as little as possible through violence, then the foundations of law and government rest more crucially on adequate education for everyone than we generally realise.
>
> (Curren, 2009: 158)

If we follow Aristotle and agree with Curren's conclusions, then there are profound implications for the education of young people. What characterises the mature adult, as opposed to the immature child, has come to be associated with the development of rationality and equated with education.

ACTIVITY 2

Discuss the following questions with fellow students:

- How would you distinguish between rationality and reasonableness?
- Which subjects or dimensions of the school curriculum would you associate with the cultivation of rationality and reasonableness? How does this connect with your ideas regarding childhood?

■ To what extent do you agree that the development of rationality and/or reasonableness should be the main goals of education and that they can be associated with happiness and fulfilment?

Locke

Some of the most abiding notions about child-rearing and education emerged from the works of John Locke who, in 1692, published his ideas in *Some Thoughts Concerning Education*. Locke argued that all human knowledge originates in sense perception so the infant's mind is a clean slate at birth, a 'tabula rasa', upon which the data of sense experience can be impressed. In discussions about instruction, the metaphor of the infant mind as a 'clean slate' has been widely adopted.

Teachers and parents today would recognise Locke's advice for child-rearing as familiar. He was a physician and made recommendations for children's health and well-being, as well as their education. Locke believed that young children are pliable and stressed the importance of 'forming children's minds, and giving them that seasoning early, which shall influence their lives always after' (32, Cahn, 2009: 180). He advocated early, strict training of reason over desire and appetite to enable parents to secure their children's compliance to their will. He believed that children should look upon their parents as absolute governors and stand in awe of them (41, Cahn, 2009: 181). He acknowledges a problem of finding the balance between a strict hand and a steady hand and concludes:

> To avoid the danger that is on either hand is the great art: the same time, to restrain him from many things he has a mind to, and to draw him to things that are uneasy to him; he, I say, that knows how to reconcile these seeming contradictions, has, in my opinion, got the true secret of education.
>
> (46, Cahn, 2009: 183)

He advocates the gradual instilling of habits and only as many rules as are necessary. He tells his readers that children's curiosity reflects an appetite for knowledge to be encouraged and is the instrument to 'remove that ignorance they were born with' (118, Cahn, 2009: 191). In terms of responding to inquisitiveness, he recommends kindness and respect, answering all children's questions, giving accessible explanations 'as suits the capacity of his age and knowledge'. Locke has a conservative view of children's capabilities, describing their minds as weak, narrow, with a natural disposition to wander, fleetingly taken by novelty. He writes: 'inadvertency, forgetfulness, unsteadiness and wandering of thought, are the natural faults of childhood' (167, Cahn, 2009: 194).

In his day, education was available only to the wealthy few – Locke presents ideas for what a young gentleman should learn and the manner in which it should be taught. When it comes to learning to read, Locke argues that great care should be taken not to make it into a business or a task. A love of liberty is something Locke regards as natural 'even from our cradles' and this inclination should be taken into account. He describes methods of persuasion and motivation, believing that children learn by imitation. In a statement we might associate with more contemporary ideas about education, Locke reports:

> I have always had a fancy, that learning might be made a play and recreation to children; and that they might be brought to desire to be taught, if it were proposed to them as a thing of honour, credit, desire and recreation, or as a reward for doing something else, and they were never chided or corrected for the neglect of it.
>
> (148, Cahn, 2009: 193)

Rousseau

Locke's ideas exerted considerable influence on the thinking of Jean-Jacques Rousseau, who produced the classic text *Emile* or *On Education*, published in 1762, seventy years after Locke's work. His account of the imaginary child Emile, a boy of ordinary ability (but wealthy), emphasises readiness as the main driver for ordering learning activities through a sequence of stages. Rousseau's preface to *Emile* provides a taste of his radical thinking:

> Nothing is known about childhood. With our false ideas of it, the more we do the more we blunder. The wisest people are so much concerned with what grown-ups should know that they never consider what children are capable of learning. They keep looking for the man in the child, not thinking of what he is before he becomes a man.
>
> (from excerpts in Cahn, 2009: 206)

Rousseau appeals for pupils to be treated according to their age. He suggests avoiding verbal lessons, stating 'the only kind of lesson he should get is that of experience' (p. 212), and advocates wasting time rather than saving it. He appeals: 'Exercise body, senses, powers, but keep the mind inactive as long as possible. Let childhood ripen in your children' (p. 213). Activities like reading were to be delayed until really needed: 'Emile at the age of twelve will scarcely know what a book is' (p. 218). This notion of 'readiness' for certain kinds of formal learning has lingered.

Rousseau describes a conflict between making the man and making the citizen, between communal and public education on the one hand, and individual and domestic on the other. He argued that the development of human character should follow nature. Rousseau emphasised the natural goodness of children. The traditional view showed a good child to be as adult-like as possible, whereas for Rousseau, the child was a primitive innocent. For him, childhood constitutes our later self and we do not leave childhood behind when we become adults. Unlike previous centuries that saw children as adults-in-the-making, Rousseau argued that childhood was a stage in life to be valued for its own sake. His view contrasted very sharply with the dominant one at the time, influenced by John Calvin, who saw childhood as a necessary evil to be passed through as quickly as possible, with minimum time spent on 'childlike' activities such as play. Rousseau is associated with Romanticism, a school of thought that regarded the rational as continuous with the sensual, rather than opposed to it, and that viewed impulses towards creativity and play as integral to human intelligence.

Archetypes and myths of childhood

Drawing on enduring philosophical ideas discussed so far, Marie Louise Friquegnon (1997) and Chris Jenks (2005) offer the following depictions of childhood archetypes, along with associated child-rearing and education:

Friquegnon (1997) characterises two views of childhood as follows:

Childhood characterised by the absence or insufficiency of adult qualities so that:

- Children are inadequate adults and the aim is to diminish and finally extinguish inadequate and childlike behaviours.
- Apprentice model serves as guide to raising children. Children are expected to imitate and obey adults without question.

Childhood characterised by innocence and playful discovery so that:

- Children are naïve and both childish and childlike qualities are given opportunities and space to flourish.
- Children should be given freedom to determine which potentialities to realise: adults should refrain from intervening too forcefully.

Based on Greek mythology, Jenks (2005: 62–5) offers the following archetypal depictions:

- The Dionysian child is wild, evil, wilful and sensual, associated with the Christian doctrine of original sin.
- Strict control is required, underpinned by rigid codes and backed by force if needed, as an affirmation of collective values.
- No room for individuality.

- The Apollonian child is innocent, intrinsically good.
- Children are separated from the adult world, they are visible but they are not heard: child-centred thinking based on valuing freedom to develop interests and talents.
- A premium put on individuality.

(After Marie Louise Friquegnon, 1998, and Chris Jenks, 2005)

Partial definitions?

Along with others in the field of childhood studies, Friquegnon and Jenks seek to challenge notions of the 'normal child'. While most societies have treated childhood as a distinct stage in life, in terms of 'defining' childhood, their argument is that human nature and society are not fixed once and for all and childhood can only be partially defined. Along with concepts such as maturity, youth, adolescence, knowledge and progress, the concept of childhood is value laden and culturally variant. When it comes to child–rearing and education, there are diverse views on which qualities should be emphasised, as well as when and how they might be cultivated or discouraged.

Final answers to the questions 'What are children like?' or 'What is a child?' seem to seek out common behavioural indicators of maturation and to require responses that mark out *differences* between children and adults. Infants are often defined by their varying degrees and qualities of dependence on adults, on what they are not-yet-able to do. Latterly, some have argued that educational practice should begin by challenging assumptions about children's capacities, and focus on listening to children and creating enabling environments and conditions. It is necessary in particular contexts to clarify the expectations and hopes of adults in roles that involve responsibility for the care or education of children. In other contexts, it will be important to work with what people, whether child or adult, have in common: what draws them together? We have to both remember and forget about age.

ACTIVITY 3

A playful and thought-provoking exercise to explore conceptualisations of child and adult in a group involves making a line on the floor with a piece of string, or on the board with a pen. At one end put the word CHILD and at the other end ADULT.

With a selection of everyday objects, pictures or labels of objects generated by people in the group (e.g. soft toy, keys, kitchen utensil, book, coffee jar, dummy, mobile phone, nappy, etc.), take it in turns to quickly position the objects, pictures or labels along the concept line.

Explore reasons behind the positioning and whether some objects might be moved or appear in more than one position.

Review your thinking about these concepts as a group.

Being childlike?

Moving away from the question 'what *is* childhood?' within the Continental philosophical tradition, we might be more likely to find a question like 'what does it mean to *be* a child?' Such a question is concerned with ways in which so-called childlike qualities (Child 3) inform *all* human experience and understanding. From such perspectives it is lived experience that informs understanding: our daily lives, what we read, see, hear, touch and feel. Our bodies also carry the memories of our lived experience, so our childhoods are never completely closed chapters; as the widely quoted Gaston Bachelard puts it, 'like a forgotten fire, a childhood can always flare up again within us' (1971: 104).

We might feel we know about childhood because we have experienced it, basing beliefs on memories of being a child. Since memories of childhood are often accompanied by very powerful emotions, we can have a sudden sense of being transported back to being a naughty, secretive, powerless, wild or obedient child, or of associated feelings being strongly rekindled in the present. These recollections are a source of personal reflection and insight. If we want to engage critically with views of childhood, we need to be able to 'park' such memories to give due attention to the claims of others. When drawing on individual stories, one can argue that there are as many 'versions of childhood' as there are human beings.

ACTIVITY 4

Consider for a moment your upbringing and think about specific examples of ways in which your recollections of your childhood tend to inform your current views about what it means to be a child and an adult.

When it comes to recounting childhoods, Gaston Bachelard reminds us that memories are 'repaired' each time we 'move' them from dreamed duration to a telling occasion; memories frequently repeated become old refrains of the personality. He suggests that children are often 'taught' the memories of early childhood, tied up as they often are with a family narrative (1971: 106–7). How often do our parents or close relatives remind us of who we are with anecdotes from our early lives?

Childhood: a lasting quality of experience

Winnicott (1971) draws attention to the idea of childhood being a lasting dimension of experience, rather than a fixed period at the beginning of the lifespan, a view strongly associated with psychoanalytic explanations of human behaviour. Reflecting on his observations of children's engagement in magical thinking and imaginative play, he proposes that there are strong connections between the realms of illusion and playfulness and the realm of creative experience: underlining a certain continuity of childlikeness in the domain of creativity.

We might also look to fictional, narrative and factual accounts of childhoods from literature, film, documentary or autobiography, including those that closely reflect a wide range of children's voices. This is one reason why many researchers and practitioners set out to include children and sometimes their close family members as active participants and co-researchers – seeking to carry out research *with* children, rather than *on* children. Drawing on a variety of sources reminds us of the multiplicities of ways in which children's lives are lived and depicted and helps to enrich understandings of what childhood means. Reading different sources enables thinking and practice to take account of plurality *and* the power of myths and archetypes, in all the ways that children are observed, portrayed and represented, through language and image.

Critics of developmentalism

Critical developmental psychologist Erica Burman has played an important part in provoking people to think about children beyond the frame of mainstream theories of child development. She writes:

> educational interventions therefore do not enter a politically neutral space but are always already saturated with cultural assumptions. Once this subject of development is depicted as alone or singular within the task of development, then other features follow. Issues of culture and gender disappear within the generalised framework; for the singular child – once abstracted from context – comes to lack such markers, but becomes 'pure' potential, development in action (and so we have all these models, stages and phases, from Gesell to Piaget and beyond).
>
> (Burman, 2001: 8)

She critiques the discourse of developmental psychology in four ways. First, she contests forms of emotionality used around children, arguing that sentimentality and paternalism are fundamentally disempowering. Second, she contests the theory and practice of normative regulation in childhood in which measurements, evaluations and judgements are made against biologically determinist and culturally biased developmental norms. Mass schooling has played a big part in this drive towards uniformity. Third, Burman wants us to interrogate both the origins and consequences of the metaphorics of childhood: whether describing children as 'our future' or as innocent, or beastly and wild. Finally, she argues that any talk of a 'crisis of childhood' must be situated in the broader picture of global economics and their impact on labour relations and family structure and organisation. She rejects the whole notion of creating a 'special category' for children (Burman, 2001). This critique of so many of the ways children have been theorised leads us nicely into the next section of this chapter.

Adultism and childism

ACTIVITY 5

■   Have you come across the terms adultism and childism?
■   How do you interpret these concepts?
■   Can you think of examples to illustrate your interpretations?
■   To what extent are these concepts useful to discussion about childhood?

Bell (1995) defines *adultism* as the systematic mistreatment and disrespect of young people. Writing about youth work in the USA, he argues that while racism and sexism are widely accepted as realities and supported by evidence in the form of literature and research, adultism is a comparatively new concept. He sets out to provide examples to illustrate its character and expression, such as widespread abuse of children and young people; modes of school or family discipline that involve threats and arbitrary punishments; their lack of control and autonomy; the legal compulsion to attend school along with everyday interactions and incidents that treat children and young people as inferior and not worthy of due consideration and respect. Bell gives examples of routine legal and institutional practices that fail to provide children and young people with the most basic opportunities to express their needs and wishes. He draws on his work with young people to outline the impact of being treated as inferior and the sense of powerlessness, hopelessness and insecurity that this tends to engender. He argues that adultism gets in the way of good relationships between adults and children and prevents good youth work and education. Bell concludes that racism, sexism, adultism and all other 'isms' tend to reinforce one another. However, while the other 'isms' are recognised:

> Adultism is a pervasive and difficult form of mistreatment to identify, challenge, and eliminate precisely because every human being has experienced adultism, whatever the degree of severity or cultural variety, and because much adultism is considered natural and normal by most people.

> (Bell, 1995)

For David Kennedy, adultism is rooted in what appear to be empirical differences among human beings, for example of size, anatomy, neurostructure or physical strength. These have led to 'the tendency to regard and treat certain human others implicitly as if they were members of a separate species' (2006: 63). Such adultism positions the child as 'difference, deviation, deficit, the unformed and unshaped' (2006: 64). The child is regarded as transitional and incomplete.

A new ethics of child: adult relations

In his book chapter 'The Invention of Adulthood', Kennedy compares adultism with colonialism, classism, racism, sexism and homophobia and calls it 'a relation with an other that is dominated by projection' (2006: 70). Drawing on the theories of Swiss psychoanalyst Carl Jung (1875–1961), Kennedy suggests that ambivalent, negative, liminal and underdeveloped aspects of subjectivity – the *shadow* – are projected onto an other. Kennedy explains how, in the case of adultism, this has played out, as 'the shadow projection on children is reified in theory by Plato and Aristotle who [. . .] create the child as a bearer of volitional deficit and dangerous instinct' (2006: 70). Kennedy adds that in excluding the child from full personhood, the adult almost succeeds in 'splitting off the shadow and colonising it in childhood' (2006: 70).

Kennedy argues that forms of adult self-understanding that can disrupt and deconstruct such adultism become possible when this psychological projection can be put aside or critiqued – through recognition of the shadow and through self-reflection. Through such development the adult can be 'in touch with the child dimension of her own subjectivity' (2006: 73). He argues that this moment is more than a personal adjustment; it is cultural and social, and suggestive of a whole new ethic of child and adult relations. Kennedy is strongly associated with the introduction of philosophy into primary and secondary schools. This chapter concludes with a brief discussion of the encounter between childhood and philosophy exemplified in this project.

Case study – philosophy for children

As a father in conversations with his young children, philosopher Gareth Matthews noticed his six-year-old daughter's capacities for philosophical thinking. The bedtime stories he read to his three-year-old son raised philosophical issues that he was discussing with students in his university philosophy classes. Becoming more aware of the philosophical nature of some children's literature, he used these stories with his university classes to convince them of his view that philosophy is a natural, spontaneous and universal human activity. Matthews' book *Philosophy and the Young Child* (1980) invited appreciation for children's sense of wonder. His writing emphasised 'the need to rethink the child, not as an ignorant being, but as a rational agent who already has the capacity to reason philosophically' (1980: 172). Matthews (1994) challenged distinctions that had been made regarding children's development and mental competencies and drew attention to the notion that philosophical questioning begins from a sense of puzzlement about the world and the widespread observation that children are disposed to curiosity and wonder, by virtue of their recent arrival into the world.

Strongly influenced by the educational ideas of John Dewey, philosopher Matthew Lipman (1922–2010) developed the philosophy for children programme in the USA. Lipman had a clear practical goal of establishing philosophy as part of the curriculum of schools, as well as the wider aim of exploring the relationship between 'philosophy' and 'childhood'. Lipman and others produced curriculum material consisting of specially constructed philosophical novels with teacher manuals, each designed for youngsters between the ages of seven and sixteen. The novels raise classical philosophical ideas and themes.

A distinctive pedagogy

Philosophy for children is quite unique in terms of its teaching approach and is not taught like other subjects in the school curriculum. Lipman and his colleagues at the Institute for Advancement of Philosophy for Children (IAPC) at Montclair State University in New Jersey devised a distinctive pedagogy to actively realise the possibility of engaging children with the ideas and themes in the novels. A defining feature of this pedagogy is the classroom 'community of enquiry'. This 'ideal' of learning through philosophical questioning and shared dialogue proposes a practical method of working in classrooms. It posits knowledge as provisional and engenders critical, creative, caring and collaborative thinking (Splitter and Sharp, 1995). The community of enquiry methodology of experimenting with ideas is a crucial dimension of philosophy for children practice. It positions children as 'co-enquirers' and teachers as 'facilitators' in the open-ended philosophical dialogue. Based on experience of philosophical enquiry in the UK context, *Children as Philosophers* (Haynes, 2008) discusses theoretical and critical considerations of using philosophy in the classroom and includes many examples of children working as philosophers.

This pedagogy is very much at odds with the dominant metaphor of teaching as 'delivery', which emphasises instruction and still seems to position the child as receiver, and her/his mind as a container to be filled. It is based on the belief that childhood is a good moment to think and talk about philosophical issues. It is a practice that both challenges the ways that many adults view children as thinkers and moral agents and invites them to reignite their sense of wonder. Recognition of children's disposition to wonder and ask philosophical questions points to an epistemic advantage of coming new into the world. It also seems to signal an ethical moment: openness by some adults finding themselves moved to listen more attentively to children's thinking.

References

Archard, D. (1993) *Children: Rights and Childhood*, London: Routledge.

Ariès P. (1965) *Centuries of Childhood: A Social History of Family Life*, New York: Random House.

Bachelard, G. (1971) *The Poetics of Reverie*, Boston: Beacon Press.

Bell, J. (1995) Understanding Adultism: A Key to Developing Positive Youth-Adult Relationships. Available at: www.freechild.org/bell.htm [Accessed on 15 March 2013].

Biesta, G. (2006) *Beyond Learning: Democratic Education for a Human Future*, London: Routledge.

Burman, E. (1994) *Deconstructing Developmental Psychology*, London and New York: Routledge.

Burman, E. (2001) Beyond the Baby and the Bathwater: Postdualistic Developmental Psychologies for Diverse Childhoods, *European Early Childhood Education Research Journal*, 9 (1): 5–22.

Cahn, S. M. (2009) (ed.) *Philosophy of Education: The Essential Texts*, London: Routledge.

Cunningham, H. (1995) *Children and Childhood in Western Society Since 1500*, Edinburgh: Pearson Education.

Curren, R. (2009) Afterword to Aristotle Selection in S. M. Cahn (ed.) *Philosophy of Education: The Essential Texts*, London: Routledge, pp. 107–150.

Friquegnon, M. L. (1997) What is a Child? *Thinking*, 13 (1): 12–16.

Gutek, G. L. (1997) *Philosophical and Ideological Perspectives on Education* (Second edition), Boston: Allyn & Bacon.

Haynes, J. (2008) *Children as Philosophers: Learning through Enquiry and Dialogue in the Primary School* (Second edition), London: Routledge.

Hendrick, H. (1992) Children and Childhood in ReFresh: Recent Findings of Research in Economic and Social History 15, Autumn, 1992. Available at: http://web.archive.org/web/20051222101311/http://www.ehs.org.uk/society/pdfs/Hendrick% 2015a.pdf [Accessed on 25 April 2013].

Jenks, C. (2005) *Childhood*, London: Routledge.

Kennedy, D. (2006) *The Well of Being: Childhood, Subjectivity and Education*, New York: SUNY Press.

Matthews, G. (1980) *Philosophy and the Young Child*, Cambridge, MA: Harvard University Press.

Splitter, L. and Sharp, A.M. (1995) *Teaching for Better Thinking: The Classroom Community of Enquiry*. Melbourne: Australian Council for Educational Research.

Stables, A. (2011) *Childhood and the Philosophy of Education*, London: Continuum.

Winnicott, D. W. (1971/1991) *Playing and Reality*, London: Routledge.

UNIVERSITY OF WINCHESTER
LIBRARY

11

Critical thinking, dialogue and communities of enquiry

Joanna Haynes

Overview

The idea of learning through critical thinking, questioning and collaborative discussion in classrooms has grown increasingly popular in recent years. To make sense of ideas and develop meaningful understanding, many educationalists argue that students need opportunities to think and talk critically, making connections between new ideas and prior knowledge and experience. What are the origins of this kind of critically engaged pedagogy? With reference to a variety of theorists in the field, this chapter explores concepts of critical thinking, enquiry and dialogue in the context of educational philosophy and practice. In the 1970s, North-American philosopher Matthew Lipman proposed that education could become transformative if all children learned to philosophise at school. He understood philosophy not only as a body of ideas but also as a set of tools or practices for thinking critically and a guide to developing an educational community where students are able to explore matters of significance in their lives; to grow morally, emotionally and socially, as well as intellectually. This chapter reflects on arguments for critical thinking and philosophising to be integral to education.

QUESTIONS

- What are critical thinking and philosophical enquiry and what ends do they serve?
- How do concepts of critical thinking, enquiry and dialogue inform perspectives on the practice of education?
- How do students benefit from teaching approaches that emphasise critical thinking and philosophical enquiry?

Introduction

This book has introduced philosophical ideas and theories that inform debates about the aims and purposes of education in the broadest sense: education that enables people (now and in the future) to explore, understand and create knowledge *about* the world, and to live a good and meaningful life *in* the world alongside fellow human beings. Philosophy is concerned with fundamental questions of everyday life: what is the nature of the world and what can we claim to know about it? What choices do we have? How can we know our selves and one another? How should we live as human beings in the world? How can we make things better?

We've shown that philosophy can be considered as a practice of how to be and how to live. In ancient times, philosophy was all-embracing, concerned with understanding physical and metaphysical worlds, as well as with human existence and experience in the world. In many traditions, both ancient and contemporary, philosophy is concerned with practices of body, heart and mind, offering guidance for well-being and for spiritual and community life. In Chapter 6, for example, we introduced Deleuze's idea of a 'philosophy of use'. In Chapter 2 we talked about philosophy changing the world. Philosophy can help us consider the aims and purposes of a practice like education. When it comes to academic and formal learning, philosophy can provide 'tools' or techniques of systematic investigation to enable theories and arguments to develop rigorously, to subject ideas to careful scrutiny, to illuminate and resolve dilemmas, and when important judgements need to be made. These methods often involve conceptual and linguistic analysis, attention to detail and meticulous, passionate argument. This chapter explores concepts and practices of critical thinking, philosophical enquiry and dialogue, and proposes that these activities should be an integral dimension of education.

Valuing criticism and criticality

Questioning, reasoning and argument are vital elements of testing out theories, sharing understanding, creating meaning and making good judgements. Philosophical methods are themselves strongly contested, suggesting that education should involve criticism *and* self-criticism. The interpretation and creation of concepts engage both intellect and affect.

Traditional approaches to teaching depend on the idea that the teacher is the main source of authority and knowledge. They are strongly associated with the liberal-humanist perspective on education: the teacher is the expert; there are clearly delineated fields of knowledge and forms of knowledge. From this philosophical viewpoint, teaching should involve the teacher working to impart that knowledge to students in a process of telling, explanation, demonstration, transmission and provocation of thinking. This kind of teaching is strongly associated with many areas of formal academic learning. Such an approach is valuable when teachers have special expertise, when there are few or no other sources of knowledge available, or when the subject matter requires careful introduction and sequencing. It can be highly effective when the teacher is a gifted communicator and students are highly motivated. It often involves the teacher explaining the key questions and problems of the subject to students, drawing them in intellectually and emotionally with the vitality and significance of the subject matter: for example, new discoveries about the nature of the universe, the challenges of climate change, accounts of the English civil war, the life cycle of bees, treatments for AIDS or schizophrenia, or techniques of creative writing. From this perspective knowledge is, by and large, something to be explained and passed on.

The exclusivity of the transmission style of teaching has been challenged. Of course there are specialists in certain fields and expertise usually carries weight and authority. Knowledge of a subject is so important in supporting and guiding others who want to learn it and in enabling certain fields of knowledge to grow and transform understanding and human existence. Human ability to use language is central to this dynamic and incremental process. This ability to represent knowledge symbolically has enabled human cultures to grow and flourish. The role of language in all areas of learning has come to be better understood in recent years. In student-centred teaching, which is popular today, learners are expected to be actively involved in finding and making sense of ideas and experience. Research, exploratory talk, questioning and discussion are usually very evident. This is associated with understanding the development of human knowledge as an ongoing and socially situated process of construction and meaning making. The proliferation of digital technologies, multi-literacies and the information revolution have also been factors in changing the ways that people learn and in shifting the role of the educator.

Changing spaces of education

Educational spaces are changing too: growing awareness of the value of education in a wider range of contexts, such as natural and urban environments, specialist centres, galleries and museums, has moved the focus away from the traditional classroom itself. Such developments were recognised as significant by the educational philosopher Ivan Illich in his *Deschooling Society* (1973). He argued that schools often did more to prevent than to enable learning and that informal networks and a variety of learning spaces would do a far better job of creating and enabling education for the majority. These ideas are still to be fully tested. The very concepts and practices of 'schooling' and 'education' need further examination and imagination.

Valuing criticism is strongly connected with valuing truths and the belief that it is through criticism that understanding grows and knowledge is revitalised. Magee writes that:

> Ancient Greece was the first society in which students were taught to think for themselves – to discuss, debate, argue and criticise – and not just to parrot the views of their teacher. It led to the most rapid expansion of understanding there had ever been and to the idea that knowledge can actually grow through criticism.
>
> (Magee, 1998: 25)

Criticism is not always welcomed in classrooms. The invitation to students to be critical, if it is genuine, is a mark of respect for students' experiences and perspectives and comes from the belief that knowledge grows through such critical engagement.

ACTIVITY 1

First thoughts – agree or disagree?

- Knowledge grows through critical thinking
- Critical thinking can resolve conflicts
- Critical thinking is relevant for people over the age of sixteen
- Critical thinking is not needed in most jobs or everyday life
- You need training to be able to think critically
- Critical thinking can be taught
- Critical thinking is needed if you want to get a good university degree
- University tutors often invite critical thinking but really expect students to agree with them.

What kind of questions about education and critical thinking does this exercise raise? Can you create further statements either to disturb or to enrich this exercise?

The legacy of independent critical enquiry

One of the philosophical 'superheroes' associated with independent, critical and courageous thinking is the philosopher Socrates (469–399 BC), who lived in Ancient Greece. Socrates' life has a mythical quality about it, partly because we rely on the writings of others, such as his student Plato (see Chapter 1), to gain access to his somewhat eccentric life and ideas and partly because of the manner of his death. Socrates was very vocal in his criticisms of aspects of Athenian society at the time: its politics and its leaders. He was eventually sentenced to death following a trial based on accusations that, among other things, he was corrupting the youth of Athens through his marketplace and street-based everyday activities of provoking questioning and engaging men in debate about topics such as justice, virtue, true knowledge and morality. Socrates died by imbibing a drink containing the poison hemlock, apparently having refused the alternative punishment of paying a fine and by doing so presumably agreeing to give up his 'provocative' activities and abide by the city laws.

It is significant that Socrates did not record his views in writing, choosing instead face-to-face engagement with his fellow citizens. It seems he was concerned about what putting thoughts into writing might do to the pursuit of true knowledge. The absence of his writing puts us in a very interesting position, as we reflect on how ideas associated with Socrates have been represented, taken up and sometimes idealised.

Risks of being critical?

In the first section of his popular book *The Consolations of Philosophy* (2000: 14–42), Alain de Botton reports on Socrates' view that people often fail to examine their everyday beliefs for two reasons: first, a lack of courage, coupled with a fear of risking unpopularity with others, leads to the mistaken assumption that what is popular is also right; second, according to Socrates, people lack a rigorous method of thinking to enable them to scrutinise the views that comprise the status quo. When it comes to living a good life, Socrates argues that this failure to examine such common-sense beliefs has profound implications for society.

ACTIVITY 2

Can you think of an occasion recently, perhaps in the context of your university studies, when you were aware that somebody's speaking out about their beliefs, against the majority view, might be making them unpopular? Or when speaking out was avoided to secure popularity?

Think of an occasion recently when you were in a situation where people's beliefs were being scrutinised – what 'methods' (if any) were adopted to examine the beliefs in question?

What might constitute a *rigorous* method of thinking? What would it involve? When does it matter? Can you write a set of instructions for your method?

In the context of education, on what occasions, if any, are intuition and implicit understanding preferable to such rigorous methods of critical thinking? Make a note of some examples.

De Botton offers us an account of Socrates' logical method for examining so-called common-sense beliefs and achieving independent thought. He tells us that 'Socrates compared living without thinking systematically to practising an activity like shoemaking or pottery without following or even knowing its technical procedures'

(2000: 21). Socrates argues that intuition alone is not enough for such a complicated business as directing our lives. Drawing on the analogy of making pottery, the Socratic method of thinking involves taking a statement of common-sense belief about the nature of, for example, justice or courage, and using a series of steps in the form of questions and examples to test the truth or falsehood of the statement (see de Botton, 2000: 24–5). This process of interrogation and logical thinking is exemplified in many of Plato's writings which take the form of dialogues between the character of Socrates and fellow citizens.

What kind of activity is Socratic education?

What does the figure of Socrates offer us as educators in terms of his views of wisdom, 'truth' and his methods of teaching? He is famous for his oft-cited declaration that the only thing he could know for certain was that he knew nothing. This draws attention to the significance of acknowledging one's relative ignorance and to the value of uncertainty in the search for deep understanding. His insistence on a life of self-examination often made people feel profoundly uncomfortable and forced them into self-doubt in front of others. By all accounts, Socrates was certainly willing to subject himself and his ideas to the same rigorous self-examination.

This approach illuminates certain ethical questions about the teacher's role in the pursuit of understanding. While Socrates appears to be non-directive, arguably his questions lead his 'partners' in dialogue to a particular place of recognising that their original claims to knowledge are unfounded. This might be considered a form of manipulation or trickery. Walter Kohan suggests:

> The so called Socratic dialogues show this path very clearly: while some people knew something at the beginning of the dialogue, nobody knows anything in the end. And this 'knowing nothing' is Socrates' trick, for it is precisely what he does know, and on every occasion it is the same knowledge, his knowledge of (pseudo) ignorance, his wisdom.
>
> (Kohan, 2008: 18)

Kohan argues that Socrates trains his students in this knowledge (*the* knowledge), leaving no space for the creation of knowledge by the other.

Not just a matter of intellect

Author of *Critical Thinking in Young Minds* (1997) Victor Quinn caused controversy among fellow educators with a teaching approach called 'provocation-in-role', developed to enable children to become confident in raising critical questions, even in the face of knowledge presented with great authority. Provocation-in-role involved Quinn presenting himself as a scientist and claiming that, as an adult and a scientist, he must know better than they did. Playing with a certain stereotype of a scientist, there was an element of humour and drama in his approach and he was very careful to gauge the responses of children with whom he worked, to make sure that his 'provocation' was not overplayed. To start with, children in his classes would appear to be suppressed by his bold claims to knowledge as an adult carrying out scientific experiments.

Gradually, as he made grander and grander claims to know better than 'mere children', they seemed to muster the courage to challenge him. His teaching would also involve a 'de-briefing' following the provocation-in-role lessons about what it means to question the views of a person in authority.

Quinn understood that being critical is not just a matter of intellect, but that overt challenges to the power and authority of others are often involved in disputes about beliefs and ideas (see Chapter 5 on the work of Foucault). More often than not, children are expected to simply accept the authority of adults. Equally, novices are wary of challenging those considered to be experts. Quinn knew that it might be easy to ask awkward questions in the relatively safe context of lessons designed to encourage critical thinking, but much more difficult to challenge and argue in contexts where other people are in far greater positions of authority than others. However, Quinn's fellow educators argued that it could never be right to manipulate students, even if it did lead to courage and critical thinking: for them the ends could not justify the means.

An orientation towards experience

In terms of evaluating the impact of the Socratic tradition on the development of human thought, Peter Abbs (1994: 16) describes it as an 'animating, deeply disturbing power' running 'like an electric current through western civilisation'. In his eloquent account of the principles of Socratic education, Abbs suggests that for Socrates education is not a collection of knowledge and skills but 'an activity of mind, a particular emotional and critical orientation towards experience' (1994: 17). He further argues: 'The noun education is [. . .] deceptive, for there is no object to correspond with the word' (ibid.: 17). Rather, education is a thinking and doing process that 'evokes a sense of personal drama' (ibid.: 17). In some educational quarters, talk of critical enquiry often appears technical, disembedded and detached from the passion and drama of human experience (see Melanie Parker's critique of the colonising of critical pedagogy in Chapter 3). Abbs is keen to emphasise the powerful connection between education and personal commitment. He describes the aim of Socrates' dialectical teaching method:

> to give birth to a desire for authentic learning. Intellectually, the elenchus, as it worked on the student, moved from strongly held opinion, to floundering uncertainty, to loss, to not-knowing, that engendered the authentic quest for meaning [. . .] Emotionally, the elenchus began with smug ease [. . .] that dissolved into unease, then into anguish, then into concern and, finally, into collaborative and reflective curiosity.
>
> (Abbs, 1994: 17)

The method is not intended as a game of logic; its purpose is primarily to foster virtue. As Abbs explains, 'teaching is an ethical activity' and education is partly about the 'art of releasing a critical-ethical process in the other, the final outcome of which cannot be known in advance' (1994: 18). What is particularly persuasive and significant about Abbs' characterisation of the figure of Socrates is the attention he draws to his particular presence, his way of being and his sometimes contradictory relationship to what he was saying. He reflects on the fact that Socrates did not record his views in writing and suggests 'books freeze the flow of movement and shed their authors, whereas teaching is always through the medium and specificities of existence and relationship and is thus unique and essentially unrepeatable' (1994: 20).

ACTIVITY 3

Imagine a world without writing and the written word. What would it be like? What does writing enable and what does it limit? Create a drawing or diagram without words in it to reflect your ideas about what this world would be like.

What do you think about Abbs' comments above regarding books, authors and the 'unrepeatability' of teaching?

Metaphors of teaching and learning

Stingray

In a paper in the *Journal of Philosophy of Education* in which she considers the role of the philosophical teacher, Murris (2008) draws attention to a metaphor in Plato's Meno, a dialogue about the nature of virtue. In this dialogue Socrates is described as being like a stingray, numbing and inducing a state of perplexity in those with whom he comes into contact. (The flattened body of the stingray allows it to conceal itself in its environment and stingrays usually have one or more barbed stings on their tails, for self-defence.) Murris suggests that the kind of 'paralysis' that results from being 'stung' could be compared to what happens to philosopher/teacher and student alike when an educational dialogue succeeds in shaking up habitual certainty or complacency and creating openness to new ideas.

Gadfly

In his book *Socratic Perplexity and the Nature of Philosophy*, philosopher Gareth Matthews (2003) discusses two further metaphors of the philosophical teacher that arise in Plato's writings. The gadfly, a type of fly that tends to trouble cattle and horses, often appears as an image in Greek mythology and in politics. In his dialogue the *Apology*, Plato compares Socrates to a gadfly, irritating and goading the 'slow horse' of Athenian politics. For Socrates this was not about argument for the sake of it, but a moral mission in pursuit of truth. In the world of politics, the gadfly describes a dissenter who is willing to challenge those in power, to question the status quo and take up a minority viewpoint. In the context of education as a virtuous activity of mind, the teacher or student who acts as gadfly is the one who presses for the most awkward questions to be taken up and who challenges the majority or popular view.

Midwife

The idea of the teacher as midwife is one of the most enduring metaphors of Socratic teaching. In Plato's *Theaetetus*, a dialogue concerning the nature of knowledge, Socrates, the son of a midwife, describes the midwife's task in the process of truth-seeking as questioning in ways that help to reveal ambiguities or contradictions that need to be resolved. The idea of the teacher assisting in the 'birth of ideas' is an appealing one. The metaphor of midwifery communicates the kind of intimate support associated with thinking about or understanding difficult ideas. If the 'birth' of thoughts is more complicated or drawn out, perhaps involving controversial questions, the teacher as midwife draws on the experience of other 'births' to provide encouragement, reduce the pain of learning and suggest alternative possibilities.

ACTIVITY 4

To what extent do you recognise these metaphors of the teacher as midwife, stingray and gadfly?

To whom or what would you compare the best and worst teachers you have known (drawings or cartoons if you prefer)?

What other analogies can you come up with to illustrate your ideas about the role of the teacher and what you think is involved in learning and knowledge creation? Make a list of different metaphors of teaching and learning: teacher as gardener, security guard, zoo-keeper, petrol-pump attendant? Student as empty vessel, vacuum cleaner, parrot or computer?

Critical thinking – and its critics!

In making the case for explicit teaching of critical thinking, some educationalists start from the view that students' everyday thinking is in need of improvement and that teaching needs to be much more demanding and engaging. Splitter and Sharp (1995: 5) describe a 'poor state of thinking competence among students and graduates'. They argue that students often struggle to think creatively and constructively, to raise questions, recognise assumptions and give reasons for their views, and to distinguish between knowledge and beliefs, for example. As discussed in Chapter 3, critical pedagogues such as Freire propose that the problem lies rather with forms of education that adopt a 'banking' approach. There are often institutional obstacles to free and open expression and interrogation of ideas and educational establishments do not always encourage students to think – the drive for more and more qualifications and processes of assessment (teaching to the test) often inhibit the development of criticality, except as a kind of carefully managed performance.

Thinking skills

Definitions of critical thinking are wide ranging. (For an accessible review of psychological and philosophical perspectives on critical thinking, see for example Lai, 2011.) Some advocates refer to specific procedures – a set of common thinking skills or proficiencies that underpin critical thinking – arguing that the explicit teaching of such skills can improve students' overall performance as thinkers and learners. They seem to paint a portrait of an ideal type of thinker. Over the last sixty years many thinking skills programmes have appeared, proposing taxonomies of skills or behaviours and a range of activities to exercise them or performance indicators to exemplify them. These resources are sometimes presented in the context of improving study and academic writing and argumentation skills (see for example Roy van den Brink-Budgen, 2000). As well as providing material for school and university students, Van den Brink-Budgen has created thinking-focused educational programmes for young offenders in prison settings, based on philosophical enquiry (see the later sections of this chapter). Such programmes as this can positively transform the thinking, achievement and aspirations of those who take part. The enthusiasm of educationalists for such approaches is certainly understandable.

Thinking persons

Splitter and Sharp (1995) argue that we should bear in mind not lists of thinking skills or dispositions but the people who learn and practise them: 'Persons are thinking, feeling individuals who think both autonomously and collaboratively. Persons, not minds, bodies or feelings, should be the focus of all teaching and learning' (1995: 9). With this qualification, they propose that thinking 'strategies' include formulating questions, making connections and distinctions, recognising contradictions and assumptions, observation, categorisation, reasoning and evaluation. They also involve listening to others, being open-minded, imaginative and committed to the value of enquiry and truth-seeking – less a set of skills perhaps than a set of attitudes, or habits, of mind and spirit.

Arguing from a philosophical perspective, Bailin and Siegel propose that the concept of critical thinking is a normative one. They suggest that to characterise thinking as 'critical' is to have judged that it meets certain standards or criteria that enable us to think of it as 'good'. For them, critical thinking is good thinking (2003: 181). Good reasons are those that warrant beliefs, claims and actions and good judgement is strongly and sensitively linked to context. They suggest that while some accounts of critical thinking rely on skill definition, most philosophically informed discussion presents critical thinking as a combination of skills/abilities and dispositions (2003: 182). By dispositions they mean qualities such as independent and fair-mindedness and respect for others in group deliberation.

Teaching approaches that focus on generic thinking skills are criticised for their claims that such skills are freestanding and transferable. Many argue that thinking is context or discipline/subject specific and dependent. They suggest it is hard to be critical in a field in which one lacks basic knowledge, and the ability to weigh up good and bad reasons and reach judgements and right actions is dependent upon good knowledge and experience. Bailin and Siegel suggest that 'the "critical spirit" component, that complex of dispositions, attitudes, habits of mind, and character traits, characteristic of the critical thinker, is [...] fully generalisable' (2003: 185).

Critical thinking equals good teaching?

For some educators, critical thinking is simply synonymous with good teaching, part and parcel of engaging students at a deep level with the subject at hand: a teacher having the confidence to enjoy students' questions and to make room for their interpretations and responses. Bailin and Siegel argue that critical thinking, which they equate with rationality, is an overriding ideal of education and paramount throughout the whole curriculum. They give four reasons for this position: it is necessary if students are to be treated with respect as persons; it goes hand in hand with promoting self-sufficiency and self-direction; it plays a central role in the rational traditions of maths, science, literature, art, history and so forth; it is basic to the fostering of reasoned deliberation in democratic life (2003: 189).

Michael Bonnett believes that thinking is at the very heart of our being and that how we think expresses our relationship with the world and sense of truth and reality. Thought conceived as a skill is a form of mastery over content from which truth is manufactured. This thinking expresses a 'disconnection between thinker and world, thinker and truth' (1995: 303). Bonnett (1995) has suggested that the appeal of a core of transferable thinking skills is that it trades on nuances of empowerment, but the idea of thinking as a set of competences is contested from both ethical and epistemological standpoints. Bonnett mounts a powerful attack on the thinking skills perspective, for its instrumental depiction of the environment, including the world of meanings, as a 'resource' for education. He rejects this view on the relationship between thinking and content, and characterises it instead as 'an open engagement imbued with a sense of the unknown' (Bonnett, 1995: 304).

ACTIVITY 5

What kinds of questions has this chapter raised for you so far about the concept of critical thinking?
   As an educator, how would you go about creating conditions for critical thinking to flourish?

Communities of enquiry

A reflective paradigm

In Chapter 10, I explained the principles and practice of philosophical enquiry with children and young people in schools and its implied perspectives on children and childhood. As one of the best-known advocates of teaching thinking in schools, and the founder of the philosophy for children programme, Matthew Lipman proposes that critical thinking and creative thinking are interdependent, occupied with the twin concerns of truth and meaning, and most likely to flourish through dialogue in communities of enquiry. This was all part of his wider vision of a reflective model of educational practice in which both teachers and students engage in independent, imaginative, complex and resourceful thinking. He summarises the dominant assumptions associated with the reflective paradigm as follows:

- Education is the outcome of taking part in communities of enquiry, guided by teachers, working towards understanding and good judgement
- Students are provoked into thinking when knowledge is presented as mysterious, ambiguous and equivocal
- Discipline and subject boundaries are presented as problematic (rather than fixed)
- The teacher's stance is fallibilistic (ready to admit mistakes)
- Teaching is based on the belief that students are reflective and reasonable
- The educational process is concerned with relationships between subject matters being investigated, not just the acquisition of information (Lipman, 1991: 14).

In developing his educational ideas, Lipman was influenced by the thinking of pragmatist thinkers Charles S. Peirce (1839–1914) and John Dewey (1859–1952) in respect of the concept of a 'community of enquiry', which they originally introduced. The need for a community of enquiry is based on the idea of the provisional and contingent nature of knowledge, embedded within a social context, and dependent for its legitimacy on agreement reached between groups of people concerned with particular investigations.

Classroom communities

In applying the concept to education, Lipman speaks of converting the classroom into a community of enquiry in which:

> students listen to one another with respect, build on one another's ideas, challenge one another to supply reasons for otherwise unsupported opinions, assist each other in drawing inferences from what has been said and seek to identify one another's assumptions.
>
> (Lipman, 1991: 15)

Lipman's account of critical thinking is 'thinking that (1) facilitates judgment because it (2) relies on criteria, (3) is self-correcting, and (4) is sensitive to context' (1991: 116). Lipman defines enquiry as 'self-correcting practice' (1991: 40). He identifies a number of skills or proficiencies that make up the practice associated with enquiry, such as the formulation of problems and hypotheses, identification and prediction of causes and effects, means and ends or consequences. He argues that it is through enquiry skills that children learn to connect the present with previous experiences and their expectations of what might happen in the future. It encourages them to be creative and put forward ideas.

The community of enquiry provides the conditions in which such criteria can be developed and thinking can be subjected to self-correction through dialogue with others. The aim of 'converting' a classroom community to such patterns of thought and behaviour is to enable the processes of self-correction that, for Lipman, define a disciplined and worthwhile enquiry.

Dialogue

Like the concept of enquiry, the idea of dialogue suggests the kind of reflective educational philosophy whose assumptions are summarised in the previous section. In the educational contexts discussed here, both ideas have intellectual and moral dimensions. A recent report on primary education suggests: 'Dialogue is central to pedagogy: between self and others, between personal and collective knowledge, between present and past, between different ways of thinking' (Alexander, 2009: 19). Dialogical teaching is increasingly encouraged at all levels of formal education. According to Alexander (2005), dialogue expresses virtues of open-mindedness, compassion, patience, generosity, fairness and persistence.

Dialogue is not linear but is characterised by 'systematically searching, reciprocal, extended, structured talk'. Dialogue involves participants in deconstruction and construction, translation, dynamic movement and the common goal of truth-seeking (Alexander, 2005). It is different from conversation, debate, monologue, chat or discussion, and happens when 'following a thread', when building on each other's ideas. 'Dia' means 'through' and, following Bohm (1996), dialogue can be described as 'a stream of meaning flowing among and through us and between us' (1996: 6). He argues: 'Communication can lead to the creation of something new only if people are able freely to listen to each other, without prejudice, and without trying to influence each other (Bohm, 1996: 3). Classrooms where this is the dominant approach to learning will be characterised by lots of oral work, skilful teacher questioning, longer and more collaborative exchanges of interaction, and more inclusive and less judgemental teaching. Dialogical teaching suggests a substantial shift in classroom culture.

Ethical requirements

A particular notion of dialogue is associated with the practice of philosophical enquiry in a community. The structure of dialogue seems most appropriate to reflect upon enquiry in the classroom, providing for homogeneity between form and content. Lipman acknowledges the ethical requirements for genuine dialogue to take place between people and cites Martin Buber's conception of a discourse put forward in his *Between Man and Man*, in which 'each of the participants really has in mind the other or others in their present and particular being, and turns to them with the intention of establishing a living mutual relation between himself and them' (Buber, 1947, cited in Lipman, 1991: 236). Lipman argues that such conditions are necessary but not sufficient for dialogue as a community of enquiry. He is keen to emphasise the logical and critical moves that make thinking and dialogue disciplined and rigorous activities. He also points to the political implications of drawing young people's attention to the notion of *community* and connects the classroom community to ideas about participatory democracies.

Lipman is by no means the first educator to make this political link between education and society. As we saw in Chapter 3, critical pedagogue Paulo Freire's adult literacy programmes were founded on a dialogical approach to teaching. He argued that this dynamic educational approach could lead to empowerment and liberation from oppression, and to greater democratisation of all social and political processes.

A note of caution

Before we get too carried away by the idea that enquiry and dialogue are the answer to all educational problems, it is useful to consider some of the reservations of those who favour dialogical education, but have observed that it has limitations. In a review of dialogical pedagogies, Burbules and Bruce (2003) articulate the limits and micropolitical tensions of dialogue when they ask:

> Is dialogue inherently 'normalizing', or can it be adapted to broader horizons of inclusiveness? On the other hand (perversely), when it does succeed at being more inclusive, is this at the cost of requiring participants to give up or compromise elements of their difference?
>
> (Burbules and Bruce, 2003)

Educationalists such as Megan Boler (2004) have also pointed out the perils and troubles of putting too much faith in dialogue as a method even if classroom communities are run on democratic principles. bell hooks (1994) speaks passionately about 'transgressive teaching' and the creation of communities that engage directly with questions of power and struggle with issues of identity and voice, with the meaning of education and with social change. Such engagement entails willingness to challenge all forms of power authority along with the discomfort that provokes. Thus, in the face of inequalities, education is directly linked to social action.

In this chapter I have reviewed a range of ideas about critical thinking, enquiry and dialogue in knowledge creation, tracing their origins in Ancient Greek philosophy and examining ways in which they have found their way into contemporary pedagogy. I have argued that such philosophical methods and practices are a good thing in education, and should be an integral part of it. These should not be treated as a disembodied and detached skill set but as part and parcel of what characterises education itself, relevant across the curriculum and in all educational settings. I have also pointed out some of the limitations of such methods when they fail to take into account students' lived experience or to engage with the difficult and uncomfortable questions of identity and voice.

References

Abbs, P. (1994) *The Educational Imperative: A Defence of Socratic and Aesthetic Learning*, London and Washington DC: Falmer Press.

Alexander, R. J. (2005) *Towards Dialogic Teaching: Rethinking Classroom Talk*, York: Dialogos.

Alexander, R. J. (2009) What Is and Could Be, *Introducing the Cambridge Primary Review*, D. Hofkins and S. Northen (eds), York: Cambridge Primary Review Trust. Available at: www.primaryreview.org.uk/Downloads/Finalreport/CPR-booklet_low-res.pdf [Accessed on 5 August 2014].

Bailin, S. and Siegel H. (2003) Critical Thinking, *The Blackwell Guide to the Philosophy of Education*, N. Blake, P. Smeyes, R. Smith and P. Standish (eds), London: Blackwell.

Bohm, D. (1996) *On Dialogue*, London: Routledge Classics.

Boler, M. (2004) (ed.) *Democratic Dialogue in Education: Troubling Speech, Disturbing Silence*, New York: Peter Lang.

Bonnett, M. (1995) Teaching Thinking, and the Sanctity of Content, *Journal of Philosophy of Education* 29 (3): 295–309.

Burbules and Bruce (2003) Theory and Research on Teaching as Dialogue, *Handbook of Research on Teaching* (Fourth edition), V. Richardson (ed.), Washington, DC: American Educational Research Association.

de Botton, A. (2000) *The Consolations of Philosophy*, London: Hamish Hamilton.

Dewey, J. (2007) *How We Think*, Cincinnati, OH: Standard Publishing.

Fisher, R. (2008) *Teaching Thinking: Philosophical Enquiry in the Classroom* (Third edition), London: Continuum.

Haynes, J. (2008) *Children as Philosophers: Learning through Enquiry and Dialogue in the Primary School*, London: Routledge.

hooks, b. (1994) *Teaching to Transgress*, New York: Routledge.

Illich, I. (1973) *Deschooling Society*, Harmondsworth: Penguin.

Lai, E. (2011) *Critical Thinking: A Literature Review*, research report for Always Learning, published online by Pearson Education. Available at: www.pearsonassessments.com/hai/images/tmrs/criticalthinkingreviewfinal.pdf [Accessed on 4 September 2012].

Lipman, M. (1991) *Thinking in Education*, Cambridge: Cambridge University Press.

Matthews, G. (2003) *Socratic Perplexity and the Nature of Philosophy*, Oxford: Oxford University Press.

Murris, K. (2008) Philosophy with Children, the Stingray and the Educative Value of Disequilibrium, *Journal of Philosophy of Education*, 42 (3): 667–85.

Quinn, V. (1997) *Critical Thinking in Young Minds*, London: David Fulton Publishers.

Splitter, L. and Sharp, A. M. (1995) *Teaching for Better Thinking: The Classroom Community of Enquiry*, Melbourne: ACER.

Van den Brink-Budgen, R. (2000) *Critical Thinking for Students: Learn the Skills of Critical Assessment and Effective Argument*, Oxford: How To Books.

12

Philosophical approaches to researching education practices

Ken Gale with Joanna Haynes

Overview

Philosophical approaches to researching education practices are many and various. It is unlikely that the reader of this book will find all the philosophical approaches to researching education practices that it might be possible to find and use within the confines of this book. However, this book is designed to encourage readers to inquire; it sets out to encourage students, as education researchers, to always be in the business of inquiry, and to be involved in forms of education practice where searching, researching and researching again become important, significant and productive modes of practice in education studies.

QUESTIONS

- How might reading and engaging with the activities in this chapter encourage and help you to work to trouble and destabilise the theory practice binary that is often promoted in education studies, pedagogy and research?
- How might a mixed-methodologies approach to carrying out education research help you to improve the quality of your inquiries?
- How might you go about questioning and reconceptualising the way in which data is represented in education research?
- How can the approach of constructing 'critical incidents' help you in taking a philosophical approach to education research?

Introduction

In writing this chapter there is no intention to conclude or to bring about closure in terms of the various philosophical approaches to education theory and practices that have been outlined here. Rather, it is written in a way that opens up a new field of inquiry that encourages the reader to always think further, to practise differently and to question what has been suggested as some of the philosophical bases of current approaches to teaching and learning in education institutions. Therefore, in making these points the chapter directs readers to some possible philosophical approaches to researching education that can be considered relevant to practices in contemporary settings. In doing so the chapter is designed to trouble and challenge what might be consider to be the unhelpful binary that has been constructed to separate theory and practice and to encourage 'researchers to re-think research processes – to pose (and re-pose) questions about the relationship between theory and methodology, the conditions under which empirical research is conducted, and its effects/affects' (Coleman and Ringrose, 2013: 2).

Therefore, the authors, in their teaching and research as academics working on an education studies programme, have tried to encourage students to engage in research processes and practices of this kind. So, for example, when engaging in work-based learning, students are encouraged to use autoethnographic approaches to position themselves within their own learning in the workplace as a means of beginning to look at working practices from different perspectives and to learn reflexively from their experience. Later in this chapter, students and readers in general are encouraged to use Tripp's idea of 'critical incidents' to encourage them to see that what is 'critical' is more likely to be made than discovered or found. Such an approach is designed to encourage students engaged in research projects on education studies programmes to inquire into their own reflections on theories and practices, to become reflexive about discursive constructions of reality and to simply try to see things from a variety of perspectives. Therefore, this final chapter and the book as a whole offer an attempt to de-mystify and question the established foundationalism of many traditional approaches to education research.

The influence of positivism

Large-scale positivist approaches to education research have been valuable in providing many important facts about the nature of education. Nineteenth-century French philosopher Auguste Comte is well known for developing an approach to positivism that attempted to construct a theory of the progress of human knowledge through a theological, a metaphysical, and a final scientific or positive stage. On the basis of discovering laws that could be used to explain social phenomena, Comte believed that it was possible to develop a science of society which he called sociology. Comte's thinking is in part based upon an intuitive logic that argues that if it is possible for doctors and physicians to discover the laws governing the behaviour of the body, surely it must be possible to discover similar kinds of laws that could be seen to explain social behaviour.

In this respect, Comte believed that this science of society could be used to cure the ills of society. For example, the important quantitative survey carried out by Halsey, Heath and Ridge and published in 1980 identified and brought to light many significant facts about the nature of inequality and educational underachievement in Britain in the decades immediately following the Second World War. While this study did not provide explanations or theories, it did provide facts about inequalities in secondary education that ultimately led to the abandonment of the 11+ examination and the tripartite system and the setting up of comprehensive education across large parts of the country.

The emergence of post-positivism

So, this final chapter takes as its starting point the highly influential work of education researchers who began to enter classrooms to inquire into educational inequalities in terms of class, gender and ethnicity. Studies by Ball (1981), Hargreaves (1967), Sharp and Green (1975), Keddie (1971) and others, often referred to as 'black box' studies, were all based upon ethnographic and interpretive approaches to research that were actually carried out in classrooms and educational institutions. These studies were highly influential in introducing small-scale, post-positivist and largely qualitative approaches to education research at this time.

Action research in education

Some writers have suggested that there are distinctive kinds of research practice in education. For example, Elliott (2006: 169) argues that what distinguishes 'educational research' from 'research on education' is 'its practical intention to realise educational values in action'. Situational understanding is very significant for educational research. In a similar vein, Griffiths (1998) suggests that practical philosophy is 'with and for' rather than 'about or applied to'. This perspective acknowledges its origins in the communities in which it acts and seeks to speak 'to something more universal, to something inclusive of, for instance, classroom teachers as well as academics, and young people as well as teachers' (Griffiths and Cotton, 2005).

In a critical research approach known as 'action research', research activities often grow out of a sense of 'mismatch' between the learning experiences teachers aspire to bring about for students, in line with their educational values, and the day-to-day life of the classroom. Research can begin when something catches our attention. If acknowledged, such moments generate questions that can lead to inquiry and modification of theory and practice. In this kind of research, the practitioner-researcher tends to be actively seeking to understand his or her context and change things for the better. Jean McNiff (1993) refers to this mismatch as a 'felt gap', or contradiction, between values and action. John Mason (2002) describes moments when something catches our attention in this way as 'noticings'. David Tripp (1993) offers us a way of working with these noticings and felt gaps through the creation of 'critical incidents' of experience.

Critical incidents

Tripp (1993) suggests that incidents in practice become significant when they strikingly appear as an example of a wider social category or dramatically contrast with previous experience. The moment of surprise, awareness or noting the distinctive character of such events is a first step, but for the episode to become critical it has to be interpreted and interrogated. An incident becomes critical when it leads to increased sensitivity to values and to re-examination of implicit beliefs and theories. Tripp writes:

> critical incidents are not 'things' which exist independently of an observer and are awaiting discovery like gold nuggets or desert islands, but like all data, critical incidents are created. Incidents happen, but critical incidents are produced by the way we look at a situation: a critical incident is an interpretation of the significance of an event.

> (Tripp, 1996: 8)

Critical incidents inform thinking and action in a number of ways. Problems can be identified. Individual learning situations can be illuminated. Change is made possible through seeing existing practice in a new light. Deeper reflection and wider social inquiry become possible when a series of incidents are recorded over time. Tripp (1993: 97) argues that certain kinds of critical incident are more strongly directed towards biographical and political understanding. These are often emotionally charged and lead to searches into the autobiographical origin of values expressed in a particular response to a situation. Such critical episodes help to describe the relationship between a practitioner and the context in which s/he is working. A series of incidents taken together can constitute an autoethnography and/or situated practical philosophy.

The following is a brief example that can be used to illustrate the idea of developing a situated practical philosophy. Haynes and Murris (2011) drew on critical incident analysis in research that evolved from their professional development work with teachers. Through their reflections on their collaborative teaching, they noticed and logged teachers' responses and concerns in the context of philosophising with children (see Chapters 10 and 11). In various ways, including affectively, teachers communicated what they found troublesome in taking on the role of facilitating children's philosophical inquiries. Haynes and Murris' analysis suggested that similar concerns and questions were raised by many different groups of teachers over time and they described these as 'recurring moments of disequilibrium'. They were able to use their insights into teachers' experiences of philosophising with children to directly inform their theorising and practice of professional work with teachers.

ACTIVITY 1

'Mary raised her right hand. After about a minute her teacher noticed, and asked her what she wanted. Mary asked if she could sharpen her pencil' (Tripp, 1993: 25).

This statement reflects an everyday incident in a classroom. Spend some time reflecting upon what the statement describes to you in terms of what is 'say-able' or 'do-able' in this classroom. What do you think are the conditions of possibility that this statement describes?

When you have completed this activity, write down how engaging in this activity has turned the description of this incident into what Tripp describes as a 'critical incident'.

Experience and education research

Drawing on phenomenology, which, as we saw in Chapter 4, is concerned with the study of things as they 'appear' in our experience and with structures of our consciousness, Max Van Manen (1997) has developed a particular approach to researching lived experience. This has been taken up by professionals working in many fields, such as nursing, midwifery, teaching and early child care. Van Manen is interested in recognising and developing the kinds of practical knowledge, often subtle and hard to describe, that are of vital importance in work such as health or social care and education. Van Manen (1997) outlines ways in which professional research can draw on 'data' such as personal experience, diaries and anecdotes, sometimes regarded as inadmissible. He encourages researchers to explore the etymology of key words and idiomatic phrases that are significant in the practice of being explored. Phenomenological approaches to research seem to be particularly helpful for understanding and creating meaning in contexts that are highly sensitive or intimate, and which pay astute attention to the corporeal, situated and sensory dimensions of experience.

Both Van Manen and the philosopher and pedagogue Martinus Langeveld have been hugely influential in the study of early childhood practice from this phenomenological perspective, which strongly contrasts with the dominant developmental approach to theorising and practising childhood. Langeveld's approach was to pay careful attention to concrete and common situations and events in the lives of children and adults in his analysis of the phenomena of child-rearing and educational experiences. Langeveld's *The Secret Place in the Life of the Child* (1967), first published in 1953, inspired many further studies into the highly private and often hidden sphere of childhood. More recently, Van Manen and Levering (1996) have offered us their phenomenological study, *Childhood's Secrets: Intimacy, Privacy and the Self Reconsidered*, which is well worth reading for any student wishing to consider a research study of this kind. It draws on a wide variety of literary and other sources, as well as anecdotes, observations and reminiscences, to theorise about meanings of childhood. The authors suggest that experiences of secrecy and privacy form a necessary and valuable part of a path towards inner competence and are part of a unique narrative of the self. Such a study is particularly powerful in the context of contemporary debates about children's lack of freedom and moral panics about threats to childhood which tend to result in policies and practices that express adults' anxiety. Approaching childhood from perspectives of diverse and multiple lived experiences might help to counterbalance the moral panics which often threaten children's autonomy and flourishing.

An anti-positivist approach?

So, this chapter is designed to trouble the linear rationality and the cause and effect reasoning of the kinds of 'march of progress' theories proposed by Hegel and others. Such an approach is based upon dialectical exchanges between different bodies of knowledge or theses which in turn bring about certain syntheses or 'developments' in rational knowledge construction. On the other hand, anti-positivist researchers such as St. Pierre (1997, 2004) encourage education researchers to foreground and research not simply the conceptually informative but also that which opens up lines of inquiry into the affective, the ethical, the evaluative, the sensate and so on. St. Pierre (1997) refers to these as 'transgressive data' and, in trying to 'undo' the subject of education, her work urges readers and aspirant researchers to consider how it is possible to engage in education studies without paying due consideration to what Schön has referred to as the problems of the 'swampy lowlands' (see below). The philosophical approaches to researching education practices that are being promoted in this chapter are therefore also influenced by Ball when he says in relation to the effects of policy on education practices:

> the complexity and scope of policy analysis – from an interest in the workings of the state to a concern with contexts of practice and the distributional outcomes of policy – precludes the possibility of successful single theory explanations. What we need in policy analysis is a toolbox of diverse concepts and theories.
>
> (Ball, 1994: 14)

Reflective practice

The 'reality' of the world of education, rather than being found, discovered or uncovered by researchers, is created, made and actively constructed by those involved in education research and policy making. In taking this view there is a need to address the question: how is education research most effectively carried out? In response, an argument can be made supporting the view that multidimensional and mixed-methodological approaches are necessary as a means of taking account of the complexities of education in Britain at the present time. Following the views of Foucault outlined in Chapter 5 the philosophical approach of this chapter argues that conventional and established forms of education research practice can potentially be seen as discursive constructions of reality. Such approaches are based upon the view that there exists a real world, out there so to speak, which is discoverable by research practices such as data collection and analysis. Taking a lead from Nagel (1986), who ironically titled one of his books *The View from Nowhere*, this chapter proposes approaches to education research that acknowledge their positionality and that, in so doing, offer views from somewhere that exists as a representation responsible for opening up spaces for further reflexive research and inquiry. Reflexive approaches of this kind encourage readers, students and researchers alike to ask, for instance, how do certain knowledge forms, professional identifications and practices based upon other education research practices and policy constructions gain legitimation in education settings?

Donald Schön (1983, 1987), in two important studies published over thirty years ago, offered for careful consideration the role of reflection within the context of professional practice. Researchers have since advanced his thinking and investigated it within numerous occupational, professional and research-based settings. Cole and Gary-Knowles (2000), for example, define reflective inquiry as a process of examining and refining practice with reference to the pedagogical, social, political and ethical contexts that influence professional work, while reflexive enquiry incorporates the reflective process and is 'situated within the context of personal histories in order to make connections between personal lives and professional careers, and to understand personal influences on professional practice'. They argue that such reflexive enquiries are always rooted in a critical perspective expressed through the 'interrogation of status quo norms and practices, especially with respect to issues of power and control' (Cole and Gary-Knowles, 2000: 2).

So, Schön's work on the role of reflection and reflective practices remains highly significant and influential. In the opening passage of the second of these two books, he says:

> In the varied topography of professional practice there is a high, hard ground overlooking a swamp. On the high ground, manageable problems lend themselves to solution through the application of research-based theory and technique. The irony of this situation is that the problems of the high ground tend to be relatively unimportant to individuals or society at large, however great their technical inter- est might be, while in the swamp lie the problems of greatest human concern. The practitioner must choose. Shall he remain on the high ground where he can solve relatively unimportant problems according to prevailing standards of rigour, or shall he descend to the swamp of important problems and nonrigorous inquiry?
> (Schön, 1987: 3)

While the philosophical approach taken in this chapter is broadly in agreement with Schön's view that reflection has the potential to prepare education and other professionals for the demands of practice, there is a sense in which Schön can be taken to task for his assertion that research in the swamp involves the education practitioner in 'nonrigorous inquiry'. It is possible to argue that reflective practices such as 'reflective observation' as used by Kolb (1983) in his theory of experiential learning, by Schön himself in the technique of 'reflection-on-action' and the 'nonrational intuitive artistry' (1983: 239) of 'reflection-in-action' and, more recently, through the diffractive challenges to reflection and reflexivity offered by Haraway and Barad are all of great significance and importance in the carrying out of education research and inquiry. While they are not fully detailed in the passage of Schön quoted above, the problems of the swamp are of the 'greatest human concern'. In education such 'problems' are the stuff of what St. Pierre refers to as 'transgressive data' (1997); they exist within the multiplicity of 'concept, affect and percept' as described and explored by Deleuze and Guattari (1994) and they are to be found within the fields of ethics, sense, intuition and so on that populate the classrooms, corridors and staffrooms of contemporary education institutional settings.

Emerging education research practices

A focused literature review clearly demonstrates that there is a growing body of highly rigorous, philosophically informed research practices that are currently being carried out, developed and applied to these affectively charged, ethically sensitive and conceptually complex domains of education practice (see for example Goodson and Sikes, 2001; Clough, 2002; Haynes, 2002; St. Pierre, 2004; Davies and Gannon, 2009; Gale, 2010 and 2014; Masny, 2011; Semetsky and Masny, 2013).

Many of these studies challenge the conventional and established view of an education research practice that simply searches for and uncovers something that is simply there. Such a view relies upon the binary classification which neatly and, in the view of this chapter, unhelpfully divides research into separate categories of data collection and analysis. The philosophical approach of this chapter proposes that research practices can also involve the actual construction and active fabrication of data through the use of creative, imaginative and personally and professionally inflected modes of practice.

> [We] must no longer accept concepts as a gift, nor merely purify, and polish them, but first make and create them, present them and make them convincing. Hitherto one has generally trusted one's concepts as if they were a wonderful dowry from some sort of wonderland.
>
> (Nietzsche, 1968: 409)

> Concepts are not waiting for us ready-made, like heavenly bodies. There is no heaven for concepts. They must be invented, fabricated, or rather, created, and would be nothing without the creator's signature.
>
> (Deleuze and Guattari, 1994: 5)

In following the reasoning of Descartes who talked of the 'malign spirit' of scepticism, it makes sense to consider that when we say we know, we must ask ourselves what that means. These philosophers are suggesting that we should not trust concepts we did not create ourselves; from a research-based point of view, it makes sense to displace a trust of concepts through the animation of distrust. So, based upon the thinking of Nietzsche, Foucault's (2002) archaeological approach to discourse analysis provides an excellent illustration of how such an approach to research and inquiry can be carried out in contemporary education settings.

Foucault uses archaeology, in a Nietzschean sense, to describe a *descent* as a means of delving into sedimented structures of language and meaning. This is carried out in an attempt to discover what he refers to as hidden 'conditions of possibility' that might have structured and discursively constructed and established meaning, knowledge and practices over time. As shown in an earlier chapter, what might be 'say-able' or 'do-able' in education settings is, therefore, dependent upon the influence of certain preceding social, cultural and historical factors which Foucault described as 'conditions of possibility'. For Foucault, this archaeology is not simply about discovering, recovering or uncovering what was hitherto covered. So, again based upon the thinking of Nietzsche, Foucault's genealogical approach to discourse evaluation can be described as *emergence*. Such an approach to education research provides a means of offering new ways of thinking and practising, of making what has been familiar for some time strange and thus offering challenges to the resistances to reflexivity offered by previously unnoticed discursive constructions.

If according to Deleuze '[t]here is no heaven for concepts', then his approach to philosophy is clearly one of use in which theories, concepts, ideas and so on are of no value if they are not used. In this respect and for Deleuze, each new concept, rather than referring to or representing something, is actually an event. Concepts that sit on shelves gathering dust have no place in the realist ontological approach of this most radical of philosophers; '[t]hey must be invented, fabricated, or rather, created'. So, this approach to philosophy is based upon the *practice* of concepts, of putting concepts to work and for Deleuze, therefore, plugging concepts in is a form of research: 'A concept is a brick. It can be used to build the courthouse of reason. Or it can be thrown through the window' (Massumi, 1988: xii). It is the 'creator's signature' that is of importance here; it is what the researcher does that is of crucial significance. St. Pierre says the following about carrying out education research using a Deleuzian approach of this kind:

> I was happy to come upon this description [. . .] and be granted permission to give up the pretence of signifying and 'making meaning' in the old way because this is exactly how I had read Deleuze (in fact, this is the way I've always read everything). I had plugged into his circuits and, without thinking too much about it, found myself plugging his concepts into everything in my life so that it has become different than it was before. I expect the pleasure of reading great philosophy is the thrill that even a non-philosopher can find in events (a life) that were once impossible.
>
> (St. Pierre, 2004: 283–4)

Therefore, according to this approach, as an education researcher your conceptualisations can be 'plugged in': concepts can be taken to contexts and used in certain ways, ways that might vary from one time to another, from one space to another. Conceptualisations can activate, animate and create contextualisations. It is important for you to use them, to do something with them, to make them work.

ACTIVITY 2

Pelias asks a very important question about the processes and practices that we engage in as education practitioners that is of particular relevance to looking critically at the Deleuzian approach to education research outlined here. Of the text, the statement, the idea, the word or the phrase, Pelias asks, simply and directly: what work does it do? He asks us to consider our practices in this way, perhaps by standing back from them and considering their effect or the impact they might have had.

> Look at a piece of writing you have a produced (some lecture notes or an assignment perhaps), or a discussion in which you took part, maybe a small piece of research you have carried out, and ask yourself this question; what work does it do? Try to assess if asking this question helps you in making a critical judgement about what you have done. Look at this piece of writing and ask yourself or a colleague: what work does it do?

Research policy and practice

Approaches of this kind are invaluable when working as education researchers because, in terms of learning from investigations and inquiries, it is important to frequently and critically ask: what does it mean to say that we know something? This question can be asked not only of what researchers do but also of the way in which the work of others is read. In relational space these others can be other researchers, other theorists and other writers in general. The task of critically reviewing the literature encountered as education researchers is extremely important in adding depth and intensity to the practices of a researcher.

Texts often operate by privileging certain features of social life while suppressing or de-emphasising others. Within a particular text certain meanings are hidden, perhaps within what might be referred to as a subtext. It makes sense to talk about encountering texts and subtexts of this kind as 'reading between the lines'. In taking such an approach to reading, it is possible to try to capture inflections, to detect thinly veiled meanings or to elicit tangible meaning from what might only be implied or inferred. So in teaching and learning, for example, it is possible that certain set texts might be taught in such a way that traditional or readily accepted 'readings' are offered and preferred and other hidden meanings and values are ignored or only paid scant attention.

Examples of this kind can be used to introduce Derrida's approach to deconstruction as a form of education research. Derrida developed an approach to language which essentially involved him in the destabilising and undoing of texts. For Derrida, the relationship between words (signifiers) and concepts (signified) is problematic. Against the traditionally accepted view of the structure and function of language, proposed by Saussure and others, signifiers do not necessarily lead us to the signified; rather, they simply lead to other signifiers. So going to the dictionary to find the meaning of a word actually only leads us to other words, which themselves lead us to other words and so on. Ball, in discussing the complex nature of the initiation, implementation and interpretation of policy in education, says:

> We can see policies as representations which are encoded in complex ways (via struggles, compromises, authoritative public interpretations and reinterpretations) and decoded in complex ways via actors' interpretations and meanings in relation to their history, experiences, skills, resources and context.
>
> (Ball, 1994: 16)

> A policy is both contested and changing, always in a state of 'becoming', of 'was' and 'never was' and 'not quite'; for any text a plurality of readers must necessarily produce a plurality of readings [...] authors cannot control the meanings of their texts.
>
> (ibid.)

Much of what Ball describes here is applicable to the operation of all kinds of texts and can be explained in terms of Derrida's view of language and the function of the text, and within the context of his theory and practice of deconstruction. For Derrida, the language we use to signify meaning is always breaking apart from what is meant. Texts are unstable and, as in the example above, can simply be seen to lead to other texts.

For Derrida to place a text 'sous rature' or 'under erasure' literally means to write a word, cross it out and then print the word and its deletion. While the word is necessary for us to be able to communicate, it is inadequate because what it signifies is always incomplete, always changing and never possible to contain within its signifying tendencies. Derrida's deconstructive methods can be effectively used within the context of our critical reviewing of language, bodies of knowledge and educational institutions. Knowledge claims are articulated through texts and, Derrida claims, these texts can always be made vulnerable through exposure and critique to a reflexive engagement with the standards, the definitions and the concepts which inhabit them and upon which they are based.

ACTIVITY 3

This exercise looks at applying deconstruction as a research practice.
Take a text with which you are familiar and:

a   Identify what you consider to be its subtexts or hidden meanings.
b   Write down why you think these meanings have been hidden: do you think this was intentional or unintentional?
c   Write down ways in which this text can be seen as both necessary and inadequate.
d   Write out a portion of the text and try to present what it says in a different way by offering a different set of meanings.

In tentatively bringing this chapter, and indeed the whole book, to a close, it is worth making one final visit back into the history of education research as a means of drawing upon some influential work that has been carried out, and at the same time making a suggestion about the work that readers of this book, in particular students engaged in education studies, might follow in the future. In the 1970s, very much influenced by the emerging theory and practices of action research and its relevance to education studies, Lawrence Stenhouse (1975), in what is probably his best-known book, *An Introduction to Curriculum Research and Development*, insisted on reconceptualising 'teachers' as 'teachers-as-researchers'. It was his view that professionally focused and committed teachers must always be thinking about, reflecting upon, experimenting and, ultimately, researching their practices in ways that always involve them in bringing new theories and the results of other researchers to bear upon their own professional practice. This continual professional commitment of teachers to be constantly engaged in researching practices is something this chapter and this book as a whole encourage students to take into consideration. Therefore, the authors of this book would be pleased to discover that before becoming the 'teachers-as-researchers' of the future, students who read this book and who engage in the activities it contains might first become the 'students-as-researchers' of the present.

References

Ball, S. J. (1981) *Beachside Comprehensive: A Case-Study of Secondary Schooling*, Cambridge: Cambridge University Press.

Ball, S. J. (1994) *Education Reform: A Critical and Post Structural Approach*, Buckingham: Open University Press.

Barad, K. (2007) *Meeting The Universe Halfway: Quantum Physics and The Entanglement of Matter and Meaning*, London: Duke University Press.

Clough, P. (2002) *Narratives and Fictions in Educational Research*, Buckingham: Open University Press.

Cole, A. L. and Gary-Knowles, J. (2000) *Exploring Teacher Development through Reflexive Inquiry*, Boston: Allyn and Bacon.

Coleman, R. and Ringrose, J. (2013) *Deleuze and Research Methodologies*, Edinburgh: Edinburgh University Press.

Davies, B. and Gannon, S. (2009) (eds) *Pedagogical Encounters*, New York: Peter Lang.

Deleuze, G. and Guattari, F (1994) *What Is Philosophy?* London: Verso.

Derrida, J. (1976) *Of Grammatology*, London: Johns Hopkins University Press.

Elliott, J. (2006) Educational Research as a Form of Democratic Rationality, *Journal of Philosophy of Education*, 40 (2): 169–85.

Foucault, M. (1976) *Discipline and Punish*, Harmondsworth: Penguin.

Foucault, M. (2002) *The Archaeology of Knowledge*, London: Routledge.

Gale, K. (2010) An Inquiry into the Ethical Nature of a Deleuzian Creative Educational Practice, *Qualitative Inquiry*, 16 (5): 303–309.

Gale, K. (2014) Moods, Tones, Flavours: Living with Intensities as Inquiry, *Qualitative Inquiry*, DOI: 10.1177/1077800413513725.

Goodson, I. and Sikes, P. (2001) *Life History Research in Educational Settings*, Buckingham: Open University Press.

Griffiths, M. (1998) *Educational Research for Social Justice: Getting Off The Fence*, Buckingham: Open University Press.

Griffiths, M. and Cotton, T. (2005) Action Research, Stories and Practical Philosophy, paper presented at conference of *Collaborative Action Research Network/Practitioner Action Research Quality of Practitioner Research/Action Research*: What's it About, What's it For and What Next? Utrecht, The Netherlands, 4 to 6 November 2005.

Hargreaves, D. (1967) *Social Relations in a Secondary School*, London: Routledge & Kegan Paul.

Haynes, J. (2002) *Children as Philosophers*, London: Routledge.

Haynes, J. and Murris, K. (2011) The Provocation of an Epistemological Shift in Teacher Education through Philosophy with Children, *Journal of Philosophy of Education*, 45 (2): 285–303.

Keddie, N. (1971) Classroom Knowledge, in M. Young (ed.) *Knowledge and Control*, London: Collier-Macmillan.

Kolb, D. (1983) *Experiential Learning*, Englewood Cliffs, NJ: Prentice Hall.

Langeveld, M. J. (1967) The Secret Place in the Life of the Child, *Phenomenology and Pedagogy*, 1 (2): 181–9.

Masny, D. (2011) Multiple Literacies Theory: Exploring Futures, *Policy Futures in Education*, 9 (4).

Mason, J. (2002) *Researching Your Own Classroom Practice: From Noticing to Reflection*, London and New York: Routledge Falmer.

Massumi, B. (1988) Translator's introduction to Deleuze, G. and Guattari, F., *A Thousand Plateaus*, London: Athlone Press.

McNiff, J. (1993) *Teaching as Learning: An Action Research Approach*, London and New York: Routledge.

Nagel, T. (1986) *The View from Nowhere*, Oxford: Oxford University Press.

Nietzsche, F. (1968) *The Will to Power*, New York: Vintage.

St. Pierre, E. (1997) Methodology in the Fold and the Irruption of Transgressive Data, *Qualitative Studies in Education*, 10 (2): 175–89.

St. Pierre, E. (2004) Deleuzian Concepts for Education: The Subject Undone, *Educational Philosophy and Theory*, 36 (3): 283–96.

Schön, D. (1983) *The Reflective Practitioner*, San Francisco: Jossey Bass.

Schön, D. (1987) *Educating the Reflective Practitioner*, San Francisco: Jossey Bass.

Semetsky, I. and Masney, D. (eds) (2013) *Deleuze and Education*, Edinburgh: Edinburgh University Press.

Sharp, R. and Green, A. (1975) *Education and Social Control*, London: Routledge.

Stenhouse, L. (1975) *An Introduction to Curriculum Research and Development*, London: Heinemann.

Tripp, D. (1993) *Critical Incidents in Teaching*, London: Routledge.

Van Manen, M. (1997) *Researching Lived Experience: Human Science for an Action Sensitive Pedagogy*, Second edition, London, ON: Althouse Press.

Van Manen, M. and Levering, B. (1996) *Childhood's Secrets: Intimacy, Privacy and the Self Reconsidered*, New York: Teachers College Press.

Further reading

Bailey, R. (2010) (ed.) *The Philosophy of Education: An Introduction*, London and New York: Continuum.
Barrow, R. and Woods, R. (2006) *An Introduction to Philosophy of Education* (Fourth edition), London and New York: Routledge.
Blake, N., Smeyers, P., Smith, R. and Standish, P. (2003) (eds) *The Blackwell Guide to the Philosophy of Education*, Oxford: Blackwell Publishing.
Cahn, S. M. (2009) (ed.) *Philosophy of Education: The Essential Texts*, London and New York: Routledge.
Gutek, G. L. (1997) *Philosophical and Ideological Perspectives on Education* (Second edition), Boston: Allyn & Bacon.
Kohli, W. (1995) (ed.) *Critical Conversations in Philosophy of Education*, London: Routledge.
Noddings, N. (2012) *Philosophy of Education* (Third edition), Boulder, CO: Westview Press.
Pring, R. (2004) *Philosophy of Education*, London and New York: Continuum.
Winch, C. and Gingell, J. (2008) *Philosophy of Education: The Key Concepts* (Second edition), London and New York: Routledge Key Guides.

Helpful websites

Stanford Encyclopaedia of Philosophy (http://plato.stanford.edu)
The Encyclopaedia of Informal Education (www.infed.org)

Index

UNIVERSITY OF WINCHESTER
LIBRARY

UNIVERSITY OF WINCHESTER
LIBRARY

UNIVERSITY OF WINCHESTER
LIBRARY

UNIVERSITY OF WINCHESTER
LIBRARY